What the exp
Bullying Boss

M000282387

Andrea Needham
International HR Expert

"This book is a must read for anyone who has ever worked. Knowledge is power and this book provides just that.

Part I provides an excellent summary of international knowledge on Workplace Bullying and additional information gleaned from Robert's practice working with Targets and organizations. He cleverly uses a descriptor, the 'Ring of Fire', to describe how isolated Targets can become. Robert's depiction, of how the diverse facets of organizations work together to attack a high performer and bring him/her down, is very real.

Part II is a lifeline for Targets. It describes how to beat the Workplace Bully at his or her own game and become a Workplace Warrior. Robert describes the knowledge, skills and abilities a Target needs in order to take on a Workplace Bully. 'Bullying Bosses' describes ways of managing these situations from a position of strength. The book gives action plans and outcomes to strive for.

This book is a necessary read for senior managers and human resources professionals who truly wish to prevent Workplace Bullying. They will learn what constitutes Workplace Bullying and how it works to break individuals emotionally and therefore impacts self-esteem and consequently productivity.

The book is an excellent reference book for Targets who want to fight the silent epidemic and expose Workplace Bullies for the chaos and desolation they cause and the lives they ruin."

> **Andrea W Needham**
> author of *'Workplace Bullying, The Costly Business Secret'*

Sam Vaknin
International Expert on Narcissism

"Thrilling book (and I use the word "thrilling" judiciously)...It is rare that a book of reference and self-help should read like an edge-of-the-seat John Grisham thriller. But this significant contribution to the study of bullying in the workplace often does.

Mueller leverages court cases and case histories into a cogent and methodological analysis of bullying tactics and strategies.

Strewn among the pages of this rich presentation are highlighted tips and quotes. The target has to discover and groom potential supporters, build a case against the bullying boss, collect potent data, craft a plan, and implement it. The author takes the victim by the hand and convincingly shows him or her how to do it.

I recommend the book to anyone who has ever been involved in on-the-job harassment, stalking, and bullying because it is both deep and practical, accurate but never arcane, eye opening and thought provoking and challenging - but never loses its empathy and compassion for the victims of this widespread and under-reported phenomenon. A gem.

Sam Vaknin,
author of *"Malignant Self Love - Narcissism Revisited"*

Dianne Ayling
Senior Lecturer in Law

This "survivor guide" is the result of many years of research, advocacy and exploration by Mueller of scenarios targets face when subject to attacks by bullying bosses.

Previous books have explored the concept of workplace bullying, (Tim Field, *Bully In Sight*, Gary and Ruth Namie, *The Bully at Work*, and Andrea Needham, *Workplace Bullying: The Costly Business Secret*), however none have prepared the target for winning the battle with the bullying boss like *"Bullying Bosses"*. The detail in this book is so good, that I am reminded of General Norman Schwarzkopf's preparations for the Gulf War.

This book is a great addition to the existing library of books about workplace bullying. It is the best in its category and likely to be for sometime to come. I was particularly impressed by the completeness of the book.

For those of you who are not or have not been targets of the bullying bosses, purchase it anyway, for as the Romans said, "Praemontius praemunitus", to be forewarned is to be forearmed.

Diana Ayling is a Senior lecturer in law,
School of Accountancy, Law and Finance at
Unitec, New Zealand

BULLYING BOSSES:

A Survivor's Guide

How To Transcend
The Illusion Of The Interpersonal

Robert Mueller, JD

BullyingBosses.com

For information, contact the publisher, "Bullyingbosses.com" (Robert Mueller) at www.bullyingbosses.com or P.O. Box 410238, San Francisco, CA 94141-0238, USA

Except for characters taken from published court opinions, no real names have been used. In the interest of accurately reflecting the general experience of Bullies, all characters are composites of several actual supervisors or employees. Except for court opinions, the genders of all characters have been used without regard to the facts being discussed at any given point, in order to reflect the reality that both men and women can be Bullies and Targets. The court decisions are generally taken from the California courts but are referenced for illustration purposes only, and not cited as statements of law that differ in different places and at different times. This book is intended to provide accurate information with regard to the subject matter. The publisher is not engaged in rendering legal advice. When a legal question, concern or issue arises, counsel from a competent attorney should be sought.

Library of Congress Control Number: 2005911392
    Bullying Bosses: A Survivor's Guide
    How to Transcend the Illusion of the Interpersonal

        1. Bullying in the workplace. 2. Harassment. 3. Career. 4. Office Politics
        I. Mueller, Robert II. Title

ISBN 0-9768293-0-4

Printed in Canada.

        06 07 08 09 10   10 9 8 7 6 5 4 3 2 1

DEDICATED TO SUSAN

ultimate challenge Target employees face is with them-
Bullies will never give them respect or approval. They will
y become reasonable or seek to befriend the Target. The
e" may be uttered, but it will never be heard. In the nor-
one would expect management to remedy the problem.
is management's assigned Bully that is misusing man-
uthority, and damaging management's human resourc-
ully's own ends, but that's not likely to happen. Except
human resource-preserving, anti-abuse employers, em-
t reasonably expect any manager to come to their aid, no
deserving the employee is, or how outrageous the Bul-

is not so much about what a Target should do, but how
ut what to do. Bullying presents difficult questions that
vious answers. Arguably, too many tactical and strategic
s will be discussed, but they convey a unified theme so
useful in understanding and implementing the others.
lar ones that best fit each employee, employer and cir-
should be obvious to most Workplace Warriors.
t Target employees need is not airy pleas for justice, but
ls and shields to wield, in conjunction with a well-con-
n for political action. As the Workplace Warriors they
ey may recognize the fight could be long,[1] destructive,
ly not successful, then quit without regard to the risks,
nsequences. Or they may do what's practically required
uver and maybe outlast the Bully until the political ele-
their timings shift, or are shifted in their favor internally,
n out appropriately.
gnificant root factor of bullying is what once was pow-
d, "violence against women." The vast majority of em-
geted by Bullies are women. Under contemporary stan-
nationally recognized definitions for workplace violence

Table Of Contents

INTRODUCTION

This is not a scholarly treatise. It s
tion guide, is unapologetically pro-Targe
get's perspective, addressing the Target's d
so far developed by scholars and professio
abuse or Bully Bossing are often too staid
gagement. It's time to become results-orie
ative, with the intent of building a politica
Internationally, there has been progress th
tective legislation. In the United States, o
topic have begun, but there's close to zerc
edy it.

For many of the uninitiated, des
riences are, at best, science fiction. Son
unbelievable, as also still happens in mar
cases. At least initially, even the Targets
that is replaced by puzzlement of a consc
point for Targets comes sometime after e
"had" by the Bully, more shame when i
yet more shame when not believed by th
to for relief and support.

The antidote to Bullying intrigue:
ic approach through the development of
on empirical observations. The objectiv
outwardly to the context with its many re
ly to the already wounded psyche. Objec
by documenting events evenly, crafting
neuvering note cards that represent the
forces into analytical and strategic forn
tion, Targets' shame lifts appreciably. Pe
ed Targets, frequently and fairly quickly
sometimes sassy, Workplace Warriors.

selves
not su
word
mal cc
After
ageme
es, to
for the
ployee
matter
ly becc

to *thin*.
have n
formul
that ea
The pa
cumsta

V
steely s
sidered
become
and pro
costs, or
to outm
ments a
or shift t

A
erfully c
ployees t
dards, in

includes acts that cause psychological damages, which are sometimes longer lasting and occupationally more expensive than physical ones. Not surprisingly, workplace bullying is a syndrome of abusive behavior that has a great deal in common with domestic violence.

Therapists are the people most likely to end up counseling abused employees just as they counsel clients on domestic issues. They are encouraged to include a larger political view in their analyses; recognizing workplace power struggles and bullying incidents as systemic problems associated with the politics of the employment world, and not problems with Targets' perspectives, emotional make up or interpersonal skills. Being attentive to business objectives, business materials discussing human relations sensibly recommend that workplace communications and exertions there be personable, but the underlying relationships function best if essentially impersonal. That's being businesslike. It is counter-productive to bring into the work dynamic, family behaviors and issues that complicate production without producing value.

Employee relations with Bullying Bosses are institutionally imposed but they are extraordinary and extreme examples of workplace conduct. Simply put, Bullying onslaughts are crude power plays disrupting production and people for individual purposes. They are impersonal but go well beyond being businesslike into an awful realm fully knowable only to the Bullies. With them, it's not appropriate or even possible for Targeted employees to develop significant personal relationships. On the contrary, the question for every concerned person is not how to improve the bullying relationship beyond non-interpersonal, but how either to neutralize or escape it.

Bullying is not about misunderstandings. It is about a perpetrator engaging in a series and pattern of inappropriate and abusive acts, targeting different people in series. It's absolutely not about the

Target-of-the-day. According to the media and the life experiences of most of us, the real world has some fundamentally anti-social people in it. These include those called "petty tyrants" operating in both domestic and workplace contexts. The existence of malicious, calculating, profoundly unreachable people may be an uncomfortable fact, but it's one that must be accepted as a basic element of life, before tyranny, whatever its scale, can be addressed.

> If you're not pissed off at the world,
> Then you're just not paying attention.
> —*Australian Singer/Songwriter, Kasey Chambers*

Workplace witnesses do not initially recognize that they are seeing a pattern and practice of malevolent behaviors. But they do naturally reel back from it. Customarily they attempt a neutrality in the bullying conflict but, by not detailing and opposing what they see or hear, they become "tacitly complicit" in it. Psychological self-defense mechanisms may limit coworkers' ability to perceive and respond to bullying incidents, but managers don't have that excuse or option. Managers are not innocent or uninvolved bystanders. They're the responsible party.

Scholars and professionals, at least in the United States, too often attempt that same neutrality. They are urged to consider the empirical evidence and disseminate their findings with the aim of maximizing public education and, ultimately, fostering social and legal protections against workplace abusers in the workplace, and thus against abusers wherever they might be. In other western countries, this has already been successfully accomplished without compromise of either academic or business integrities. People suffering from workplace abuse deserve energetic support of intelligent and disciplined kinds.

Abuse does not become acceptable just because it occurs within a hierarchical workplace structure, instead of in our more democratic streets and homes. The existence of an employment hierarchy does not excuse any particular employee with supervisory authority of violating an employee's dignity or compromising their health and safety. On the contrary, particularly persons given authority within hierarchy over supervisors have a duty to investigate and where appropriate, take corrective steps.

This action guide attempts to support and guide leadership-oriented managers who honestly exercise their duty of due diligence to protect their employees from harm caused by their agents. By rooting out Bullies, these managers protect not only employees but also their employer's mission, and bottom line, from compromise by renegade supervisors in pursuit of ill-disposed, private missions of "conquest," over what are otherwise *management's* human resources. There can exists no business justification for purposefully damaging Target employees, particularly not given today's health care costs, and also not given that the employees Bullies chose as Targets tend to be among the most loyal and successful employees in the performance of their job duties.

Managerial action must start with the adoption, as a health and safety matter, of a policy that announces management's position against the abuse of its employees. Bullying behaviors are not acceptable in their workplace. That policy must include a protocol that swiftly removes apparent Bullies from positions of power over others. The examples of Hewlett-Packard Company, Coxcom, Inc., and "Datamine Limited" will be discussed. With formal policy in place, managers are urged to listen to employee complaints, including those not formally made but found or elicited, as well as conduct a global assessment using existing employment cost data as indicia of where potential Bullies might be operating within their company.

Bullying, the damaging for human resources for personal reasons, is an avoidable business cost.

Just as in addressing domestic violence, the first priority must be to protect even allegedly harmed employees from even the prospect of further harm. It is not necessary, and is perhaps unethical to allow abusive behaviors to continue occurring, until a psychological "understanding" of the Bully's actions and motives is accomplished. Whenever because of employment data or a complaint, it is reasonably suspected that a person with supervisory authority is abusing a subordinate, the tentative but immediate removal of the alleged abuser, with a presumption of innocence, is the soundest and safest course of action. Initially, the business focus can't primarily be about the supposed guilt or innocence of any given individual. The higher priority for managers has to be to protect the employer's operations generally as well as its several or many at-risk employees regardless. This prudent approach allows for no further cost to the employer, harms and allows no harm to come to any one.

In due course, the company can then proceed with an inquiry to determine the relevant facts, and remove apparent ambiguities. Unfortunately, Bullies are skilled at making themselves invisible to their superiors, charming them while terrorizing select subordinates. Because of this, subjective assessments are generally not adequate. Instead, competent investigators of bullying behaviors depend upon the collection of evidence demonstrating, or not, patterned behaviors as analyzed objectively.

As renegade supervisors, it's in Bullies' self-interest to hide what they do to the fullest extent possible, to claim innocence and high purpose when prompted, and to obfuscate at all times. While they are in what are safe settings for them, they may be prone to bragging about their behaviors, they do not normally expose themselves in formal circumstances, including not participating in workplace surveys. No matter what, the generally amorphous and confusing answers they give to questions in every context tend to defy quantification, and are thus not appropriate to either survey methodologies or informal questioning. Whatever a Bully does, he or she "games" it. Finding and evaluating Bullies requires formal investigation. There is one thing they are consistently clear on: the battle they bring to both Targets and employers is a political one for power, and not for either relationship or production.

What this author also brings to the table is the study and application of labor law in a wide variety of workplaces, together with a lifetime studying the political and military masters, applying their theoretical lessons as practicalities in a host of different settings. My theoretical construct explicitly differentiates between myriad hard and soft tactics, developed and utilized over the years, with soft ones being generally more productive for the weaker party, the Target employees.

As a former attorney, I investigated a couple thousand cases of employees in workplace distress. Most included at least some form of bullying; many were predominately bullying, and all were instructive for these purposes. When the Bullies initiated an official action with legal consequences, such as employee discipline in certain settings, litigator access to the workplace became possible. Personal interviews with co-employee and other witnesses were conducted, as well as reviews of the customarily elaborate documentation. During the course of this discovery process, there was the opportunity to develop workplace appraisals, including identifying and factoring into the analysis the various cultural influences involved, be they general, occupational, and institutional.

At hearing, Bullying Bosses are subject to the rigors of cross-examination where their every known word, present and past, is matched against each other, as well as compared to the documentation and the testimony of others. Through these "tests by fire" held under compulsion, one can develop a good understanding of how

Bullies function and, to lesser extent, who they are as people. From repeated and aggressive participation in these hearings, I came to understand the various supervisory influences involved, both legitimate and honorable as well as those particularly intense few that were not.

> ...the lesson for me was that one becomes most effective when one is speaking out of one's personal experience and one's action grows out of the understanding of one's immediate personal experience.
> —*Dr. Judith Herman author of "Trauma and Recovery."*[2]

Importantly, in my professional capacity, I came to know, quite intimately, a handful of Bullies. I knew them for years as colleagues on different sides of labor-management relations, but always as adversaries. I was made a Target by some of them, over considerable periods of time with serious consequences. Currently, as "The Bullying Boss Counselor," my employee clients and I together perform system analysis (not psychoanalysis) to discover power flows and disconnects in the workplace as they relate to each relevant individual involved. From there and together, we develop a strategic plan for action. For employers, the steps of the analysis are the same, however without the personal guidance of an employee client but with enhanced access to witnesses and documents.

From these processes rooted in the hard evidence, Workplace Warriors can fairly quickly come to understand that the Bullies are not the towers of strength they pretend to be, but are instead superficial, anti-personal, and profoundly isolated individuals. As will be discussed throughout, observation teaches that the Bullies do not exactly engage in anti-social conduct for the conscious purpose of harming society, although they clearly cause it and its people harm.

If anything, they regard themselves as the protectors of society. They live their lives, and perhaps earnestly work to protect the rest of us in society without the experience of being a part of society, without connecting to the people who surround them daily, or important ones afar.

Observably, it's in the tension in their selves between vigorous protector and seemingly ignored alien, that their boasting behaviors come from, as well as their abuse behaviors from the start. Their methods are impersonal, indirect, inhumane, and yet, maybe oddly, these are the best means of communication available to them—all the while working to render their Targets isolated rather than they. For Bullying Bosses facing what is for them a forever foreign environment, Targets serve as freshly killed game ostensibly for the "tribe," and as scapegoat for them personally at the same time.

It's not with meeting the Bully or the onslaught of the bullying that Targets become Workplace Warriors. The transition from Target to Warrior comes from growing into an acceptance that the Bullies exist, and that they do so without regard to any particular employee. The bullying is not personal and it's certainly not about the latest employee chosen as Target. With the larger perspective, Workplace Warriors begin to think in the strategic terms that balance coping and resisting over time. They learn how best to build and foster political relations with people at work and outside in the community as well. From these, they gain both the inner and external strengths necessary for taking affirmative steps towards creating their own relief. This is not just about political swords and shields to fight bullying battles, it's also about the heart and soul to back them up. It's about becoming fully conscious; then working for the win, that is *life itself.*

PART ONE
THE MANY FACES OF BULLYING

1

UTTERLY ALONE

THE RING OF FIRE

Anna was on the wrong end of an ugly Bully grilling—and not for the first time. As with the others before, it didn't seem that Wayne had planned it, but it started out small and he quickly lit his words into a firestorm. Wayne surprised Anna from behind when she was staring intently down at her work papers, proofing them to beat an approaching deadline. She did not turn around. Her cubical was one of a pair of quads, roughly in the middle of a large office, with a dozen other employees working that day. Wayne wasn't yelling, but talking just loud enough for everyone to hear every tense word. He came out of nowhere and attacked Anna for issues she had nothing to do with, and seemed to be making up things as he went along. He breathed heavily down on her and stared at her with malicious intent.

"Your work is unacceptable, absolutely unacceptable." Wayne hissed bending forward at the waist. Anna remained seated, already stressed and getting more so. "Where did you go to high school?" he asked.

It seemed a rhetorical question to a woman who graduated from a two-year college program with honors. It was the purist of insults, having no facts or reasoning. Anna didn't move, certainly not to look up at him towering behind her. She pretended to continue proofing her papers, even making a few corrective marks. "Well, it's time you went back," he said. "Forget it. They can't make you any smarter than you're not."

He turned halfway around without going anywhere. He'd challenged her intelligence, a hot-button issue for her, recalling childhood. She didn't engage him, but felt the same tortured, victimized emotions that she remembered from her days contending with her abusive father. Notions of "justice" and "injustice" were prompted by each repetition of challenge. Like a stalker, Wayne just hung there, waiting for a reaction. He said nothing more, but he wouldn't leave.

This particular chastisement was unprofessional, even abusive, but subtle compared to most. As Wayne continued to stand behind her, blocking her exit, Anna felt trapped in her tiny workspace; a prisoner in a cell. "Escape" was a word suddenly important to her. A deathly pall had fallen over the entire office. Her cubicle had become her solitary confinement. And for what? Her job performance had long been documented as excellent in all areas. She felt ashamed and isolated. Was Wayne signaling that he intended to fire her? How would she meet her bills? She had two kids to consider. A sickening feeling came up in her gut.

Wayne just stood there, twisting her insides into knots. He was not touching her, but he was close enough, and it felt creepy. Anna later likened it to *"a death by a thousand cuts."*

Anna could only make out what was within three feet of space around her and her Bully. For that time, her entire universe was that small. It was getting hotter than Hades in the tight little *"Ring of Fire"* that he had created for her. It was seemingly the most intensely negative interpersonal experiences she would ever have, and he possessed all the power. He was the boss, and seemed to have the authority to behave however he pleased, and he was using his position of power to unfairly criticize her work, her integrity, and her character.

As is common with a lot of bullying cases, Wayne didn't give Anna the courtesy of telling her what her error might have been, so there was nothing she could say or do in defense. So she said nothing, keeping her back to him in uncharacteristic submission.

A minute before this occurred, she was going about her work productively, but now the action was moving very quickly without anyone moving at all. She knew from past incidents that if she happened to make a defense, he would twist and turn whatever she said against her. She wasn't going to repeat that mistake again.

Outside the walls of her cubicle, no one could see any of it, but their imaginations filled the gap. It could only be bad. Wayne's message to Anna and all of those in earshot was, "This fool's had it." She was officially ostracized, someone to avoid for the sake of office politics or suffer the consequences. She'd been successfully isolated from her coworkers, tied up inside a very tight girdle, ringed in heat, and devoid of air. The temperature just kept building.

For months, behind Anna's back Wayne had insinuated negatives about her to other employees—comments that were insulting, degrading, and dehumanizing. To her face, he'd put her "one-down" every chance he got. Her emotional responses were many but it was her profound sense of constant vulnerability that was paramount. He'd questioned her competency to be in the workforce at all.

When Wayne isolated Anna from her peers, he essentially threatened to evict her from their archetypical "village," raising the specter of her starving to death in the forest outside its gates. She seemed to be facing her own mortality. She could report and claim whatever she pleased, but she knew that no one would believe her. Not even her co-employees watching these incidents unfold could comprehend what they were hearing or seeing. They were blanked faced, stunned. It was just too much. It was no wonder she was confused, and fearful.

For most Targets like Anne, it's to be expected that their escape from their Bully will come only by leaving their jobs one way or another. That's the bad news.

WORK POLITICS IS NOT OPTIONAL

20 Million[3] or 1 in 6 Employees[4]
Affected by Workplace Bullying,
In the United States

Here's the good news: that Ring of Fire of Wayne's was artificially generated and largely illusory. It may have been of the Bully's design, but was sustainable only by Anna's reasonable, but false, sense of smallness. If Anna was going to find relief from her Bully, it would not be found inside of the little Ring of Fire in which he had once again trapped her and where he was the biggest thing going.

Relief, if it were found, would be discovered as she grew politically beyond the Ring's tight confines. She'd gather information and people around herself. She would become politically too large to ever fit back inside that small Ring again. Through strategic thinking leading to action, she could become a moving party, "working" her new and larger world. It will have become a world at least partly of her own making.

The workplace is an intensely political place. There exists a common illusion that good, hard, and productive labor will protect a good employee from all the nonsense that others, such as Bullies, may bring into it. It doesn't. It can help, it can even hurt, but there's no substitute for playing it smart. Workplace politics are not optional, but playing them well is. Employees can't change Bullies' minds or who they are as people, but they can change themselves from Target and victim into Warrior by growing beyond them. Sometimes in crisis, "wisdom comes suddenly."

ANNA'S TIPS TO TARGETS:

Engage yourself
beyond the confines of the three-foot Ring of Fire.
Enlarge your pool of supporters
and information.
Then watch as your Bully and his fury shrink.

If Targets have good enough reason to stay at their job, at least for the time being, then they need to defend their right to be there. Most days, we are accustomed to exercising our rights such as speech and love, as if they were unchallengeable entitlements, but that's illusionary. Having rights and defending them—or at least being prepared to defend them—are inseparable. Rights are not only birthed from the crucible of conflict, but that's also how they're protected. To sleep undisturbed in bed at night is certainly their right, but it's also subject to intrusion by criminals and noisy neighbors. It's a right defended by walls, doors and locks. It's a right protected by mutually convenient social customs and laws backed up by guys and gals wearing blue and carrying guns. If a cat wails into the night, eventually we'll call someone. They're not free and not to be taken for granted. Rights are edgy and that makes workplace politics edgy as well.

With Anna's current poverty of information and contacts, she could probably only see Wayne on the hateful, not altogether real, interpersonal level that he presented himself on. There was nothing personal between them. Work was supposed to be business. Clearly, the Bully had no interest in becoming Anna's friend. He sought her conquest—which is a different thing altogether. What was real was political conflict.

Bullies seek to control other people for reasons that are entirely theirs, and exploit their management given authority to do so. But they're not particularly interested in the employer's mission either. It's just the opposite, they have their own mission: to conquest and control subordinates. The good news is this: Anna may not be able to escape her Bully and his hostilities in the near term, but she can make his Ring of Fire largely dissipate by outgrowing it politically.

FRIGHTENED, FIGHT, FLIGHT

The big question always asked by Targets is: "Should I stay or leave?" This is a reasonable question, but it underestimates the circumstances. Sooner or later, everyone leaves. And, most Targets ultimately find leaving to be their only escape from their Bully. The more practical question is: "When will I leave and on what terms?" Until then, they'll fight back to the extent that they can do so gainfully. The rest of the time, they'll duck for cover and build political reserves. They'll strive to survive and maybe even thrive, but always with their eye on the exit doors.

For a lot of people, by the time a Bully intrudes into their work lives, they've already earned certain good things by virtue of their efforts and time served. Dale worked as a tax analyst the same employer for nine years. He was vested in an excellent pension plan that gave him a powerful incentive to hold on to his job. Over the years, he moved up from one office to the next, and finally landed in a good one on the fourth floor that looked out on nearby treetops.

He'd developed personal and professional relationships that were hard to sacrifice, particularly when he'd done nothing to deserve losing them.

It seemed that he and his Bully Bryan held each other in a death grip. Dale had been rudely struck by Bryan's challenges and had struck back as well as he was able to. His self-respect had been compromised, making it more difficult for him to look for work and escape. It also gave him additional impetus to fight for peace to return. In every way, it was hard for him to step to the side of that flurry and too easy to continue standing there toe-to-toe, until one of them, preferably his Bully, dropped.

For most people, the responsibilities they have on the job and at home can also keep them feeling pinned in that negative situation for too long, sometimes for a very long time. Leaving the workplace may not be an immediate option. Their bills need to be paid, their kids need to be fed. Larger career plans may require finishing a certain project, winning a critically important contract, or using their current job—as awful as it is—as a stepping stone to get the next job. As true and legitimate as all these concerns can be, they can also develop into a never-ending quandary, artificially preventing Target employees' departure when departure is the only reasonable thing to do.

Leaving would be made easier if there was the option of moving smoothly into a new job. It can be scary to jump empty-handed into an employment void, particularly when feeling weakened or damaged.

But as a matter of self-preservation, Targets must exit an abusive situation as soon as practical and possible. No matter what awaits them, at least there will still be a true sense of personal identity and integrity that they can take to their next job.[5] It may be counter-intuitive, but once departed for a time, Targets almost invariably report back that leaving was the best thing they ever did. They not only landed on their feet, but they landed better than they could ever have imagined.

If they leave on their own time, they probably will have had enough time to document the Bully's activities, as well as an opportunity to confront him or her, even if only indirectly. As they go out the door, aided by some of the specifics below, they may deliver copies of their report and compiled evidence documenting the bullying events to just the right manager and coworkers of their careful choice. Their report will have inherent credibility because of its thoughtful and professional presentation that is also then free of a personal agenda. By the time anyone reads it, the former Target will be long gone and not looking back.

Until that final day, Targets are well served to consciously adopt the roles and attitudes of Escapee and Victor in some combination—but not allow themselves to fall into martyrdom. Once employed elsewhere and standing on solid ground, they'll no longer have to be management's Best Worker, as a management offense. They'll no longer have to be a Workplace Warrior, as a Bully defense. They'll regain confidence and their self-identity as a valued contributor to a preferred company's goals, as they were meant to be.

2

SOME BULLYING VARIETIES

COURTING

With the benefit of hindsight, we know that Bullies do not normally attack a Target impulsively. On the first day they walk in the door to start a supervising job, all subordinates are equal candidates. Typically, they scan the workplace, consciously looking for their first adversary to create, take on for conflict, and then control.

Their eyes eventually land on the Target-of-choice. Maybe they notice his or her good work performance, dedication to management's program, or personal strength, and take these qualities as proper cause for their personal, political, and professional eradication. Through any other lens, these attributes are valued as unequivocally positive. But it could be something having nothing to do with work, like the sweater the Target just happened to be wearing. Bullies have gone active in response to all these things and a great many more.

It's also clear that Bullies generally take no overt action at first. They are calculating predators, not fools. They are likely to court,[6] or at least size up, the Target, and scrutinize his or her several strengths and weaknesses before actually striking. "Keep your friends close and your enemies even closer," they've been heard to say. Bullies have few or perhaps no real friends.

Having never met such an individual before, it's only when it's too late that most Targets realize they have been scanned for points of vulnerability. Seeking ever more angles on their chosen Target, and sometimes to intimidate him or her with their authoritative standing, Bullies have been known to use their influence to coax the reluctant but still unharmed Target to join them for a meal, drink, or special meeting. Bullies communicate with others indirectly and impersonally, in this case through courting rituals rather than by either personal connection or businesslike conversation.

It's possible a Target may notice their Bully manipulating others, and so they may become aware that they, too, are being manipulated. Quite often, when looking back Targets remember "feeling" that something uncomfortable but unidentified was wrong. It seems that most, wisely avoid getting sucked into a Bully's predatory promises, praises, or ever-so-subtle, but pointed, threats—instead taking each as warning signs. For Targets, keeping their job just got a whole lot tougher.

MAKING PATTERNS

Bullying harassments are virtually never singular events. They're cumulative. In all workplaces, there are difficulties and problems. An outsider hearing about a single bullying incident would probably assume it was a case of either work or interpersonal problems, like any other when, in fact, these incidents are artificially generated and aggravated by Bullies.

The proof of bullying can generally only be found by examining the patterns of their behaviors. By viewing all the little incidents in conjunction with the larger ones, patterns emerge demonstrating a "course and conduct" of bullying. This is why it is very important for Workplace Warriors to create and collect documentation for each bullying episode. It may at first seem like it will be emotionally painful to sit down to write up an incident, to relive its anguishing details.

Actually, the exercise of writing has proven able to clear away the confusion and soothe the pain. For as long the emotional reactions to prior incident, no matter how reasonable, are allowed to run loose in memory, the confusion will remain. The pieces will never quite fit together.

Sweat the small stuff. It is often the smallest incidents that become the most important, illustrating a pattern of bullying that might not otherwise be apparent. Later, there'll be suggestions for documenting events as painlessly and productively as possible, like jotting small notes on incident cards instead of writing elaborate journal entries. There will be suggestions for working with those documents and others to create the clarity Workplace Warriors need for themselves and to maximize their ability to communicate with others, such as with their partner, selected coworkers, and even some select managers, as well as outside professionals such as attorneys, unions, and community groups.

ANTI-SOCIAL ACTS

There can be no definitive list of harassments. Bullying can come in many forms. A certain behavior might be bullying in one setting, and not in another. Workplace Warriors take the broad view. For each Bully, in some way, all the incidents being suffered are related to each other. It's just a matter of defining each bullying event in a standardized way. Simplicity and consistency are the keys to making patterns apparent.

Targets' starting place is to identify each abusive incident by its broad type as it is occurring, to be written down later. From there, it will be obvious which bullying types and circumstances their particular Bully favors generally, as well as those he or she favors specifically with them as Targets and notable others. From the regularity of Bullying Boss patterns, Workplace Warriors are better able to place themselves within workplace events and so more consciously function both defensively and offensively.

Just as importantly, the patterns as documented make it apparent to others that the employee faces not merely a couple, odd personal conflicts with a superior that can easily be dismissed. Instead, they make it obvious that he or she faces a campaign conducted over time, by the Bully as an aggressor, who engages in quantifiable, anti-social behaviors of specific types. With this clarity, the challenges of others questioning a Target's emotional disposition become irrelevant. The focus shifts from Target, to his or her documentation, to wrongdoer. As proof of the patterns layer upon each other, the Target's complaint becomes increasing hard for anyone to ignore. If the documented patterns include incidences of the Bully deviating from the employer's mission in other ways besides bullying, the indictment becomes all the stronger.

There are three general types of harassment charted below: isolating acts, official acts, and twisting acts. Each constitutes an anti-social behavior and they work in a cumulative fashion. Unfortunately, before a Target realizes that they should be plotting the Bully's patterns, there will already have been several incidents.

ISOLATING ACTS	
Creating a climate of fear	Campaigning against
Isolating	Gossiping negatively about
Ignoring	Spreading disparagement
Icing out	Spreading rumors about
Excluding	Sexuality smearing
Excommunicating	Scapegoating
Taunting	Demonizing
Teasing with hostility	Treating rudely
Humiliating	Glaring at
Degrading	Grimacing at
Compromising confidences	Vexing & Annoying

First, there were the isolating activities that Bully Vickie used against Target Karen. Vickie didn't really think about any of it; going after someone personally was second nature to her. She'd done it many times before. What she was doing had a dual purpose, but she didn't really think about that either. Kyle, Joyce and Paul were her immediate audience, an employee group that Karen belonged to at work. Vickie sought to separate Karen from them, and maybe even win their respect or admiration for herself. She did think about that. By the singular act of targeting Karen, she marked Karen as separate from the others.

By challenging her both professionally and personally, she also destroyed, to an increasing degree, Karen's reputation and thus furthered her separation from her group. At the same time, Vickie caused Karen to experience self-doubts, creating an internal split between Karen's true self and the one the Bully presumed her to be.

These activities alone might have driven Karen to quit or, much less likely, submit to Vickie. But Karen remained. Nevertheless, Vickie had laid the foundation for more expansive undertakings. If Vickie decided to take an official, supervisory action such as dismissing her, Karen would have already been isolated, besmirched and weakened, making her easier to take down. Karen would get no support from Kyle, Joyce, or Paul. There would be no lingering hard feelings for Vickie to deal with after Karen's demise. It was "divide and conquer," with the Target divided away from her fellow employees.

OFFICIAL ACTS	
Downgrading	Negative performance reports
Reducing	Selective rule enforcement
Removing	Bumping
Displacing	Adverse action
Changing or denying an office	Disciplining
Changing role or assignment	Retiring

Vickie's second type of harassment was an act utilizing her position of authority as the supervisor. She took off her leather gloves to put on her official supervisor's hat. Vickie's intention was to make the executive decision to discipline, downgrade, or dismiss the Target Karen.

She chose demotion and drew up the papers accordingly, complete with fabricated charges of gross insubordination, alleging that Karen "talked back" during their last three encounters. Despite being false, the formality of charges for the first time brought some definition to the struggle, and that was good, but it also pushed Karen further on the defensive. Through formal charges, Vickie had in yet another way communicated indirectly and impersonally with her staff as well as her fellow supervisors and managers.

As expected, when they heard about Vickie demoting Karen, Vickie automatically garnered the managers' and other supervisors' support. They didn't have to know what was really going on, and far as they could tell, Vickie was simply doing her job as a supervisor. They expected the same support from Vickie when they disciplined their subordinates. In their minds, the official nature of the act was enough to prove that Karen was a bad employee as well as a bad person.

Beginning with isolating acts, Vickie isolated Karen from her peers. With her official act of demotion, she furthered Karen's isolation from her peers as well as away from the other supervisors, and the manager. At this point, Karen was alone. Effectively, she was no longer a person, no longer someone to treat with dignity.

TWISTING ACTS	
Micromanaging	Unrealistic work demands
Providing false information	Excessive work not reassigned
Withholding critical information	Stress used to push performance
Withholding critical resources	Testing loyalties
Withholding credit	Stalking
Toying with raises, bonuses	Black Balling
Toying with vacation requests	

By now, Karen was in a greatly weakened state, and Vickie took advantage of it. Her third type of harassment was twisting acts. She tore up Karen's emotions in ways so odd they were incomprehensible to Karen, and everyone else as well.

To Karen, it seemed like everything was crashing in on her. Even her connection to the outside world was getting seriously compromised, and her larger notions of how the world was supposed to work had been thrown into chaos. At work and outside, people and places were taking on appearances foreign to her. Karen was losing her good humor. Targets can't let this happen to them. No matter what predisposition or vulnerabilities an employee may or may not have to be targeted, it's the Bully who goes about the business of separating and negating employees from their fellow human beings.

SOME BULLY TYPES

Subtle Bullies, like Vickie, can be the most emotionally cutting and devastating Bullies. On some mornings, Karen wondered how Vickie could just breeze right past her in the hallway without exchanging a look, much less a courtesy. Once, Karen was at a large meeting where neither of them had much of a role, but from across the table, she could see Vickie glaring at her, Vickie's eyes slightly crossed as if she had Karen in her crosshairs.

Women bosses are generally respected as being more accomplished at subtle bullying and men Targets more immune. Among Bullies, Subtle Bullies are known to be the masters of understatement, cutting to the quick with just the right glance or toss of hair that all can see, signaling that the Target has been ostracized. In an open meeting, a Subtle Bully may simply but poignantly disregard what the Target says, as if he or she wasn't in the room—or even turn his or her back on their Target, becoming both an authoritative and a physical barrier separating a Target from the others. Subtle Bullies are quiet and curt.

Subtle Bullies make biting comments and criticisms about petty work issues and personal appearances. A Subtle Bully might negate a Target's work role by cluttering this employee's to-do list with pieces of disconnected junk or redefining his or her position vaguely as "special projects." The Bully might go so far as to send a Target on personal and obviously petty errands, with parting comments suggesting that it's all he or she is good for.

Abusive Bullies, like Rodger, are employees with supervisory authority who tend to hound a Target employee without mercy. They get too close physically, with or without significant drama. If they are of the cruder sort, they may appear more deranged to some, and less so to others. *Crude Bullies* may demonstrate their agitation with louder than normal voices and animated gestures, such as waving their arms. The occasional expletive or expectorant might get thrown into the mix. Their particular bullying may be episodic, followed by an apology the next day. Remarkably, employees are quick to forgive Abusive Bosses and sometimes construct excuses for them, but nothing can change their wrongfulness.

Raging Bullies, like Rodger once again, are Abusive Bullies who act out with particularly great and loud drama. They tend to intimidate everyone in the vicinity, not just the Target. Rodger would yell when other people talked. With some hard foot stomping against the floor, he could make the whole place thunder around him, controlling others through his demonstrations of self-grandeur. If their Targets are lucky, Raging Bullies will contain their rage while at work and save their thunder for the home. Even if Raging Bullies contains it, throughout the day, they will frighten employees as they stand or sit steaming with an angry face and taut body.

Echo Bullies, like Ruth, appear to be normally balanced and mature individuals who come to report to a Bully, then mimic those bullying activities in their relations with their own subordinates. They are just a guilty as any other Bully, but they have the capacity to return to normally appropriate social behaviors when their work assignments eventually separate them from their own Bully, and perhaps away from the extraordinary institutional pressures that may have accompanied that Bully. There are many ways supervisors respond to manager Bullies, but, by definition, only Bullies respond by bullying others.

Ghost Bullies, like Mark, are institutional operatives, perhaps from headquarters or the parent company. They remain at arm's length from their Targets, guiding, supervising, and mentoring lower level and local bosses in bullying techniques and tactics. Ghost Bullies are stalkers.

Satellite Bullies, like Eleanor, are individuals of stature in the workplace, industry, or community. They may be unwitting participants in someone else's bullying but they are Bullies themselves. A primary Bully, maybe also a Ghost Bully, and can double his or her bullying effectiveness by motivating a bystander to bully the same Target. The primary Bully takes only a second or two to prod an issue of special sensitivity for a particular Satellite Bully, in Eleanor's case that meant men who abandon their children. Thereafter, Eleanor took every opportunity she could to undermine the Target within the professional group that she and the Target were both members. She functioned independently, but effectively.

SCAPEGOATING

Sometimes what generates or flavors bullying activities is an ancient drama called "scapegoating." Scapegoating has a powerful capacity to fuel the Ring of Fire, giving it a particularly malodorous quality that is inappropriate in a contemporary and mature society. It's normal for workplaces, employers and employees, to have problems with or without Bullies being present. In scapegoating, the Bully channels that collective angst against a single human being, the scapegoat, thus relieving general unease at the expense of a sacrificial person.

> **Scapegoat:** 1 a goat over the head of which the high priest of the ancient Jews confessed the sins of the people on the Day of Atonement, after which it was allowed to escape: Lev. 16: 7-26...
> 2) a person, group, or thing upon whom the blame for the mistakes or crimes of others is thrust
> —*Webster's New World Dictionary (Third Edition 1988). Simon & Schuster.*

When a Workplace Warrior reaches out to talk to people at work and outside, and maybe push the search engines a bit, he or she may discover that the employer, department, or Bully is being challenged by competitors, creditors, regulators, politicians, litigators, suppliers, customers and clients. In the absence of leadership, a lot of loose angst is generated in this mix that has to do something or go somewhere.

The Bully might also scapegoat a Target to channel away supervisory angst connected to his unit's work. The big boss, Raymond, had a perfectly legitimate problem with the quality of work in Bully Wayne's unit. Raymond properly put some heat on Wayne. In turn, Wayne improperly deflected it downward onto Anna when he publicly claimed that she made an allegedly serious error. Sometime later, after he'd thoroughly hammered Anna for her imagined transgression in front of the angst-ridden group, Wayne proudly reported back to the big boss Raymond that, by challenging Anna, he'd done his job of straightening out the problem. He also made everyone feel better.

That time, the buck stopped with Anna, but it could have hit her Bully also. An employer's command culture may even use scapegoating as a substitute for leadership just as it might sometimes use guilt-tripping. And there were times when big boss Raymond would exploit *odd-man-out* Wayne as his own scapegoat to vent his own angst. When management made Wayne its scapegoat, Wayne made Anna his.

A Bully might also scapegoat a Target to channel away his angst over his own performance problems. On an every day basis, Bully Wayne felt the workplace challenge that he imagined was caused by his high-producing subordinate, Anna. There were days when Wayne thought management would discover the fraud he generally was and knew himself to be. Anna was his Target, and so she was also his scapegoat.

On a Wednesday afternoon, manager Raymond casually commented that he liked what Anna did on her last assignment. The manager didn't mean much by it, except as a light compliment to Wayne as the responsible supervisor. Instead, Wayne interpreted Raymond's praise for Anna as a threat to his job, and took it as an urgent warning signal. He imagined that his fellow supervisors also interpreted it that way. In his mind, Anna had put him "one down" in front of all of them, and she wasn't even in the room.

As scapegoats go, Anna was a "the tall tree that catches the wind," and so seemingly had to be cut down to a more manageable size. When Wayne returned to Anna's work area that afternoon, he verbally lashed out at her on a series of issues. Once he'd scapegoated her, he felt more secure in the world for having done so.

It's not always the tall trees that get targeted as scapegoats. Sometimes, less often, a Bully needs a quick and easy kill to make a political point to others. For such purposes, any easy conquest works. That might mean picking on someone who is already isolated and inherently meek. The isolated employee has no platform from which to fight back, and the meek employee won't fight regardless. Brenda was a meek employee and so was an easy Target for that one difficult day when Wayne came back from a management meeting, feeling threatened and fuming about a ding to his pride rather than something actually related to the work. Through his scapegoating activity, Wayne's message-of-the-day was proclaimed to everyone— he confirmed his authority and power over his realm.

When the scapegoated Targets Anna and Brenda walked out the door that night, Wayne had effectively set it up so that they were taking the workplace's political garbage out with them. It was all Anna's fault, or it was all Brenda's fault: Anna was compromising quality, Brenda was a low producer. Brenda was the one that weakened their competitive position.

Bullies also scapegoat employees to offload problems from their outside lives. Bully Wayne's wife got angry with him at breakfast regarding his failure to make intimate connection with her. He said little, but steamed. Once at work, Wayne went after Anna about a late report that was delayed by circumstances beyond anybody's control. By the time he was done with his tirade, he'd demonstrated his double disconnect from women, both his wife and Anna. Importantly, by challenging Anna for reason entirely his, he'd also demonstrated his third disconnect—from his employer.

Anna's coworkers did not come to her aid. By remaining silent, they actually became involved, serving as the Bully's audience rather than the Target's witnesses. But Anna didn't sweat fools lightly. Even while under fire, she was making mental notes of each person's particular reaction. When she got home, she added her new data to the file she had already started, then broke down all the work-related elements of people, places, and things into their component parts on her note cards.

By accurately objectifying these varied factors, Anna deprived the negative elements, such as her Bully, their emotional power. That left the positive elements, such as her potential allies, visible for discovery and attention. Throughout the time she was being bullied and after, Anna was looking for tactical allies, workplace intelligence, patterns, and advantages.

DEMONIZING

Demonization is far more insidious than scapegoating. Although in both cases an individual is targeted for essentially political purposes, scapegoating is not necessarily premeditated, while demonization is.

In scapegoating, there's a preexisting angst that needs attention, and that angst is concentrated on a sacrificial individual (race, nationality, sex, sexual preference, occupation, etc.). In demonization, an individual is targeted specifically. Any existing angst there might be is secondary, and if there is none, some will be generated.

Scapegoating is mainly about somebody processing a negative emotion. Demonization is about somebody targeting a somebody. A Bully is certain to scapegoat employees *generally*, but demonize a Target *specifically*. Through scapegoating and demonizing, Bullies communicate with employees in yet another way that's indirect and impersonal.

Demonization is standard fare when the leadership of a large country seeks to invade another country, especially when lacking the support needed for military action. To the public, invasions are rude and offensive, even if sometimes seen as a necessary evil. Invasions are frequently regarded as bullying on an international level. The Target leader is sometimes falsely, or at least unfairly, painted as threatening to the people of the larger country, and possibly to humanity as well. The charges made against that leader will be structured artificially to shock the audience: He or she may be painted as a corrupt and unsavory politician, the leader of a drug cartel, or serious human rights violator. Most people are reluctant to partake in destroying human beings but they are more inclined to bully or destroy a demon.

When demonized, a Target's usual knee-jerk response is to challenge it head-on, publicly discounting everything the Bully has said as baseless and without merit. That may be the most obvious way to solve the problem, but it isn't generally an effective one. There's a structural problem to consider.

In most cases, biases start against the employee, as well as with anyone who has been charged, particularly employees of lower rank. With each defense the Target makes, he or she sounds all the more guilty. The greater the piety employed, the greater the presumed guilt. To worsen further matters, each time he or she defends against a specific allegation, it's necessarily repeated in the process. The same negative message thus gets broadcast twice, then thrice, and then many more times thereafter.

Experience teaches that both scapegoating and demonization are hard to beat. But just because a Bully places these tactics front and center in his or her campaign, does not mean they have to be in the middle of the Workplace Warrior's. Yes, the demonizing is probably the personal violation that hurts the most but as the Warrior's plan develops, there will appear several issues and fronts that are, as a practical matter, more powerful in their impact, and more defensible as well. Warriors choose for themselves what issues to fight for, fronts to approach through, and timings to move with. Instead of heightening the negative impact of scapegoating and demonization through protests about injustice that go nowhere, one can take to the high ground to take advantage of its big picture perspective.

This doesn't mean the Workplace Warriors or anyone else forget what's happened. These things still get factored into their strategic plan, including the positive and negative aspects of each element. But it is winning, or least surviving gainfully that matters. The victors write history. By winning, if that's the outcome, the Workplace Warrior will have cleared him or herself of all charges.

3

DEFINITIONS AND DESCRIPTIONS

SOME STATISTICS

Although women are as likely to bully in the workplace as men, Bullies of both sexes are significantly more likely to target women than men. Bullies and their Targets may be of the same sex and same sexual orientation. Sexual harasser bosses are also Bullies. Indeed, there seems to be a not yet quantified sexual undercurrent running through all workplace bullying.

SOME STATISTICS:

84% of Targets are Women.
82% of Targets Ultimately Lost Their Jobs.
81% of Bullies are Managers.
50% of Bullies are Women & 50% Men.
98% of Bullying is Witnessed.
—*Drs. Gary & Ruth Namie.*[7]

SEVERAL BULLYING DEFINITIONS

There are a great many definitions of a Bullying Boss and workplace abuse depending on the country and professional setting.[8] Each country that has adopted protective legislation (i.e. Australia, France, Norway, Quebec (Canada) and United Kingdom[9]) has a different legal structure and definition. In some countries, the terms *bullying* and *mobbing* are synonymous. *Mobbing* is better reserved for those circumstances when several co-employees abuse an employee, often at a Bully's instigation.

Within the psychoanalytic framework, workplace abuse is inferentially defined in terms of the behaviors, the apparent intentions behind the behaviors and trauma it causes, and for which therapeutic intervention is appropriate. These trauma symptoms include depression, anxiety, disassociation and others that will be discussed.[10] They are the same symptoms associated with domestic violence as well as for Post Traumatic Stress Disorder (PTSD).

In traditional legal analysis, workplace bullying may rise to the level of a tort, giving an abused individual a cause of action in a civil lawsuit for intentional infliction of emotional distress or, more modernly, an occupational workers' compensation claim. Within the framework of modern anti-discrimination laws, sexual, racial, and other forms of illegal harassment have differing and sometimes complicated definitions, but they can be instructive in understanding workplace bullying more generally. As in the psychiatric context, the courts look to the intention behind the harassment and not just the trauma and other damages resulting from it. Courts are powerful places that respect only powerful cases. In the particular area of sexual harassment lawsuits, courts require that the harassment be "severe or persuasive."

In one appellate court case, two art students, Jeremy Ringermacher and Ariel Rosenberg, of CalArts, posted a drawing depicting an 82-year-old female administrative employee, Mary Herberg, in a vulgar and sexually explicit way. Their drawing attracted attention from the student body, caused controversy, and generated artistic and political debate. The drawing was taken down within twenty-four hours. Ms. Herberg sued for sexual harassment. The appellate court held that, "Although doubtless upsetting, it was not severe or pervasive harassment." The court pointed out that a single incident could not be considered sexual harassment unless it was accompanied by egregious conduct, such as a physical assault or threat of one.[11]

In another case, a different appellate court found there was illegal sexual harassment at a major hotel, MGM Grand, because the harassment was severe or pervasive. An openly gay male employee, Medina Rene, was repeatedly taunted by his gay co-employees who called him "sweetheart," subjected him to crude jokes, gave him sexually explicit gifts, showed him pictures of men having sex, caressed and hugged him, grabbed his crotch, and finger poked his anus through his clothing.[12] Theses circumstances were extreme by any standards.

In more generalized workplace bullying, the motives, the particulars of the offending behaviors and the degree of harmfulness are all irrelevant to its definition. It's enough the abuse occurred. As Anna learned, *a death by a thousand cuts* is a death just the same.

In the traditional labor-management framework, workplace bullying is seen as an occupational health and safety issue with a very different focus: prevention. In this context, contemporary definitions of workplace violence include both physical abuse and often more damaging psychological abuse. "Violence at Work," published in 1998 by the International Labor Organization (ILO) of the United Nations, originally defined bullying, as perhaps most people originally do, as including both behavioral and intent elements: "offensive behavior through vindictive, cruel, malicious or humiliating attempts to undermine an individual or group of employees."[13] Later, the ILO adopted the European Commission definition re-casting workplace violence in essentially behavioral terms: "incidents where persons are abused, threatened or assaulted in circumstances related to their work, involving an explicit or implicit challenge to their safety, well-being or health."[14]

On February 2, 1996, in keeping with evolving, international definitions for workplace violence, the U.S. Department of Labor's, Occupational Safety and Health Agency (OSHA) floated, but later abandoned, a proposed regulation that would have required employers to report incidents of workplace violence. Importantly, OSHA's proposed definition of workplace violence included all acts causing either physical or psychological illness or injury, "regardless of fault or preventability."[15]

A BUSINESSLIKE DEFINITION

To facilitate managerial efforts to remedy bullying in their workplace, prospectively, a business definition is called for. It must be narrowly crafted in operational terms rather than in the external constructs of law, psychoanalysis or medicine. For these purposes, a Bully is an employee with supervisory authority who deviates from the legitimate employer's mission, with behaviors having the appearance of pursuing an independent mission (a campaign; repeated events) to secure power or control over a subordinate employee by means regarded by general community standards as anti-social.

A BULLYING BOSS:

» Deviates from the employer's designated mission,

» Seemingly to pursue his/her own mission for power or control

» Over a subordinate employee

» With behaviors regarded in the general community as anti-social.

The focus of the businesslike definition is on quantifiable behaviors and not motivations, malice, or harm. It leaves room for a great deal of political, psychological and other relevant analysis, but, ultimately, a workplace Bully is a renegade supervisor who engages in anti-social behaviors, compromises human resources, adds zero value to the operation, and causes the employer calculable and considerable costs. If the current numbers in circulation are even close to right, there are a great many bullies out there masquerading as management's charming chums while pulling down their bottom lines.

Functionally, this definition addresses the matter as an occupational health and safety issue within the traditional labor-management framework. It points to the creation of workplace policies and cultures with zero tolerance for both physical and psychological violence. It is never businesslike or legitimate for anyone to use the largeness of institutional authority to bully, harm, or hound a smaller, politically weaker subordinate employee. If there are genuine problems with subordinate employees, and there frequently are, there exist legitimate procedures that, unlike independent bullying, include consideration of the employer's interests.

This businesslike approach examines the alleged Bully's adherence to, and deviation from, the employer's mission and rules of conduct through bullying and in other respects as well. By its attention to business values and being based on behaviors, it offers language that managers can work with when faced with a bullying circumstance that can seem baffling when narrowly observed as an independent, interpersonal incident. Being businesslike, it suggests that Workplace Warriors employees shift their deliberations forward from pained, personalized analysis and pleas for justice to more businesslike and hopeful strategy-making.

TO UNDERSTAND BULLYING, FACTOR OUT THE TARGET

The first clue that these disturbances are not interpersonal disputes is that they make no sense on their own. On the contrary, they confound. But they do make sense when the scope of inquiry is enlarged to include the political dynamic within which the Bully is functioning. When it's examined as a whole, a quite different, non personal, bullying-reality emerges.

To aid the analysis, it helps to factor out Target employees altogether. The bullying is not in the least about them, except as victims. They're not really involved as precipitating elements. (More on this later.) From an institutional perspective, Bullies choose their Targets essentially at random. If it hadn't been today's Target, it would have been someone else. The same was true of the Target before and will be true for the one to come after. [16] Targets are so irrelevant to the syndrome that when they remove themselves from the workplace by quitting, taking their supposed psychological difficulties with them, the bullying continues.

It's probably most illuminating for business purposes, and ultimately it's most productive, to define bullying as a social type, as opposed to personality types that tend towards the enigmatic. Bullying is not a single and maybe passing aberration of an individual, it's a way of being; a lifestyle. Generally, lifestyle behaviors can be defined in clear terms, are similar to those of others of an identifiable group and tend to be immutable, at least in the near term. Contemporarily, and depending on any given lifestyle's impact on operations, most employee lifestyles are ignored or accommodated, but some can't be and their adherents are necessarily removed.

Accommodation is generally made for new mothers who understandably tend to get distracted for a time, as well for recently retired members of the United States Marine Corp. with their "ram rod" style of doing things and relating to people. Employees with lifestyles defined by unrelenting drug or alcohol problems are often removed, as are those who have outside interests or second jobs compromising their performance.

From a non-bullying perspective, the bullying one is not much of a lifestyle but it is theirs and, to hear them, they are adamantly proud of it, just as other people are proud of their own. Members of most any lifestyle group communicate (indirectly and impersonally) his or her group-based identity to the world, establishing, "I have an identity," "I exist," and, "I am important." While virtually all do this benignly, through coordinated clothing choices or owning a particular car or boat, Bullies communicate theirs through abuse behaviors.

As a lifestyle, bullying is not about any particular incident or event. It's a lifelong dedication. It's a programmatic vendetta flavored by personal malice. And it's not limited to just a certain someone, but reaches out against an entire class of people that Bullies regard as their inferiors–people lacking their entitlements, particularly those that seem threateningly close to impinging on their sense of supremacy over their lessers. A lifestyle of bullying employee human beings requires removal.

IT'S NOT ABOUT DEGREE, IT'S ABOUT TYPE

The best test for judging a Bully is not one of guilt or innocence associated with any particular behavior. That test would render merely bad, tough and rough bosses indistinguishable from the Bullies. The difference between these others and a Bully and is not one of degree but of a particular type.

For these immediate purposes, it doesn't matter so much how high a certain supervisor raised his or her voice on Thursday. These other, non-bullying supervisors might be known to wrongfully raise their voices in frustration or anger, but they tend to be motivated by a concern to fulfill their organizational duties in pursuit of a legitimate business end. Any one of these others may very well be deserving of some combination of affirmative and negative remedial actions. But by definition, if they have the capacity to connect with others earnestly, to learn lessons and grow from them, they are not Bullies. These others, the Rough Bosses, are criticized. Bullies are pathologized. What these others do may be bad, but what they do is not "about them," it's about the work itself.

Bullies are most easily distinguished from the others by their focus: "It's all about them." They might charm, curry favor or connive others, and they might criticize wrongfully, challenge personally, and charge at Targets politically, but they do not *connect* with others. By this workplace definition, they do not have the capacity to feel others, much less feel concern for their well being. They squash where others would lead. They humiliate where leaders would use their basic capacity for empathy to hear employees, comprehend their difficulties with compassion, and then devise an appropriate solution benefiting the employer they're both responsible to.

> impersonal: …2a. Showing no emotion or personality: an aloof, impersonal manner. b. Having no personal reference or connection: an impersonal remark. c. Not responsive to or expressive of human personalities: a large, impersonal corporation.
>
> connection: 1a. The act of connecting. b. The state of being connected. 2. One that connects; a link: made a connection between the two pipes. 3. There appeared to be no connection between the two crimes.
> —*American Heritage' Dictionary of the English Language: Fourth Edition. 2000.*

Being impersonal Bullying Bosses can be observed communicating only indirectly through the languages of rules and hierarchy; displays of status symbols and Targets as trophies; as well as by issuing charges and Fatwa's against employees when others with supervisory responsibilities would stop, look, and listen. They affect status instead of sharing a sincere handshake. They issue citations at others rather than converse with give and take. Bullies are unrelentingly not personal people.

Bullies are not particularly interested in business solutions. (More on this.) They prefer artificially generated conflicts as platforms to beat down, isolate, and ultimately, if successful, secure domination over a subjugated person. That is the short form test. What Bullies do is always "all about them."

CHAPTER

4

INSTITUTIONALIZED BULLYING

INSTITUTIONAL BULLYING

All workplace bullying is institutionalized abuse. Bullies' degradations are not an exercise of their personal power, intelligence or wisdom, if any, but rather an exercise of positional power given to them by management, and funded by the institution that employs them. Without at least the tacit support of the managers, a Bully couldn't function as one. They exploit official authority, procedures, and resources to indirectly and impersonally communicate with managers, employees and others through institutional channels. All these belong to management, making the managers responsible for their use and misuse. Managers have an outstanding duty of inquiry.

Employees are accountable to their supervisors, and CEO's are accountable to their boards and shareholders, but somehow in the mix, when it comes to personnel matters, supervisors are usually and largely left unaccountable. Managers frequently excuse themselves from checking on their subordinate supervisors, saying they don't want to invade their turf and undermine authority. In actuality, those managers are precisely paid to perform the duty of supervising the supervisors they're responsible for. However, because managers often place themselves in opposition to employees and have other, seemingly higher-level problems, they write off this particular managerial duty as pointless. When it comes to dealing with employees as employees, Bullies function in a large, organizationally blind area where they're not only free to do as they please, they please to do harm.

Managers are scared to death to face a gathering of employees, afraid to end up on the wrong end of something that looks like a quasi-union meeting complete with its demands for better wages and working conditions—and in the case of Targets, for harassment-free working conditions. Yet, these same managers regularly face scrutiny by their peers and superiors at gatherings of fellow managers. Their CEO has to face his or her board, the stockholders, the financiers, and the press, and these can sometimes be brutal. The only real difference for managers in facing lower ranking employees is their perceived lack of worthiness.

OFFICIOUS BULLYING

Bullying activities may or may not be recognized by the managers as occurring in their workplaces, but they're not invisible. If Bullies fail to drive an employee away unofficially through direct abuse, they'll exploit official disciplinary procedures and organizational resources. In union, civil service, arbitration, and court settings, these disciplinary proceedings can be elaborate and expensive. They generate a formal record with transcripts and exhibits documenting bullying.

That record, if reviewed, demonstrates that Bullies are manipulating managers to their own ends. The record sits right in front of the managers, and they see it there, but instead of reviewing it and then confronting the Bully about it, they hire big gun lawyers to make what was already a bad, Bullying-Boss workplace situation, into a permanent, institutionally-endorsed course of action. More political conflicts leading to legal conflicts will follow and the managers don't mind. If no action or responsibility is taken, then no risk has been taken, and likely no harm will come to managers personally or professionally.

Their attorneys don't mind either. They get paid hefty hourly fees to inflate the Bully's charges against Targeted employees. A Human Resources manager would get rolled over flat if he or she did his or her duty to the institution by standing against abuse—in opposition to the managerial and attorney forces. There'll be more discussion about the attorneys and Human Resources later. Of course, the managers have an "out," and it rings in their special sense of morality, which is derived from their generalized presumption of guilt for employees they don't really know.

In a particular Targets' case, that presumption is artificially aggravated by the Bully's smear campaign, a campaign conducted in measured doses over a period of months or years. Demonization is central to bullying. In doing case work, it becomes obvious that when many, if not most managers see the immediate errors in what their Bully is doing to a Targeted employee, they ignore what they see.

Ms. Smothers was a high-ranking management representative with full-time responsibilities reviewing disciplines and discharges of large numbers of employees in evidentiary hearings. Exactly 100 percent of the time, she found against the employee. When confronted with the logical absurdity that every single employee charged could be guilty exactly as charged and without any mitigating factors present—her response was, "If they're not guilty as charged, then they're at least guilty of *drawing attention to themselves* and, for that, deserve what they got." Ms. Smothers was an unapologetic Bully. By financing her malfeasance, her employer financed a counterproductive program of officiously-styled, institutionalized bullying against its most precious resource, its employees.

SCIENTIFIC BULLYING

Carrying other forms of institutionalized bullying to their logical conclusion are those rare employers who have rationalized otherwise amateur bullying processes. Just as companies in the 1930's used psychoanalytic tools to revolutionize advertising by appealing to consumers' subconscious, these modern companies use psychological tools to make Targets' employment painful down into their subconscious. They standardize bullying to make it, in their minds, the most reliable and efficient means available for ejecting employees as targeted individuals, representatives of disfavored work groups or disfavored demographics.

Bullying is likely a basic business practice in their core operations, and thus becomes a part of their internal, employment practices also. These ruthless employers accomplish their malevolent goals without dismissal proceedings, severance agreements, litigation, or significant-to-them complaints of unfairness from either departing or surviving co-employees. By striking Targets far below the emotional belt, they callously induce Targets to quit. What cost there is—and it is considerable—is born entirely by the Target.

Rather than dismissing Scientific Bullies as the anti-social anomalies they are, it's helpful to examine their extremist protocols to gain a parallel perspective on traditional bullying. They've taken the time, spent the money, and acquired the experience to perfect workplace bullying. They feel no shame and are not the least bit embarrassed. On the contrary, they imagine their activities place them above individuals more backward, less scientific than they.

For these purposes, they are. By reviewing their protocols, it's possible to develop a wider and more objective understanding of Bully Bosses that is not readily apparent from the anecdotal study of amateur cases alone.

As typical in Scientific Bullying, this composite of cases began with headquarters sending a scout, like Mark, as an organizational operative into a workplace. However, Mark was not there to take a supervisory post. He visited only intermittently, staying in the background and operating as a Ghost Bully. In traditional bullying, these elements are reversed: management sends in what it thinks is a supervisor but is actually an active Bully.

Once on location, Mark remained aloof while making evaluations of the individuals he found there. He smartly ducked responsibility for his actions by staying a good long step away from the scene, controlling events through others like a puppeteer. He took care not to leave "footprints" that might later prove his anti-social and possibly unlawful behaviors. Amateur Bullies don't have this luxury. Working in close quarters with non-bullying peers and subordinates daily, they leave "footprints" with each step of every campaign.

Mark's assignment was to identify employees as potential Targets. He was confident that he would never become a Target himself. Mark and his colleagues were organizationally guaranteed safety from their own kind, so they could do their nasty work with impunity and efficiency. In traditional bullying, management's choice not to get involved addressing bullying activities effectively affords the amateur Bully that same, institutionalized immunity for their wrongdoings.

As a scout, Mark's job was to report back to headquarters using the employer's standardized profiles for each relevant employee, including Lori. Of course, Mark tainted each profile to achieve his preferred outcome. As it happened, and despite scientific pretensions, Mark despised Lori. He never met her. He never even spoke to her, but he thought she dressed a bit too sharply. He felt challenged by the status statement he saw in her clothes and the competent and confident way she carried herself.

In traditional bullying, there are no scientific pretensions: a perceived challenge to the Bully's status or control is all that is required. While in the traditional, bullying is necessarily a deviation from the employer's mission, in the Scientific version, it is central. In neither form of bullying do the responsible managers check their subordinate's appraisals or activities.

The profile Mark chose for each employee automatically begat a pre-established protocol at headquarters. Headquarters instructed Mark (this is a Bully quote) "to torture Lori out." A profile for "competence" begat a protocol for "torture." Torture would create trauma for Lori, and it's the experience of trauma that would eventually drive her painfully out the door. To those supposed Scientists, cold and limited to the superficial by disposition, and to no other human being, it was all very sensible. The institutionalized profiling/protocol procedure of Scientific Bullying tracks the traditional bullying's courting routine.

In the Scientific, a declared intent to "torture" triggers a sequence of events, while in the traditional its import is limited to a boast. The thrust of both Scientific and traditional bullying is to isolate the Target, but the Scientific isolates with razor sharp execution while the amateur wields a blunt instrument. Because Scientist Mark worked from a silent distance, Lori never saw the bullying coming, but she probably wouldn't have seen a traditional Bully coming either. Even for Targets, both bullying types are hidden from view behind the seeming impossibility of their existence.

For Lori, the Scientific Bullying started with a cold shoulder from each of the mostly new, supervisors and manager. It was so absolute and icy that it was as if Lori didn't exist at all. She could look down and with her hands feel the human warmth of her body, but stony stares said otherwise. She felt as if she had received their formal, bureaucratic version of last rites. She was all but dead. In contrast, amateur Bullies revel in the negative exchange. That's where they can give their malice the exercise it needs. Lori soon received a written notice of her transfer to her employer's version of Siberia, an outlying office with a bad reputation for being dirty and dangerous. Her commute times had been artificially increased to health-compromising ends.

With the transfer, all of her duties had been stripped away with no new ones substituted in, leaving her sitting bored and frightened in a strange place with no work, files, or furniture—apart from an old and empty desk, a squeaky chair, and a suspect telephone. Any paper she sent in their direction, such as reports on lingering matters and requests for new assignments, disappeared into nothingness. Lori no longer existed. Traditional Bullies have also been known to do these things but not so comprehensively.

Lori was receiving messages from an ally and also from a supporter still working at her old office. It was reported to her that the manager and supervisors had ridiculed her at a meeting just after she left, and then again at two others. Traditional Bullies do the same, but less consciously. In ridiculing her, they took their behind-the-scenes direction from Mark, each using exactly the same words—Mark's words. Through the uniformly scripted speech, they sought to achieve the appearance of credibility through repetition. Most anything said often enough begins to take on the appearance of truth. Traditional Bullies work alone, but they also repeat themselves quite a bit.

The Scientific have a great deal of experience from scientific trial and error to learn from, and base their finely tuned protocols upon. None of their attacks focused on the substance of Lori's work efforts. That would have allowed for a debatable "he said, she said" dynamic, in which either party could have been right or wrong about a substantive matter. Structurally, an attack on her merits would have also created a political feedback loop in which Lori would be at least impliedly included, functionally resurrecting her back into the fold whether she could defend herself or not. Scientific Bullies know better than to do that but there is one exception. If the Target successfully creates a feedback loop by laying a charge against a Scientific Bully that cannot be ignored, "Charge A," then, confusing matters and neutralizing the charge at the same time, the Scientific Bully will counter against the Target with the exact same charge, "Charge A," no matter how bizarre. The original charge, such as sexual harassment, is lost in a "theater-of-the-absurd." In all these things, the amateur Bully would have been clueless.

Under most circumstances, the Scientific Bullies content themselves with ridiculing the format of Targets' papers, as well as their grammar and spelling. Lori's competence was attacked in terms too general to allow rebuttal. Amateur Bullies also tend to ignore competency issues. Competence is a "done deal" known in measured in results. There's nothing left from which to get the good feeling of control. Although on a less radical level than grammar, the amateur Bully similarly, and inherently vaguely challenge employees' work processes. With seeming sincerity and for all to see at each meeting, Mark's functionaries pegged Lori's previously exalted work at the sub-high school level.

Although actual political and emotional damage was done to her, nothing real was said so she couldn't counter with a meaningful response. Lori was nobody, banished to nowhere and thoroughly stained. She was about to be broken as well. No amateur Bully could be this strategic in his or her bullying as a Scientific Bully.

From the beginning, Lori found herself lost in the hurt of what seemed to be an interpersonal morass. After all, she'd historically been recognized as one of the better employees. The new manager had probably been misinformed, she initially thought. On the contrary, the official profile Mark gave headquarters to prompt Laurie's torture was one of employee excellence. That meant she was a potentially influential individual with independent assets, possibly or probably functioning outside the control of headquarters. Except for staff directly beholden to headquarters for pay, power and prestige, headquarters preferred compliant employees to competent ones, and viewed the two types as mutually exclusive. Traditional Bullies view employees generally, and especially Targets, in that same way.

Demonization is at the heart of both Scientific Bullying and traditional bullying, but the amateurs are not entirely conscious actors, and not as sharp as the strategically thinking Scientific. To be demonized is to be dehumanized. Both sorts of bullying deny the Target of his or her personhood.

Lori had become confused to the point of immobility. She was like a doe stuck staring blankly into bright headlights of a bullying machine. As in all workplace bullying, Lori was personally offended, but apart from Mark's original and injudicious distaste for her, it wasn't in the slightest bit personal. When Scientific Bullying is viewed mechanically, as a subject it's not a challenging one to fathom, like astrophysics, the arts, or spirituality might be. It's simple arithmetic: bullying by-the-numbers. Scientific Bullies fashion themselves to be "scientists" when nothing about them makes them worthy of the title. If they are scientists, they're mad scientists. They're certainly every bit as pathological as traditional ones.

If a Target should, against all odds, find him or herself facing Scientific Bullying, his or her days in that job are numbered. In politics, as in the military, the smaller party can sometimes defeat the larger through preparation, cunning, and excellent timing, but only if the larger party is not enormous, well-studied and even more cunning. Meanwhile, the amateur, traditional Bullies do many of the same things and in the same order as the Scientific, only much less competently.

GANGLAND BULLYING

Gangland Bullies are also rare but can be found in inherently brutal work environments, such as the state prison systems that have become a large American industry. Their anti-social activities are systemized like those of Scientific Bullies. But unlike Scientific Bullies, they don't coldly and professionally apply psychoanalytic principles. Gangland Bullies function more loosely in line the occupational cultures in their rough and tumble prison environment.

The principle lesson to be learned from these prison-guard Bullies has to do with the element of enhanced unbelievability of events in a prison *generally*, and of the bullying treatment of employees *specifically*. Many of the things that happen behind prison walls are unbelievable to the point of being unmentionable even in these pages. But "unbelievability" as a masking element functions essentially the same for all Bullies. The second lesson has to do with the importance of occupational cultures made particularly apparent by radical, prison environments. After examining the exaggerated values of occupational cultures of prisons, no one is likely to underestimate their importance when examining them in other settings.

For these purposes, there's a third lesson. Gangland Bullying illustrates the structural weakness inherent in most, if not all, managerial review processes for disciplinary matters. If an employer has an internal review process, its purpose is to compel managers to review the disciplinary practices of their supervisors on the merits, as the representatives for the larger institutional interests. It's a form of check and balance, and sometimes that's the way it works.

More often, however, the review process actually aggravates the abuse of employees rather than protecting them or the employer's interests. The problem is that reviewing managers typically do not perform a meaningful investigation and so bring little or no value to the process. Instead, the manager merely stamps the pending action with his or her approval, thus adding just his or her managerial power and authority to whatever abuse might already exist.

In Gangland Bullying, managers sometimes add their own bullying to whatever lower-level bullying may have already existed. Most prison managers were once hardened prison guards accustomed to contending with hardened criminals. These managers approach their managerial review tasks contentiously. There are, of course, exceptions, but in that cultural setting as with many in the mainstream, for most everything, "It's the good guys vs. the bad guys." Any person faced with charges, whether inmate or "free staff" employee, is "a bad guy." What may or may not have begun as personally motivated bullying, may become bullying during management review.

In the prison system, as in other traditional personnel systems, the disciplinary process goes through a number of steps: from allegation, to investigation, to proposed action, to review of that proposal, to action, and then possibly to an appeal. At each step, the local prison supervisor reviews the matter, then submits it to a manager for consideration. With each step, there exists another possibility of bullying at either end. And, if there's a Bully involved at both ends, the bullying multiplies exponentially.

The general lesson here for all responsible managers is this: no management involvement at all is better than a pro-forma non-review. Where there is no earnest management review, the institutional interests are unrepresented regardless. Responsibility conveyed on a manager, but not exercised, exacerbates whatever bullying there might be by enhancing the authority behind the bullying.

The long-term lesson for everyone is: no matter what laws or employer policies and procedures there might be, there can be no substitute for competent and engaged leadership. Very obviously to any observer with a direct view of bullying people and events, most or all Bullies can't help being the subtle or crude brutes they are, but management has no such excuse.

5

GOLD MOUNTAIN: THE EMPLOYER

Section One

The Management Team

MANAGEMENT TEAM AND BULLY NETWORK

Bullies might or might not be on the management team, but if they are afraid of anything in this world, it is the management team. Normally, the employer is an abstract and amorphous entity. It's the institutionalized form of its principle stakeholders whether they are stockholders or the public-at-large. The management team is the daily embodiment of the employer and defines the employer's mission. Its members tend to be secretive. Employees may consider it "conspiratorial" when management's actions are negative to them but, for them, it is usually just "business." They almost certainly don't know the affected employees.

Yet, who is, and who is not, on the management team can sometimes be a mystery, even to the managers. Nevertheless, one of the very few things a Bully and a Target have in common is that both work for management and seek its support, and for very good reason. The employment destinies of both are tied to management. In all likelihood, management team members interpret any confrontation or problem an employee might have with a Boss as also being a confrontation with them. In these difficult circumstances, the Workplace Warrior needs to proceed thoughtfully and by circuitous routes.

Bullies directly and indirectly lobby management for everything they want. With a Target in sight, what they want and lobby for is the Target's demise. Bullies seek to separate Targets away not only from potentially supportive co-employees, but also any potentially inquisitive managers there might be. That's a relatively easy task, given that the managers have probably never talked to the Target and regularly talk to the Bully. As in other contexts, the Bully runs a negative campaign of disparagement against the Target. Predictably, none of the managers will make an effort to investigate the validity of anything said.

Repeatedly it's seen that a Target's alleged isolation standing alone, whether natural or artificially imposed, can be quickly considered proof enough for management to view him or her a problem. The Target will appear to be, and will probably be described as being, "not a team player" or even "hated by everyone." Once that's established, then it's also established that the Target's departure is in order, and can probably be done with few feathers being ruffled. For management, it's not quite a "win-win" solution, but there's no noteworthy loss either.

It may not look like it from an employee's bottom-up perspective, but the management team is actually beyond Bullies' control. Even if the Bullies are actually on the management team, they will almost certainly have enemies among its members for reasons having nothing to do with the Target. The managers look out for themselves. For untrusting control freaks like Bullies, that's got to be unnerving. The management team is something they stay up at night thinking about.

Like a worried customer made vulnerable by scarcity, Bullies are dependent on a single supplier for power, through a single supply line. In contrast, Workplace Warriors who, as employees, function on the lower and organizationally horizontal plane, have many. A management team can turn on the Bully, rather than the Target, at any moment. In that moment, the Bully's close proximity to them suddenly becomes vulnerability. A Workplace Warrior's strategy not only has to include building a political foundation for support, ultimately, it will include the most workable strategy possible to divide-and-conquer the Bully apart from the management team, before the Bully does the same to the Workplace Warrior. That's a tough task.

Outside the management team, Bullies may have a network of contacts and independent sources of information they've groomed over the years. Managers can often times be researched, if their profile is sufficiently high. But most members of a Bully's network are probably well below the Internet's radar screen, yet they are always worth check on. Regardless, they are a part of the Bullies' support system, whether their intentions or good or ill. If Warriors listen closely to Bullies' words and track their movements, they may discover who those people are, and then can choose whom to avoid and whom to find an advantage with. Many of them would be repulsed if they knew what the Bully does to people. Many of them are truly innocent, misinformed, or simply misguided. Others are not.

When a Bully last came barging into a Targets' work area, he or she was implicitly (if not actually) backed by all those mentioned above. Solidarity of the management team is presumed. To a greater or lesser degree, by virtue of their appointment as bosses, management gives them to a place in the loop. The only loop employees can be a part of is a loop they create for themselves. That last exchange the Bully initiated with the Target certainly felt personal to the Target, but its thrust and import were much bigger than that.

It matters a great deal to employees whether managers are strongly led and united. That's the difference between management teams that are focused on their goals and effective in realizing them, and those in disarray and unable to respond to circumstances, including being unable to respond effectively to a Bully Boss predicament. If a Bully thrives in their management team's environment, the team may lack leadership or be just as toxic as the Bully. If toxic, then there can be no internal interest, climate or mechanism for a corrective action to protect either the organization or its employees from Bully highjack. Short of a miracle, one almost necessarily coming from an outside source, employees in this toxic circumstance are in trouble beyond workplace redemption.

FOUR BUSINESS IRRATIONALITIES

In recent years employers' have been plagued with skyrocketing workers' compensation and other health-related costs. More than just hanging traditional "safety first" posters, employer's have gone to expansive lengths to reduce these costs. In addition to sponsoring expensive legislative initiatives, they have examined their workers' compensation costs from every direction, excluding those associated with bullying. Yet we know from studies conducted by the United Nations, human resource experts and others that this illicit practice is widespread, that it adds zero value, and that it is profoundly expensive, but it's also been an illusive practice to document until recently.[17]

Beyond the tendency of Bullies to render themselves invisible politically, the costs they create for the employer tend to be obscured by the sheer variety of them spread across several categories rather than appearing obviously in just one. They are apparent in everything from a loss of production[18] and the better personnel,[19] to absenteeism, health care costs, litigation costs, and workers' compensation. Managements' not just failure, but disinclination to examine and control these avoidable costs is irrational.

QUANTIFIABLE BUSINESS COSTS OF BULLYING:	
Loss of Production	Litigation
Loss of Key Personnel	Absenteeism/Sick Leave
Employee Turn Over	Workers' compensation

By sponsoring rather than remedying psychological abuse, managements also behave irrationally by violating their own "Zero Tolerance For Violence" policies. Those policies protect the employer from enormous exposure, and are not wisely shunt to the side. As with physical violence, psychological violence (discussed above) can affect targeted employees in varying degrees but, perhaps, its cost affect on the workplace as a whole is a larger one to consider as well. Looked at from the positive direction, employers that truly utilize team-building concepts already understand the importance of group dynamics very well.

Displaying anti-businesslike irrationality a third time in the face of bullying, managements have equally strong policies prohibiting discrimination against women yet most regard "bullying," which principally effects women, acceptable. Managements' ultimate act of irrationality is that, in crisis, they virtually always and aggressively, if need be, support the expensive, non-value adding Bullies against not only their employees but also as against the employers' mission.

Apart for the rare employers, like Comcox Inc. and Hewlett-Packard Company, cases that will be discussed later, management in the United States has said little about workplace bullying. In the United Kingdom, purposeful abuse of employees, whether physical or psychological, has, indirectly, been made unlawful. A U.K.-based human resource magazine, "Personnel Today," has run a thoughtful set of articles with techniques helping management identify and correct, costly bullying problems. In sharp contrast, no article on bullying can be found in its American counterpart, "HR Magazine." American management has been largely moot on the bullying issue, one central to their organizational integrity.

» What facts do American managers already have about Bullies, and what are their current opinions? In what ways do those opinions change when they're given basic materials on the subject? Before they will move to stop acts of workplace abuse, do they first require there be developed an academic foundation for understanding it?

» Do they see workplace abuses as a potential or real business costs? Are the abuses and losses of clients and employees both seen as avoidable costs, or just the former?

» In addition to complicated and differing sets of rules prohibiting harassment when it's specifically motivated by sex, race, etc., would a singular policy prohibiting all workplace abuse be both more practical to work with and protective of the institution?

» Are they concerned their own positions might be challenged by bullying allegations if there were an anti-abuse policy?

Managers are not without their personnel experts. In *Workplace Bullying: The Costly Business Secret* (Penguin 2003) by Andrea W. Needham, an international human resources specialist, she presents an accounting methodology for employers to use when examining what bullying costs them. She also presents a program for creating a "Bully-free organization." In her closing chapters, she examines employer models, including, "Datamine Limited—A Best Practice Company."

Management is, of course, the responsible party for whatever abuse occurs based on its authority. But the erroneous judgment of too many managers to dismiss each Bullying Boss conflict as merely a one-on-one, irrational, and interpersonal affair is so commonplace that it is hard to find all these individuals entirely culpable—however tempting that might be for Targets. Much like magicians more purposefully do to cover the practical workings of their trade, the immediacy of bullying dramas draw managers' attention away from the empirical evidence found in the event's context that define an event as a bullying one.

As repeatedly observed, even if a manager inquires about a bullying allegation, Bullies might claim that they are the real victim and that the Target is the real Bully. Amazingly, and despite the obvious power differential between the two of parties, the manager will predictably believe the Bully—no questions asked. For management, with its head buried in the sand, it's often the convenient way to go.

Worse, a manager might see the Bully in the same "heroic" way the Bully sees him or herself. Bullies are emphatically clear that they believe they are doing the secular equivalent of "God's work" by properly addressing, albeit perhaps harshly, a "problem employee" that's "stepped out of line," is "totally out of control" and/ or is "trouble." Each Target in series gets essentially the same self-righteous condemnation hurled at them, regardless of person or circumstances. As an actor, the Bully is the only common denominator. Managers who take remedial action to address abuse have proven to rare. The Drs. Namie estimate that only seven percent of Bullies end up censured, transferred or terminated.[20]

Unfortunately, when faced with a Bullying Boss, few employee Targets prevail. In all probability, Targeted employees will loose their valued employment, experience severe economic losses, and suffer a long-term detriment to their career. Targeted employees and witnesses alike suffer not only losses of production, but negative, sometimes devastating, consequences to their mental and physical health. All of these are cost items for the employer as well. Under our contemporary social values, bullying is inexcusable. For each of the same reasons, it's also inherently anti-businesslike.

TAKE IT LIKE A MAN

As stated, the political heart of workplace bullying is violence against women but, it's not just about gender—it's also about role. As employees, Targets are subordinates. As traditionally defined, the subordinate role is the feminine one. In contrast, Bullies are superiors within an employment structure. Thus, they operate in the traditionally defined masculine role and a hierarchical structure derived from the paramilitary one. Some would say that the whole point of the employment hierarchy is to apply negative stimuli in order to motivate employees to work, and to work as directed. Nothing else will. They might say that without bullying, our entire economy would collapse and even the so-called Targets would suffer the results. Even in this post-feminist period, it might be said employees have to "take it like a man."

Instead, it could also be said that the central pillar of any organizational structure, derived from the paramilitary one or otherwise, is an attentive and active leadership. That is in direct contradiction to the Bully style of imposing abstract dictates from afar, and from organizationally on high. Workplace abuse may, as a practical matter, sound like a functional shortcut substituting for leadership but it's neither effective medium-to-long term, nor acceptable. Where there's bullying, leadership is either absentee or in short supply.

> You can love people by correcting and criticizing them, but you have to make sure love is utmost. The encouragement comes from care, concern and love. The discouragement comes from contempt.
>
> —*Cornel West, author of "Democracy Matters"*

As made clear during legal discovery processes in employment cases, managers generally function under the traditional illusion that by protecting the Bullies in their company, they're also protecting the employer and themselves. No thought is given to protecting the employer from a deserted supervisor.

The leadership alternative for them is to investigate these matters in defense of the employer's mission from its potential compromise, in the process of protecting its human resources, its employees, from personal abuse. Instead, managers effectively help their Bullies hide behind their veil of managerial prerogative rooted in their private property rights as the owners of the workplace. For many managers, it's demonstratively less about the alleged Target and the alleged Bully and more about maintaining the appearance of their being the supposed managers of events. For them, it's an "Us v. Them" dynamic rather than an internal systems failure.

Aggravating that contentious dynamic is the same polarity functioning on the Targets' side as well. By the time employees understand they have been made a Target, they have probably already lost whatever respect they may of once had for management. Subjected to bullying, it's easy for Targets to loose track of the important role played by chain-of-command as it related both to themselves as well as the Bullying Boss. Management sent a Bullying Boss to them, has ignored their pleas for relief, and is responsible for the continuing abuse of themselves and probably others. In the legal sense of the word, they're "guilty" as charged. It is tempting for an employee to rebel against the entire management team as protest against what's obviously *their* Bullying Boss. But it is relief and not proving any managers' guilt or innocence that really should matter to Targets. Unfortunately, a Target's bad attitude and rebellion is very likely what management sees—or more likely hears about from a cold distance. Just as the contentiousness exists with both managers and a Target, so does the prospect of becoming, and remaining businesslike. Businesslike for the Workplace Warrior is conducting an objectively based study and campaign. For managers, it's conducting an objective inquiry.

But there's also a structural and cultural wall separating managers and their subordinate employees. While they see themselves as high, strong, and intelligent, they consider their employees to be their opposites in each regard. Because the vast majority of supervisors are competent in their duties, and tend to "stay on point" in pursuit of organizational objectives, most any supervisor is seen as "one of them." But that can't be assumed in every case, yet, employers tend to operate on the basis of that erroneous assumption.

The managers in bullying afflicted workplaces have probably heard and ignored the rumors about their Bully. Ideally, one or more of them would be prompted by those rumors at least to collect briefing materials on workplace Bullies generally, then dig out the facts personally. Absent managers taking the initiative, with a Workplace Warrior's careful planning, general sociability, and good luck, he or she might find a way to flank around the Bully to send a "Bully Boss reality check" into the managers' meeting room.

It's remotely possible, although unlikely in any direct way, a Workplace Warrior who is attentive to managers' concerns may find a lever to motivate one of them to act responsibly. Managers' concerns are typically their own survival (friends and foes), their own responsibilities (capabilities and capacities), and their own placement in the pecking order. The pecking order itself, as a functioning machine, effectively has its own concerns beyond the sum total of its participants. To the fullest extent possible from an employee's limited perspective, with or without a political lever, at every turn Workplace Warriors will be mindful of each manager's self-interest in all its complexity. If they have absolutely no idea what any particular manager's concerns might be, it's better to have a well-considered deduction, smacked with gut feelings, to work with, than nothing at all.

WORKPLACE CONFUSION

A bullying workplace is a place of confusion. It's utterly baffling to those who work there, and inexplicable to those outside. The starting point for that confusion is, as repeatedly noted, the inherent unbelievability of the bullying events. This element of unbelievability creates a dark screen behind which the Bullying Boss can act with impunity and deprive the Target of the support that any individual being maltreated would expect to receive. To most people, inside or outside the battle zone, bullying sorts of things simply don't happen in our civilized world. They might seem to happen in backward countries, but certainly not in our developed and sophisticated one. But it takes only a very few abusers in society generally, making a relatively small impression, for them to have a large impact in the workplace.

For illustration purposes only, if one assumes that abusers make up just one percent of community residents, then the number of Bullies who gravitate into the workplace to become supervisors will be a multiple of that number. It naturally attracts them. The workplace is, for them, an abuse amusement park where they are officially given legitimized authority to do what-Bullies-do. They get to exercise their malice and enjoy the good feeling of controlling others, while receiving pay and prestige in the process. Once there, it protects them. Being character types who define themselves by external markers, abusers who find their way into workplaces are granted a title and prestige within a hierarchical institutional context. On the other hand, for however long they remain outside the structure, as seen from within their own framework, they are not quite anybody, and are certainly not getting their due. But gravitational pull is not the only multiplier to consider.

Once inside, a Bully might have three supervisory jobs in his or her career, and supervise an average of fifteen employees each, spread over the term of each job. Then each Bully has a negative impact on three employers, and forty-five employees. No bully or abuser that remained in the community could dream of having that kind of impact. But even that number has to be multiplied to account for the intensity of their negative impact on personal others and operations. In contrast to most community contacts with abusers, workplace relationships are involuntary and of significant duration. However rare they may appear to be in the community and thus to reasonable minds of that community, their quantifiable impact on the employment world can be enormous. The element of "unbelievability" protecting Bullying Bosses is, in part, due to a confusion created by systemic differential between human relations within community context, and those of a working one.

Of course, most any untrained individual investigating a bullying allegation will be skeptical. Not just Targets, but also all employees under fire at work claim they're being harassed. After all, they are under fire. It can sometimes be difficult to distinguish a genuine Target of bullying activity from the large pool of other employees claiming and believing that they're being harassed when their superior may actually be addressing, in a professional manner, a genuine, work-related difficulty, such as a subtle developmental difficulty interfering with his or her ability to complete certain assignments or a substance abuse problem.

As noted, and exasperating the inherent confusion of bullying is that tendency of well-meaning people to limit their inquiry to a single, seemingly interpersonal incident. That frees the Bully to enjoy his or her skills as a master manipulator without being contradicted by the contextual reality. Unless confronted with specific evidence demonstrating a pattern and practice of abuse over time, predictably a Bully will wiggle away from responsibility for their latest incident on a declared pretext that's just credible enough, when heard alone, to pass muster.

A supervisor being queried may also have a "mixed motive," one legitimate and the other bullying, the Bully can exploit to bullying ends. Once again here, in society, in general, and at work in particular, there's an unfortunate bias that suggests that people charged with something are presumptively guilty of it. Accordingly, managers hearing a Bully's negative reports about any employee too quickly latch onto what might seem like simple and easy to imagine behavioral or job difficulties while closing their ears to the larger, Bullying Boss implications.

Even before damaged, Targets are earnest but, on their own, tend to be inherently unreliable witnesses. They want to understand what's happening to them and they go to great lengths to fill in the gaps found in events beyond normal, social understanding. They have strong feelings about the bullying incidents, and may offer cogent explanations, but generally don't have a sufficiently broad understanding of how the employment dynamic works, a dynamic with values defined by the management culture, and not by the community that they absorbed theirs from. This is evidenced by Targets' bringing from the community a political value for "justice," into a place it doesn't fit. They may never understand why their protests are being ignored; after all they are talking about the basics of right and wrong, and so they make yet more cries in the name of "justice," but to no avail. It's a cross-cultural misunderstanding that tends to confuse.

As an example common among hourly employees, employees generally learn how sick leave works during high school when being sick required collecting a doctor's note to excuse them from attendance. In the workplace, that is frequently also required but it does not excuse the employee from a failure of production. Managers focus on the work they, themselves, are responsible for getting done, not on the individual they charge with doing it. There are labor arbitration cases holding that employees can be guilty of "excessive absenteeism" and subject to discharge even when they've truly been sick and have not yet expended their accrued, employer-sanctioned sick leave. To the surprise of employees, but not bosses, when such an employee is terminated allegedly "for cause," there may be a community sense of injustice but not necessarily workplace bullying.

Targets also tend not to understand the true perspectives of the people working around them. At an interview, Targets often and earnestly report they have the strong support of coworkers when interviews reveal they don't. With everyone's livelihood at stake, and with a widespread desire to be as agreeable as possible in a loaded environment, coworkers generally choose to be polite and positive when talking to a coworker Target, even if their affirmations are not necessarily the truth of how they see things or who they are.

The act of engaging in emotional resistance can, on its own, create a psychological bias in an employee's perceptions.[21] Beyond that, the act of political self-defense in the workplace creates biases that employees sincerely don't seem to be conscious of, as reasonable under the circumstances. They're defending themselves as individuals subject to anti-social conduct, as well as defending their immediate jobs, continued income, and long-term careers. Their ability to provide economic support for themselves and their families has been placed at risk. Home mortgages, rent, and car payments have been threatened. Dreams and ambitions that were previously on track, like their children's educations or a special trip, have been rudely stepped on. Their identity as productive and respectable members of society has become uncertain, and their previously solid work and social roles have come unraveled. It's not that they are dishonest, it's that their human spirit has been compromised and will likely become more damaged as time goes on.

Targets' ability to communicate their plight is maybe always compromised by the structure of its development and presentation. As will be discussed, Targets piece together a story line to describe their experience in uncoordinated spurts, as immediate responses to bullying incidents, rather than being worked into an organized timeline that can be effectively communicated. Legally and politically, "The Story" they tell is virtually always counter productive in the workplace, but it's normally the only thing a Target knows to offer, or anyone else knows to ask for.

Just as outsiders dismiss the bullying stories as fantastic, insider witnesses do much the same thing through psychological functions. Examples observed and those repeatedly reported in the literature include employee-witnesses who disassociate from the events or more simply become numb. Some suppress their experiences through depression. Some become anxious and maybe hyperreactive. Some get disoriented, while others experience varying degrees of anxiety.[22] It seems that our brains are sometimes smart enough to exclude information that might immediately damage us. Some call these common insider and outsider reactions to bullying "denial," but that vastly underestimates what is taking place.

Malice in a bullying environment baffles most everyone by being simultaneously ever-present while largely also being undefined, maybe indefinable. It's both harmful and effectively invisible to onlookers and participants alike. Without an objective understanding of the specific role played by a Bully's malice, understanding a bullying workplace is impossible. When, for the first time, Bully Benjamin entered his new workplace to become its supervisor, there was calm production. Despite his authority, no one paid much attention to him. They had work to do. Work and work life continued as they always had without any work problems needing his involvement. For a Bullying Boss, that's a political problem. Malice rose inside of him. Within weeks, he'd picked out his first Target.

He scapegoated Chris, a young, large and meek man responsible for maintaining the computers. Chris had always done his job competently despite old equipment, but the age of the computers left him vulnerable to a series of bullying events. Benjamin was a stalker. He was crude. Never before had there been malice in that workplace; all of a sudden it was a part of almost everything. If Benjamin's criticisms were right, Chris could do no right. Everything he did was wrong.

Within a month, mass confusion had set in. The employees looked bewildered. Chris was just Chris. So what? Many employees appeared to be in a dreamy state, fundamentally lost, not quite connected to a world suddenly and inexplicably turned hostile. If they were interviewed then in standard fashions, the data would have been just as confused.

OBJECTIVE INVESTIGATION

Bullies may boast of their bullying accomplishments with surprising aplomb, but, as already mentioned, they do not offer themselves up for official scrutiny. As they proceed with their bullying, they shroud what they've done and why, concealing who they are as people and as supervisors. On the other hand, Bullies do surface under certain circumstances, and can be examined then. Bullies are combatants. As touched on, they are most likely to surface and expose themselves during the course of open battle when they're compelled to give testimony under cross-examination, and the veracity and accuracy of their testimony can be challenged by the documents and testimony of others. With proper background materials and as a proactive step, this can also be accomplished far more economically through interview processes.

Under these formal conditions, Bullies tend towards formality in their behavior, affecting an affinity with the other authority figures in the room when there may be none. As with the Target, they have their own "The Story" which also grew incoherently in spurts, and is usually also incoherent in its delivery. When questioned professionally, such as when subjected to cross-examination, their "The Story" typically becomes discombobulated. Any hope there might have been in discovering the facts from them, disappears, but a bullying reality emerges in the form of a particular confusion.

Bullying Bosses can, like most people, be researched. Company records, public records, newspaper archives, and online search engines are valuable tools in gaining a good understanding of who they are, beyond the image they project of themselves. Under certain circumstances, and in light of the large economic and personal stakes involved, the services of politically savvy, private detectives have proven to be cost effective and their results invaluable, especially for interviewing former employees of Bullies and other outsiders.

The objective for an investigation can't be to understand Bullies, but, more modestly, to root them out, just as would be done for any other avoidable cost. For responsible managers who put loyalty to the employer and themselves above loyalty to a cohort gone bad, their Workplace Warriors should be treated as champions to be encouraged, not pariahs to be neutralized. They're the ones who, at cost and risk to themselves, issue sentinel wakeup calls explicitly informing management that a Bully is compromising its human resources, thus also implicitly signaling that a Bully has hijacked some portion of their operation generally for his or her own destructive pursuits.

PART TWO
SWORDS AND SHIELDS

CHAPTER

6

PRELIMINARY ADVANCES

THE DISTINCTIONS BETWEEN ADVANCES, DEFENSES AND RETREATS ARE LESS IMPORTANT THAN THE COMMON PURPOSE THEY ARE PUT TO.

Section One
Isolation and Independence

BULLIES ISOLATE TARGETS

No man is an island, entire of itself, every man is a piece of the continent, a part of the main ... and man's death diminishes me, because I am involved in mankind; and therefore never send me to know for whom the bell tolls, it tolls for thee.

—By John Donne
Meditations 17, "Devotions Upon Emergent Occasions" (1624)

Isolation is the central political problem for Targets. To deny Targets support and to demoralize them, Bullying Bosses seek to separate them from their coworkers and supervisors, as well as outsiders such as customers and clients. Making that task easier, some Targets are naturally independent from others for personal, cultural, or structural reasons. No matter what predisposition a person may have to being targeted, the Bullying Bosses are the moving party striving to segregate Targets from all others. While the Target's pre-existing employment state is social, the Bully's activities are inherently anti-social. The culpability is all theirs.

As with sharper dogs, Bullies favor a cunning rooted in predatory instincts rather than being fully cognitive. The process of inclusion and exclusion in, and among social groups are a basic part of social dynamics. Clubs and cliques are familiar to most, their functioning going back to the very beginnings of human social networks. The Bullying Boss takes full advantage of these social rites, which are simultaneously ancient and contemporary. There is no need for them to consciously plot to isolate a Target, and coworkers do not need to consciously ally with a Bullying Boss. Exclusion and inclusion are primal. When they are done, they're simply done.

MOBBING

Political axioms like "divide and conquer" and its corollary, "united we stand," may be used to the point of sounding cliché, but they remain the central operating principles in politics, whether electoral, military or other. Military commanders recruit and conscript troops united for battle, then seek to isolate, or find already isolated, enemy clusters for neutralization. Bullying Bosses likewise build their support networks, adding allies and contacts, while dividing Targets away from all. Once isolated, the Target is ripe and vulnerable. "Conquering" is the next thing on any Bullying Boss's agenda.

Targets' isolation is at its worse when their coworkers engage in "mobbing" against them, often covertly inspired by a Bullying Boss. It's an ugly thing. The fact that it happens at all is a poor commentary on our development as a civilization, but it does happen. When it does, mob members effectively become co-Bullies, thus perhaps decreasing the chances of being bullied themselves, at a Targets' expense. They may take some personal satisfaction from being on the dominant team and thus, in some attenuated way, obtain the prestige associated with management. Some become smugly pleased with their newfound superiority over the Target.[23] After all, everyone outranks a Target.

PERSONAL INDEPENDENCE

Sometimes independence is a natural part of Targets' make-up or is built into their duties, thus making them more vulnerable to conscious isolation by a Bullying Boss. That doesn't mean that there's anything wrong with these Targets. They need not necessarily be social people to do their particular jobs. Or, they might even be essentially social but tend to function best on their own. People who aren't comfortable with being assertive, even when it may be required by circumstances, may be especially vulnerable. High achievers may likewise be at higher risk by being separated from coworkers because of especially challenging tasks required of them, or perhaps they get so focused on their work that they tend to exclude themselves from social niceties. Someone who the Bully regards as more intelligent, propertied, popular, good-looking, ambitious, with an attractive spouse or exotic lifestyle, is sometimes informally set apart from the others. Until the bullying, these had all been good things in life. However, once it starts Targets can no longer afford to go it alone.

Bradley had always come to the office just a bit early, anxious to get to work. His outgoing supervisor had given him an assignment with enormous responsibility, and he had every intention of getting the results expected of him. He took pride in his work even though he worked alone without the public accolade he would have earned, had his project included others. He worked independently with no difficulty. Every day, he came in the front door, said a quick hello to the security officer, walked up two flights of stairs, said another quick hello to the other early birds socializing around the coffee maker and eating bagels and donuts. He liked them all well enough but he didn't come to work to chat. They liked him also but thought him a bit aloof, maybe a bit full of himself. That was fine, everyone has his or her quirks.

WHAT WOULD ANNA DO?

Everyday, she picked out someone she hadn't talked to for a while. Being fully attentive, she asked, "What's going on with you these days?"

A few months after his new boss took over, Bradley noticed a change. Before, he had always passed by the others, and was greeted by them uneventfully, but now he faced an uncomfortable silence. He didn't know why but did know he had more important, projected-based considerations. He tried ignoring it, but it was becoming increasingly difficult. It was puzzling. He did not yet know that his new supervisor was a Bullying Boss, or that such individuals existed. Supervisors, it seemed to him, should be pleased rather than threatened by subordinates with intelligence and excellent performance records. Bradley didn't know then that the Bully was lobbying the others to see his natural independence as anti-social and arrogant. His entirely appropriate independence had become his isolation. Bradley knew that he'd been rendered vulnerable. He did the only thing he knew to do; he buried himself in his work when he could have reached out to the people around him.

Preexisting isolation might be present, which might have nothing to do with the individual as a person or employee. Already established cliques of coworkers can be a problem for Targets, without anyone necessarily thinking about it. There might be a cross-cultural divide separating a female Target from her male-dominated environment, or an employee of Mexican heritage set slightly apart from her Anglo coworkers. There need not necessarily be hostilities or any ill will, such as in mobbing, but there may be a difference and a distance that a Bullying Boss can exploit. Without much thought, Bullying Bosses methodically aggravate existing schisms, create new ones, dividing and conquering for their private benefit—and to everyone else's loss.

Naturally independent employees, and those set apart by circumstances, often believe their value as employees and their maturity will allow them to ride above the fray, unsoiled by the political perversions of others. Not anymore. Bullying Bosses work hard to push Targets off the social foundation of their work group. They force them into indefensible positions in the center of things then execute a program of persistent rudeness. A Workplace Warrior's choice is not really about whether to try to weather the storm or take on the storm-maker. The only real question is: Will these things be done on the Bully's terms or their own?

Section Two
Allies and Others

While circulating around to coworkers and others, Workplace Warriors identify people who might be or become allies, supporters, contacts, constituents, opponents, and enemies. Only tentatively, they'll write these tags on the note cards that represent them as character elements. But labels, of any type, can only be useful for analytical purposes; they are not exactly "true" descriptions of individuals. They're always subject to change and are best thought of dynamically rather than statically. After all, change of a positive sort is the goal.

ALLIES

Allies are gold, fairly rare, and to be treasured. Workplace Warriors can't work alone. Having even one ally gives the Warrior at least one trusted workmate to bounce ideas off of, to accept criticisms from, and to work in concert with. They are valuable, and must be protected by keeping the relationship just out of the Bullying Boss's sight. As Warriors canvass, they probably will not find a ready-made ally but rather a couple of prospective allies, or maybe supporters, they can groom into their roles with personal and sincere attention.

Warriors look for reliable allies with whom they can establish a common cause, but probably not friends. It's said, "Friends and money are like oil and water." Friends are the people employees join with outside of work. Allies seem a lot like friends but work relationships are fragile, made vulnerable by the inevitability of workplace changes. Friends stay friends regardless of where they or Warriors work. Of the two sets, actual friends are the more cherished, which is why Workplace Warriors keep their social weight outside of work with the people who are consistently supportive of them.

Where there are existing allies, their support must be consciously maintained and never taken for granted. The most dependable allies are those that the Warrior has already stood in battle with, shoulder-to-shoulder, with neither forsaking the other. Some allies may be actually, but not consciously, created by the Bullying Boss through the maltreatment of them or others, including the Warrior. These allies may not find reason to align with the Warrior but can be helpful nevertheless. "The enemy of my enemy is my friend."

POTENTIAL ALLIES

A potential ally might be discovered in the heat of battle when it's the easiest to tell who the people with feelings and fighters are. When a Bullying Boss was last dressing a Target down publicly, he or she might have looked out beyond the Ring of Fire to see a witness obviously offended by the Bullying Boss's mistreatment of another human being. The Warrior and special witness might establish a tentative, but discernable, bond. Taking nothing for granted, the Warrior would make sure they got together privately after work and on that same day.

Potential allies might include people who live their lives naturally aware that we're all bound together in our human interdependence. They might be active in community, church, or school affairs. On the job, they're the ones most inclined to work with others on a project, a team, or for a cause and so they might also be willing to work with the Warrior. Unfortunately, most people aren't like that.

Mythical Target Jacqueline's Bullying Boss, Mr. Johnson, hounded her all day long – bullying made worse by the extra orders they had to fill and the extra hours they had to work. As Jacqueline moved from one spot to another coordinating packing processes, Bullying Boss Johnson and his venom followed her. At each station, additional employees were exposed to his abuse and her humiliation.

Sara was among them but she differed in that she was not confused in the slightest. Instead, the stance she took was wide and unmoving. She was visibly outraged by the bullying incidents. Jackie saw and made note of her reaction. She had known Sara for the entire three and a half years that she had worked in their downtown office. Sara was tough, an amateur athlete of several sorts. She took no guff from anyone though she lacked some of the social graces. Jacqueline had felt comfortable with Sara and hoped she felt the same way but they had never talked about anything that mattered. Jacqueline knew that at least their liberal perspectives and enthusiasm for bicycling matched. She enjoyed the commonalties they shared but was not blinded by them.

In chatting with Sara in the copy room, Jacqueline learned that she worked out at the same gym on Saturday mornings, but they made no arrangement. Jacqueline wanted their meeting to come together casually and spontaneously. Sara didn't need to know in advance, or figure out later, that their meeting each other was purposeful and its purpose was political. Jacqueline had no intention of talking about the bullying or Mr. Johnson. Not yet. She was more interested in evaluating Sara as an ally.

Jacqueline intended to listen to Sara with empathy and understanding to everything she said. In a perfect world, the two of them and several others would share the same points of concern making it possible for Jacqueline to devise a plan common to all. In a world less than perfect, Jacqueline knew that flexibility would be required to find and develop a common issue, if one could be found at all.

Jacqueline left Sara to her work having a good feeling about her and looking forward to talking to her at the gym. If their relationship looked positive, she'd try to groom Sara, cultivating their relationship into an eventual alliance. As a subtle recruitment and to show leadership, Jacqueline intended to discretely share with Sara some pieces of what she'd come to know about the workplace. However, she wouldn't share anything personal about others that she'd gathered. That might be seen by Sara and any other right thinking person as a compromise of confidences.

SUPPORTERS

"Contacts" is the term that best describes most of the people Workplace Warriors talk to or listen to. Mainly they serve as sources for information, so the more information they're in a position to collect, the better. On rare occasions, a Warrior might enlist a contact to do something, like introduce the Workplace Warrior to someone that might be of political value.

"Constituents" are the people that may or may not have a relationship with a Warrior, but who are affected by the Warrior's actions. Constituents are among the people that Warriors consult before taking action to determine what the consequences might be for them and to accommodate their concerns, as well test a plan against their particular notions of believability and reasonability. That's how constituents and contacts develop into supporters.

"Supporters" are closer to the Warrior than contacts or constituents but are not quite as reliable as allies. The difference between a contact and a supporter is that a supporter has actually done something, or is ready to do something of aid and value to the Workplace Warrior. That could mean speaking up for the Warrior in front of others or merely sharing particularly pertinent news. A supporter may identify with the Warrior's plight, see validity in the Warrior's actions or, maybe more likely, have his or her own reasons to be active and helpful. The Warriors don't always know who has spoken up in their defense as a supporter. Behind closed doors, a supervisor, a customer, or client, might reflect upon something the Warrior did of value that the Bullying Boss would never convey but maybe should have.

ENEMIES AND OPPONENTS

"Enemies" are very few in number but disproportionately large in impact so it can appear like there are more of them than there actually are. Keeping tabs on their true political size is critical to staying emotionally even and to plotting the best course around them. "Opponents" are not to be confused with enemies. Enemies actively dislike the Target while opponents are motivated by self-interest rather than malice. Their focus is on the issues, like a struggle for scarce institutional resources or personal recognition. Contacts with opponents tend to be conversational but circumspect whereas those with enemies are entirely devoid of meaning. The guy who gives a Target strained looks from the other department might merely be an opponent while the Bullying Boss is definitely the enemy.

ADDRESS OPPONENTS DIRECTLY

Allies, contacts and supporters must be groomed, which mostly means making a point of talking to them regularly to hear what's on their minds, but enemies and opponents should not be ignored either. They may never become allies but the information they share in conversation can be useful. More importantly, making regular, personal contact with them tends to humanize each party to the other. Intimacy shared, however small, will disarm opponents and enemies in some degree. It will at least take the edge off.

Jessie worked in a nasty shipyard with enormous, steel hulls bigger than many buildings. It was a dangerous place. Welding sparks and cutting torches lit the place up on all sides. Chipping hammers banged loudly against plates, damaging human ears. The hulls were 100,000 tons heavy, 1,000' long, and well over 100' plus high. Across the stern from him, there were a pair of older white guys, Carl and Jim, having lunch, tightly paired together and silent, as always. They fit perfectly in the shipyard, looking a bit like gray skeleton hulls themselves. Jessie had heard they had developed a grudge against him for no reason he could figure. If true, their presence made that deadly environment all the more dangerous.

Normally, Jessie ignored them as well as he could but with the Bullying Boss on his case, he couldn't afford to have enemies from any additional quarter. He decided to lean into the problem rather than back away from it. At some innocuous point in the middle of the break, he strolled over to them to ask for advice. He asked where he could get the suspension of his hard hat replaced. It didn't really matter who he talked to but, with them being senior, they were among the logical guys. No more than 20 words were exchanged and he walked away having connected with them. Job done.

A couple of weeks went by. For the first time, Jessie was assigned to work with Carl and Jim. They were required to work high up in a deep hold. To get to their assignment, they had walk on wood planks paired together with nothing else between the men and the deck 90' below. Being cautious, Jessie walked behind the other two. Being distracted, one of his feet slipped between the planks. For just a few seconds, he was headed straight down but by grabbing hold of a plank on each side, he wasn't really going all the way. But at the time he found himself suddenly dropping the first few feet of the 90 more below. There would be no compromise if the softness of his young person's body smacked against the hard steel plating at the end. Nevertheless, the eerily speechless partners who may have had a grudge against him, had already spun fully around, grabbed Jessie firmly, hugging his limbs tightly to their bodies. Having showed them respect just a couple weeks earlier may have made the difference.

Workplace Warriors are safer having friends rather than enemies and they can't really ever know which is which from a distance. Maybe more than anyone, Warriors may want to talk to those they think might be their enemies, possibly finding an opponent they can work with instead. Both enemies and opponents hold valuable information, often the most valuable, because it comes from places and people outside the Workplace Warrior's political reach, maybe from within the Bully's circle, and because of their contrasting way of thinking. In all cases, showing respect beats cowering.

FORMER TARGETS

Former Targets who worked for the Bullying Boss can be the very richest source of workplace gold, but talking to any of his or her former employees is also of enormous value. They are in a position to corroborate the Target's experiences generally, but more importantly they will likely have recollections of specific bullying acts that match those the Target has been subjected to. Their corroboration down into the specifics is highly probative of a pattern and practice of abuse.

In each department the Bullying Boss has worked, there will be senior employees who know the names of former employees, maybe Targets, who had problems with the Bully. They'll be most likely to share what they know if asked obliquely. In general conversation they might be asked to describe how "things were back in 2003," or about a particular past project. Customers, suppliers, and regulators may also be forthcoming with names. The employer, probably the secretaries, will have old phone and address lists in their computers or in files. Online searches, together with up-to-date phone books, can be helpful finding current phone numbers and maybe even addresses. Sometimes it may appear daunting to identify and find one or two of them, but in this information age, it's not.

All former employees, and not just Targets, will have the benefit of workplace history giving them invaluable insights about it generally, and possibly the Bullying Boss specifically. While first talking with one of them about who they know still at the job, and what they're currently doing, the trust levels can and probably will build to a point where the former employee will probably be the one to broach the subject of the Bully. Let that run freely for as long as it has legs.

When the Warrior and the former employee, "click," and they probably will, the Warrior can share one of his or her incident cards or a witness statement describing an event with the hope that he or she will specifically corroborate the experience by remembering one just like it from the past. Ideally, and most likely if there are lingering hard feelings, with just a few words the witness will fill out their own incident card describing a matching event they witnessed or suffered. If the witness has a story to tell and agrees to talk while a recorder is on, that's also good but working with tapes can be unwieldy, and getting transcripts is expensive. Witnesses are frequently reluctant to write down dates, names, and the like unless they can be remembered with precision but generalizations are fine, such as "Sometime during the summer of 2005." The less the current Warrior speaks and the more documentation that he or she brings to the table, the more freely the witness's remembrances will flow – even if it's not all directly about the Bullying Boss.

TAMING THE IMAGES OF OTHERS

When a Target was the last standing in a Ring of Fire with their Bullying Boss firing degradations, it probably seemed, at first, to be an interpersonal experience, and the Target took it personally. At that early point of great confusion, thinking objectively was probably impossible. To help, there is an easy and amusing technique called "objectification." It's simple. For the Bullying Boss and other relevant people, including Targets, a Workplace Warrior assigns each a refreshing archetype name, like that of an animal, that best characterizes his or her personality and style. It's uncanny how accurately these archetype names tend to describe the people they're reflecting.

Objectification strips workplace actors, particularly the Bully, of their actual personality, which can be complex with nuances beyond what objective analysis can work with. In particular, the Bullying Boss's generally overwhelming political and personal power tends to create emotional confusion and cloud thinking. In contrast and in a flash, the archetype name crystallizes who he or she truly is without distractions.

On first blush, and if a Target is feeling particularly victim-like at the moment, he or she might identify as a Chicken, a Cow, a Doe, a Flea, a Lamb, or a Mouse. If so, the services of a good therapist may be needed for this Target more than most. On a better day, the Target might identify with a Bear, a Bee, or a Donkey. After constructing a strategic plan with an action just ahead, a Workplace Warrior, which is also an archetype, might find greater identity with a Fox, a Tiger, or a Porcupine.

Across from the Warrior at work, he or she might see three sheep huddled together and may find a use for them, but only after things are already going his or her way. These characters will, in accord with their nature, follow most anyone's lead, including both the Bullying Boss and Workplace Warrior's. As long as things are going against the Warrior, these characters can be expected to follow the Bullying Boss – assuming that they do anything besides graze contentedly. For the short term, the Workplace Warrior would probably limit him or herself to working with them as a precaution against Bullying Boss inspired mobbing, maybe eventually winning them as supporters.

Ashley was a new hire and mostly unknown to Warrior Tom. He'd only worked with her twice. Although he was prepared to change archetypes at any point, he thought it mostly likely Ashley was a tiger. It just felt like the right thing to call her. She seemed to be a scrapper and that could be helpful during a Bully Bossing incident. Lillian, the older woman nearby, had been there forever and sometimes she seemed like a bear undisturbed by the Bullying Boss, the Warrior, or anyone else. But to Tom, it felt more right to call her a hawk. She minded her distance, and saw everything. If Tom took the time to groom her as a supporter or maybe an ally, she could be useful for what she saw and maybe for giving advice on occasion. Stretching it only a bit and thereby finding potentialities where they had been few, he imagined that if he proved himself particularly deserving, her metaphoric talons might also come in handy.

It might seem to some people that animal designations are contrivances. They are. So are the essentially non-personal workplace roles and designations such as receptionist, supervisor, and CEO. The designation of Target made by a Bullying Boss is entirely contrived. The big difference is that these animal designations are created by Workplace Warriors and used by them for their own benefit—as a tool for analysis and planning. The other difference is that they sometimes lead a Warrior to a better understanding of the individual described. Whether formally written on note cards for strategic planning purposes through maneuvering, or informally thought about during the workday, they create an opportunity for a fresh start in any employee's thinking,

Section Three

Surrounded, Not Ever Alone

MAKING THE ROUNDS

If isolation, either natural to Targets or artificially imposed by Bullying Bosses, is the central problem, then joining with others is the obvious solution. This is something that many people do casually and competently, some have to work at, and some intensely independent others just don't do. But Targets' employment defense against a Bullying Boss requires it. Reasoned argument is not going to be enough, no matter how powerful.

However large or small, everybody and everything creates a series of ripples in the universe. Workplace Warriors might not see the ones they create as they go through their day, focused on their duties, but the laws of physics teach us that all their actions send out energy, changing the things and people around them. Ripples are also coming their way, as well as washing back and forth over everyone involved, and also many who are not directly involved. It's cause and effect. Each thought, desire, duty, and action generates ripples and waves that have their own characteristics, such as being productive or unproductive, friendly or hostile, tight or loose, and all affect Warriors' fate. To the extent that they are able to observe objectively the causes and effects of events around them, they'll make good use of the favorable ones while negating or maybe channeling away what is undesirable. They'll be better able to function on a larger scale, one that includes everyone's perspective and impact.

When suffering the isolating effects of bullying, Warriors can feel like they're all alone in the world. In fact, they're surrounded by persons and personalities every bit as rich as they need for them to be. Sometimes embattled Warriors have to back up a few steps from the commotion to appreciate each in his and her fullness, followed by engaging with each one personally. It's worth the bother. Bullying Bosses and Workplace Warriors are competing for their support. As Targets turned Warriors make their rounds, casually socializing with people one at a time, they are particularly looking for each one's complaints, connections to others and agendas. Basic information is collected. More informally, Warriors identify the precise social and work roles people have as well as the feelings they have for each of the others—or might later be encouraged to have, particularly including their feelings for the Warrior themselves and their Bullying Boss.

In the beginning, the central focus is on developing and improving relationships with others involved or affected by the Bullying. While personal relationships are generally discouraged for workplaces, in bullying environments where social isolation is the problem, personal communications and earnestly made contacts are made necessary. That requires nothing more than simply being attentive to, and later documenting, the personal concerns and attributes of each. Canvassing is basically being neighborly. It's just a common courtesy but it's one too commonly neglected.

ANNA'S TIP TO TARGETS:

Reach out to the people you work with, but not to sell your problem to them. Instead listen and learn about their concerns.

Bullying Bosses know employees, supervisors, and managers from other work areas because they go there. So can Workplace Warriors, but not so obviously. Bullies know something of their stated concerns and fears because they've heard their complaining and maybe seen what they've written. The Warrior's initial forays may not provide ultimate relief but have two important and interrelated purposes. The first strategic purpose is to forestall any further loss of political standing in the workplace, and the second is to collect the their initial data set as objectively as possible.

At first, these contacts seem simple enough for Warriors to keep track of in their heads, but as their web of contacts increases and becomes complex, particularly as the nuances and interconnections start accumulating, they'll need the note cards for each of the individuals to keep track of what they're learning. They make it possible to make physical comparison of issues and connections, missing nothing. They're lightening fast to make and lend a precision to their thinking that their memory alone can never match. At best, memory can provide incomplete, imperfect, and abstract remembrances of events while cards speak definitively, demonstrate interconnections visually and, very importantly, they may be the only way to illustrate the blank holes between, the ones that need filling.

STRENGTH IN ATTITUDE

Irene was an older woman with a great deal of precious seniority earned. Her new supervisor, a young woman named Linda, felt challenged by her, and so challenged Irene's position in an early confrontation. Irene was not about to let anyone take that away. "Having been around," she was particularly savvy in social matters. The respect Irene had for her coworkers was genuine, but politically useless if not acted upon in some way. She talked to employees one-by-one. During the course of each personal contact, she demonstrat-ed her capacity for empathy, her respect, and the strength of her re-solve – with significant good will returned back to her in kind.

It was Linda's first job as a supervisor, and she knew nothing about the inner workings in her new office. Worsening matters for her and everyone, she was so tightly wrapped in her ambitions that she would have missed both all the details and the larger picture re-gardless. She saw Irene circulating among employees, but she didn't know enough to know it was unusual. She ignored it. As far as Lin-da was concerned, she had the title "supervisor" and that was that. But Irene's authority wasn't just found in her position. It was built into the mature person she'd become and earned the right to be. All along, she was more a Workplace Warrior than Target.

Most people are attracted to strength, and few will challenge it. By getting around and making true connections with her co-workers, the strong Irene preemptively denied her Bullying Boss the opportunity to rally her coworkers against her. Irene was not only making new business contacts, she was (in political terms) "show-ing the flag." She created a soft and social rallying point around her-self. She was at all times positive, creating a climate of good will, in stark contrast to the toxins her Bullying Boss spewed. When it's all said and done, if Warriors win anything, it's because they pulled on their innate capacity to be "just folks"—something Bullying Boss-es can never be.

BE ATTENTIVE

It never hurts to compliment people, and that includes an em-ployee's enemies. But not the Bullying Boss, who can't believe any-thing said anyway. It's just not possible. To be heard, and for the sen-timent internalized, a compliment has to be true about some specif-ic thing. Its function is not to manipulate the other person but, like a handshake, it's a showing of personal respect, a ritual. A failure to compliment when it's deserved is an insult. Whenever someone does the employee a favor, such as giving support in a crisis, or sharing tips about the Bullying Boss or the larger workplace, the Warrior will not take that coworker for granted. The Warrior will find a way to express, then later show he or she is genuinely grateful.

If employees are attentive to the employer's mission and cast themselves as the company's Best Worker, then coworkers and superiors will likely regard them positively, as a bright contributor rather than the dark dampener that victims can too easily become. Workplace Warriors pay attention to what their workplace audience sees in them, and what would be better for them to see? Do they see calm confidence, or fear and hurting? Do they see appropriate emotional connections, or inappropriate detachment from them? Do they see someone they subjectively feel to be loyal, or a traitor? When a Workplace Warrior communicates, do they hear clarity and credibility, or cloudiness and confusion? Is he or she seen as a person doing business and being businesslike, or maybe someone not professionally engaged? None of these can be left to chance. They must be matched to a plan establishing a productive course of action.

With a newfound, consciously developed positive attitude, Workplace Warriors engage in no evil. They do not lie or promise what they can't deliver. They protect other people's confidences even if they don't protect their own. They don't insult people either to their faces or behind their backs but they do remember who among them does. Workplace Warriors have bigger things on their minds. They do not engage in idle group griping, which functionally serves to dissipate group angst into useless oblivion. They either then assume leadership responsibility of the group, harnessing that angst for focused use then, or dissipate it themselves for productive purposes later. When they speak negatively, it's for a planned for purpose at a planned for time.

Aesthetics are the big picture feelings found in, seemingly, the little things. Workplace Warriors think not only about the times and places things normally occur or might better occur, but also the general ambiance of each as they affect or might affect those involved. If a confrontation is inevitable, where, when, and how will Warriors be the safest when it happens while perhaps maximizing political hay in the process? (More on this.) They take a few moments to consider clothes, lighting, positioning, colors, sizes, textures, emotions, smiles, and groans. If a meeting that includes the Bully will probably be difficult, maybe that's the day to wear a suit—for reasons unrelated to work, of course. Just as in a stage play, the regular workplace props, like certain files, books and boxes, are consciously considered for political use. Demonstrating a presence no less than an accomplished Shakespearean actor, Workplace Warriors present themselves to the Bullying Boss and everyone else with an air of clarity and confidence. *"All the world's a stage..."*

WHAT DOES ANNA DO?

She actively promotes values and vision generally as well as attends to the little things from the color of a shirt to the colorfulness of an event.

Warriors making their immediate work area attractive to the people they work with is helpful. That starts with keeping their door open, literally. It's more inviting to others to keep their the work area reasonably neat and, if possible, having a chair or two cleared off so visitors will be almost automatically inclined to sit down. Big plants also help. Posters should be chosen for their appeal to others more than as a statement of their individuation separate from them.

Doris was a master of hospitality. She consistently maintained a dish filled with candies for her coworkers chosen for their preferences. That was always a winner with sugar enthusiasts. "It's easier to catch a fly with honey than vinegar." She never failed to please her coworkers when she, every so often, passed around cookies or brownies "left over from a party the night before," even if there was no party. Social niceties work the same way. When someone approaches a Warrior's desk or workstation to talk, it just has to be a good idea stand up with a greeting and to shake hands. If Warriors do, then they make the work environment a better place for everyone, fostering links with others and at no cost to themselves. Little things matter in a big way.

ANNA'S TIPS FOR TARGETS

Note how is the Workplace Warrior perceived by each:

» Coworker.

» Bullying Boss.

» Outsider.

» Manager.

Note how are her workplace habits perceived?

Hard at work or making wandering trips to:

» Restroom.

» Smoking Area.

» Coffee Machine.

» Cafeteria.

Her clothes communicate:

» Self-Respect

» Unity with Others
  (and with a dash of leadership)

INDIVIDUATION AND AFFINITY

Travis was both extra tall, so he drew extra attention, and quite young, actually quite immature, so the attention he drew wasn't always favorable in the warehouse. He was a hippie of a sort, wearing blue jeans, flannel shirts, and cowboy boots that established his identification with his outside life and friends. His coworkers wore tough industrial clothes that held up under warehouse abuse. His attire was in everyway appropriate to his outside life, but dysfunctional at work. Until he drew the negative attention of his Bullying Boss, all of this was fine, and sometimes even amusing to his older coworkers. But once the Bullying Boss started coming after him, these differences became difficulties. Work was becoming uncomfortable from every direction.

Over time, as he bought replacement clothes, he increasingly tended to make more practical choices, and that also meant clothes more in social sync with the people he worked with. He didn't make a political plan to meld in better, or to be less of a lightening rod for bullying. The work itself compelled his adjustments. Predictably, his shift in attire didn't slow down the warehouse Bullying Boss coming after him, but with his inadvertent showing of respect for his older coworkers and increased identification with them, they became closer and more protective of him in paternal and maternal ways only youth gets the benefit of. Their support mattered.

PROCEED GENTLY

Taking to people with conscious purpose may not be a natural thing for some people to do. Bullying Bosses don't share that reluctance, are probably already doing that job and doing it openly. While they're gossiping generally, they're also gossiping about their Target. But employees are subordinate and thus the weaker party so they have to be clever and careful. With respect for the enormity of what they face, they'll not be deterred but will proceed softly as they penetrate the workplace as thoroughly and deeply as possible. No matter whether they're circulating socially, collecting data, or lining up supporters, all of what they do must occur below the Bullying Boss's radar to the greatest extent possible. Otherwise, some form of negativity will get bounced back against the Target employee as well as possibly against they people who they're known to talk to. Before a Target has reason to reach out, their Bullying Boss has probably already prejudiced the environment with his or her negativity, that can be discouraging, but, the Warriors' approach is positive and their influence will grow.

There's power in numbers. The fight is over whom, the Bullying Boss or Workplace Warrior wins leadership, or at least holds the greater sway over the body politic. That might not seem fair or even doable, but if not done and the Bullying Boss wins, then Targets will end up feeling and being even more alone and oppressed as time goes on. The Bullying activities will have gone unchallenged. They'll have conceded the political win. Targets will be damaged, possibly ending up on workers' compensation, disability or simply depressed and unemployed. Regardless of any other circumstances, if the battlefield is to be conceded to the Bully, it's time for targeted employees to leave that job regardless. But if they reach out and make real contact with people, they just might ride through the bullying storm, or last long enough so they can to land on their feet there or maybe somewhere else that's actually desirable.

Canvassing, networking, and organizing can be particularly challenging affairs for most people to start. How well they do depends upon how relaxed and comfortable Workplace Warriors are or can become with themselves, and then the people around them. Fairly quickly, it becomes second nature. So much so that sometimes, when canvassing energetically for information and networking enthusiastically for support, it's tempting to pressure co-employees to disclose their thoughts or to write witness statements when these might be premature. It's often better to wait patiently. Actual events as they unfold, subject to the Warrior's ongoing commentary, are more powerful teachers than pushy arguments made by Warriors or anyone else. "Baby steps."

WHAT WOULD ANNA DO?

» She approached the Bullying problem methodically, like other work projects.

» She was dedicated to being a Workplace Warrior, while looking for other work.

» She unburied herself from work demands maybe self-imposed or unnecessary.

» She investigated, made a goal, crafted a plan, coordinated resources, and then executed her plan.

How many people Workplace Warriors ultimately canvass depends on how their worksite sets up. They'll certainly talk to everyone they have personal contract with during the day. Beyond that, the greater their reach, the greater their understanding and the strength they gain. Workplace Warriors eventually extend the reach of their canvassing beyond the immediate worksite, stealthily making contact with workers in other departments and maybe outside people in their occupational field. Leaving the workplace to get an outside view can be a powerful learning experience in the same way people sometimes have to leave their country, then view it from the outside, before they can truly understand it. Warriors leaving their work area to view it from the outside not only widens their viewing parameters—it deepens their understanding of where their inquiry began.

While Bullying Boss may or may not be on the employer's management team, Workplace Warriors can informally put together their own team by simple canvassing and listening. And no one will be the wiser, not even the teammates. With just a few covert lunches and coffees, they'll discover the positive and negative relationships between each of them. They become the workplace holder of its collective wisdom with all its facets of connections, concerns, ideas, and motivators. They won't change the world, but they'll change their immediate work climate for the better.

DISCOVERING WITNESS STATEMENTS

Most of the research and documentation discussed here can seem like a hassle, something employees shouldn't have to bother with in the first place. But it's all actually quite easy with one exception: collecting witnesses statements. It's not that these take great effort. It's that they require the courage to try and the finesse to pull it off. The approach and skills Workplace Warriors use to secure a witness statement are very much the same as discovering and grooming allies, except that the goal is narrower and the probable length of the relationship shorter.

Mostly, it's just hard to ask knowing that co-employee witnesses are apt to be reluctant to commit themselves in writing, but Warriors' word alone is not going to be enough against a superior's. If they go it alone without a least a few corroborating statements, Warriors could end up not only disbelieved, but humiliated. Whatever difficulty they might have in braving their way over to just one coworker to talk at least informally about an incident, that difficulty falls far short of being humiliated. Just the opposite. If the approach is made with an open mind and heart, it can be invigorating.

By merely talking with a coworker witness, even if the Warrior doesn't actually end up with a statement, he or she will at least learn the coworker's perspective. The Warrior will come out of the discourse ahead. It bears repeating, it's amazing how each witness to an event sees and remembers what transpired quite differently. The only way to know another person's viewpoint is to ask them. In a discussion, the Warrior may, or may not, decide to also communicate his or her version of an event with the witness and maybe influence how he or she see things in ways that are honest and productive for both.

Target Eva knew from Shelia's comments that she was disturbed by Bully Ryan's conduct and made a mental note to talk to her about it. Although still charged from that afternoon's confrontation, Eva knew better than to approach Sheila while Ryan was still around and in his bullying mode. Eva merely wanted to hear Shelia's view of the incident, ideally in the comfort and security of her home. There, Eva could also find out if Shelia's husband was more or less supportive of her efforts against the bullying or, instead, find Eva's presence threatening. If there, Eva could address whatever concerns there were together.

Instead, Shelia preferred to meet Eva alone at a cozy restaurant not very far away where they met after work for dinner and drinks. In the moment they sat down, with Eva still charged with adrenalin from the bullying fight, Eva wanted to get right to it. Her thirst was not for the margaritas but for Shelia's insights and information. But she remained patient. Eva took deep breaths to relax. Very importantly, she consciously allowed her self to become less focused and so more receptive to whatever Shelia already had on her mind. She didn't want to scare Shelia away with her post-incident intensity or by pulling out a bright legal pad. If Eva eventually discovered there was something worth writing down, she could use the tools found at the restaurant.

While waiting for their drinks, they shared an uncomfortable silence but Eva didn't let herself get flustered. She tried to think of something light and distracting to talk about. She couldn't. A silence that powerful can sometimes indicate what's being held back, and what's coming, are similarly powerful. Eva mildly took another deep breath. She was fully prepared to let Shelia's offerings, if any, unfold. Until then, any request Eva might have made for a witness statement would have been premature, confusing, and properly rebuffed. Then Eva wouldn't have known what Shelia might have had to offer her and so not known what to ask for, if anything.

When the server brought their drinks with a bit of chit-chat, the conversation silence between Eva and Sheila broke. Shelia moved just a little bit toward Eva indicating she was ready to speak. It turned out that her father was something of a Bully himself. Shelia had the whole thing down from recognizing the surprise-nature of the attack Eva suffered, to Ryan's constrained but threatening body language and his teeth-clinched scolding. Shelia understood what Eva was being put through, maybe better than Eva. At that right and most intimate moment, Eva pulled out what she'd written up for her own witness statement concerning that day's incident. It was no more than a half dozen sentences. Names and quotes, mostly. Eva was not asking for much. As Shelia read it, she knew exactly what Evan needed without the confusion that comes with a necessarily vague, verbal description of what's being requested. As a shortcut, Eva had thought about writing a statement for Shelia merely to sign, but that wouldn't have worth much. There would have been no Shelia author-ship and very little commitment. Eva wanted the real deal.

With her own statement on the table, freshly read by Shelia, Eva brought up the idea of Shelia writing a statement to back up her own. Eva's worked well as a guide for Shelia but it wasn't some-thing for Shelia to merely copy. Eva needed Shelia's full power and not a hollow contrivance. As expected, Shelia didn't see the incident exactly the same way Eva did, but that was fine so long as it was both helpful and true to her. From the beginning, Eva had assured Shelia that only the truth would do. Eva also assured her that she wouldn't be using Shelia's statement unless it became absolutely necessary and that almost certainly meant never. Eva merely had to preserve the record while memories were still fresh. A month or later will be too late. Shelia understood.

Finally, it was time. Eva dug a cheap pen from her bag but it didn't work so she borrowed one from the next table. On the back of the restaurant's placemat, Shelia wrote no more than six sentences describing Ryan's conduct with quoted slanders and the names of other witnesses. It was over in a matter of seconds. The incident had been painful to live through, but writing those few words was pain relief. Eve couldn't have guessed how forthcoming Shelia would be. Just like a salesperson that closes a deal before losing personal contact, Eva knew from experience that if she had to, she would have insisted that Shelia give her something written before she left the restaurant. Even if Shelia left, making sincere promises to write something when she got home, it would never happen. Eva would have ended up with nothing. Instead, once the two of them connected and things got going, Shelia had no reluctance to jotting done a few notes. When she signed and dated it, she did so with vigor. Eva left the restaurant with Shelia's excellent statement tucked inside her bag.

KNOWLEDGE, ISSUES, CHARGES

As Warriors visit each person on an initial canvass, they don't ask for anything from anybody except a chance to hear them out, to learn what's on their minds with their natural powers of empathy and compassion fully engaged. Maybe the first person they talk to with conscious intention, but in entirely comfortable way, will be named Florence. What does she think about the latest production issue? How does she feel about her own manager, her coworkers, the new production requirements, her commute, and her kids? What can the Warrior do for Florence? What can the Warrior and she do for each other and others more?

As understanding develops, Workplace Warriors often find the common issues, concerns and ideas among employees. Maybe they'll discover there's a jointly held issue concerning the condition of the rest room, security in the parking lot, flex time for parents or payroll accuracy and procedures. The best issues, in non-union settings, are those that are strictly business, designed to enlist the support of management for an obviously worthwhile goal rather than challenge it. Ideally, it will directly further the employer's mission. Even if these concerns don't address the bullying directly, they will, if successful, greatly enhance the Warrior's power and influence as preliminary to getting his or her bullying concern addressed. Bully Bosses are about power. Workplace Warriors under fire can't survive without power of their own.

ANNA'S TIP TO TARGETS:

If you allow it to be "all about you," you lose.

Things that people feel inclined to share will eventually have value, but not necessarily value that will be apparent right away. Workplace Warriors just keep listening and taking mental notes. Later, they write them up. There's no need for Warriors to talk about his or her Bullying Boss, but the contact persons might. Let them do the talking. Warriors content themselves with soft generalities illustrating only the outlines of what's going on. What remains unsaid can be even more significant than any literal charges they might make. The potential allies they're talking with have their own imaginings about the Bullying Boss. Their notions, which are of their own making, are more powerful to their minds than the necessarily bizarre and inherently unbelievable charges of wrongdoing the Targets were previously and unsuccessfully making with their The Story.

For Workplace Warriors, and at first it may not seem like it, the positive climate they share with the others can become larger and more powerful than most Bullying Bosses' negative fury, in part because it's essentially invisible. The Bullying Boss, if he or she notices anything, will be concerned "there's no telling what the Workplace Warrior's talking about." Confounding the Bully completely, the Warrior isn't talking about much of anything. They're listening. When he or she later organizes the note cards around a table, it will be obvious who connects to whom, why and how. They will see whose complaints and agendas match, or can be made to match. These are what generate political influence. They may or may not give the satisfaction of being directly related to the bullying but they are powerful, political currency for the Warrior to share or spend when the time comes. Information is power.

In Warriors' informal but serious survey of the field, they scope out and record who has guts and who does not, as well as discover people that might be helpful in specific ways. Some of the new contacts will never become allies but helpful nevertheless. They might meet insider experts who know their employer's production and service protocols, its position in the market, management's larger problems, and maybe where it's headed next, with or without the Bullying Boss. They might meet people experienced in their employer's personnel processes and how best to avoid or make use of them. They might merely gather the names of inside and outside contacts they had never before heard but are worth talking to generally. One of these contacts might be the one who eventually delivers Workplace Warriors' materials to a carefully selected manager, without dangerously exposing themselves by "going over the head" of their Bullying Boss.

ANNA WOULD CANVAS:

» To Show Respect For Others.

» To Collect Information, Agendas and Ideas.

» To Identify Pre-Existing Social/Work Networks.

» To Discover Unifying Issues *(Bullying Or Not)*.

Tactically, canvassing is a Warriors' flanking maneuver around Bullying Bosses using workplace issues as their vehicle and the responses as fuel. If an attractive, unifying and doable issue can be fashioned, it may be time for Workplace Warriors to establish a modest measure of leadership before what remains of their political capital dissipates any further. The tactical goal for any political action is simple: to cause virtually any kind of motion by at least a couple or more people. In non-work politics, motion likely takes the form of people coming together for a campaign of some sort, or just to distribute written materials. In a bullying workplace where the purposeful isolation of Target employees is the problem, it's enough if the motion takes a purely social form, such as inviting selected coworkers to lunch or celebrating birthdays. It's not much of a stretch from there to sponsoring a more overt but cautious political motion, maybe in the form of a jointly signed memo seeking a workplace change or, better, seeking a meeting with a manager to discuss a particular and positive change. It doesn't so much matter to the bullying fight what the action is so long as the Workplace Warrior demonstrates leadership that is followed by results people regard as positive.

ANNA'S ISSUE AND ACTION:

> » Unites Coworkers.

> » Furthers Employer's Mission.

> » Under Warrior's Leadership.

> » Reasonable/Justified By Numbers.

> » Generates *"A Motion."*

> » Ultimately Successful.

The structure of this Workplace Warrior social/political tactic is exactly the opposite of the preexisting strategies of both Bully, who seeks to isolate directly, and the former Target, who effectively self-isolates through repetitions of his or her "The Story." The Warrior's canvassing strategy is an indirect one that smartly ignores the Bully's Ring of Fire – a construct that is tough to escape by force – and the bullying that's difficult to even to talk about. Instead it directly addresses the political constituents of both Bully and Warrior contenders, the workplace audience, on issues of import to them, in their terms, perhaps reaching a result that benefits them.

MARIO THE ORGANIZER

If left to their own devises, Bullying Bosses can bring the morality level of an entire group down to new lows, perhaps approaching the Bullying Boss's own. For Targets, the workplace can seem like it's become an experience in personal damnation taking on proportions well beyond the Bullying Boss's intrigues. That's all the more reason to become conscious, and play it smart.

Mario, an atypical Target, had been offered a job on a project beginning in three months. It had better pay but a long commute. Except for his Bullying Boss Bill, he preferred to stay with the job he had. Between them, Bill had the authority. He held the keys to everything that mattered at work. Mario was a nice, competent, and good-looking guy but didn't have the keys to anything. His coworker group had devolved from a productive team into a mess lacking both direction and coordination. They were caught in the middle between Mario and Bullying Boss Bill and did their best to stay out of the way. At first, it was hard for Mario to imagine why Bill was so intent on winning their favor while casting disfavor on him. None of that had to do with the job. As far as Mario was concerned, the others had been useless but he tried not to get a bad attitude about it. If Mario was going to do something, it had to be soon, while his job offer was still pending. If Bill thought his coworkers' opinions were important, then so would Mario.

Before Mario conducted his initial canvas, he counted only two coworkers in 16 that saw things as he did. It seemed like the rest had written him off as deserving what were becoming Bill's almost daily blitzes but, having not talked to them, it was impossible for Mario actually to know what they were thinking. What Mario did know was that, in the workplace, he had a favorable rating of maybe just 12 percent. That wasn't as bad as it might have seemed. Up until then, the conflict had been entirely one-sided, with Bullying Boss Bill doing all the firing and the Target Mario silently taking all the blows. Mario casually worked his way around to talk to all 16 coworkers. By doing nothing more than reaching out the others to hear their concerns, he doubled his favorable rating to 24 percent. That was a vast improvement, but not enough to make staying with the job bearable. That's why he was smart to keep his emotional and social weight in the community and had been looking for a better job all along. With both of those secure, he dared play hardball with Bill.

Mario would have liked his coworkers' active support but would have been happy if one or two merely stood up as his witnesses, maybe even write up a couple of quick witness statements that he could add to his file at home. He shifted his concentration from his daily tasks to those around him, examining every mood and movement. Being naturally political, he looked for patterns that would disclose an advantage he could leverage against Bill's reign of terror. By being the aggressor, Bill was making hits but he was also exposing vulnerabilities.

ANNA WOULD ORGANIZE:

» To Build Social Cohesion.

» To Forestall Mobbing.

» To Establish Leadership.

» To Promote Anti-Bullying Values And Actions.

At an afternoon staff meeting, he looked each employee in the eye and, in each, saw the same confusion, as always. At least their being confused was something akin to being undecided. Mario's examination was cut short by Bullying Boss Bill moving into a barely controlled rage over a scheduling issue he imagined had to do with Mario. Bill slapped his hand down hard on table then stormed out, not in the least embarrassed. Right there and then, and in front of the stunned staff, Mario put pen to paper to write it up. But he was the only one who did. Of course, he was the only one that had a job in the offing. For this incident, like the others before it, it was just his word against Bill's with no one else prepared to put their jobs on the line for some other employee. Of course, with a Bully in charge, all their jobs were on the line regardless.

Mario wanted to up the political ante to consolidate his new 12 percent gain, and maybe make some additional progress, but he hadn't really found a common and non-threatening cause around which he could unite his coworkers and, besides, they weren't ready for that. He decided to conduct a second, entirely casual yet conscious canvass, but this one would include his distributing political swords and shields to coworkers. Mario had been compiling loose notes describing Bill's behavioral patterns, his several cogitative holes and his many hot-button issues as well as his emotional blind spots. With his notes piled, he played around with various comparison charts and found some interesting patterns as the pieces came together in the mass of details of times, date, places, and quotes. He discovered that *behaviorally*, Bill was repeatedly most volatile just before manager meetings. The reports he prepared for the meetings were a *hot-button* issue for him. That's also when he was most likely to confuse which employees were responsible for which tasks—a *cogitative hole*. As a result, he tended to spread blame randomly, with Mario being his first choice for scapegoating but no one was spared completely. His anger created an *emotional blind spot*.

With his second canvass, Mario again chose not to spend what little political capital he had to fight for his own and so far ignored issue about Bill's bullying. Instead, he distributed "wealth" in the form of digested information to his coworkers. The next meeting had a completely different tone. Mario's coworkers stared at Bill with a certain distance and newfound confidence. Instead of victims wrapped up in Bill's dramas, they had become businesspeople with an objective view of his antics. Predictably, Bill lost track of work assignments. Instead of his coworkers being offended by his lack of respect for them as professionals, they saw a *cognitive hole* of his having nothing to do with them. As usual, Bill sent blame in every direction including Mario's. Instead of the employees feeling threat headed their way, they saw Bill's anger as a point of vulnerability, an *emotional blind spot.* Getting no reaction from his audience for the first time, Bill fell silent rather than going ballistic. On that day, he was the one who felt disrespected while the employees experienced no threat or vulnerability. With their new understanding, discovered and articulated by Mario, they knew that the anger they were witnessing had everything to do with the report due at his upcoming managers' meeting as his *hot button issue,* and was not about them, and was not their problem. His negative *behaviors* just before that meeting were predictable and, indeed, had been predicted by Mario.

Bully Bill fell quiet while he fumed. He was coming to understand a power shift had occurred. He was playing to a dead room. The political "motion" taken by these employees was one of accomplishing a self-protective, personal distance and unified distain involving no words and requiring no one go anywhere. Where there had been a monster defying definition, there was sitting a petty tyrant with no one to tyrannize. The problems that had been "all about Mario" had become "all about Bill." The general mood and two more employees shifted politically in Mario's direction. That gave Mario at least a 37 percent favorable rating with the momentum for support from the group as a whole on his side. Increasingly, Bullying Boss Bill stayed in his office and out of sight. Instead of isolating Mario, he was isolating himself. If Mario had been able to keep his job with only two coworkers tentatively supporting him, his threefold increase was powerful indeed. Yet, sometimes, winning just the support of just one individual, with leadership qualities, can be enough to do the trick.

Coworkers are Workplace Warriors' political constituents. Warriors who fail to be attentive to their constituents, do so at their own peril. What do politicians do? They shake hands, smile a great deal, kiss babies, give tokens of gratitude and smile some more. They may or may not be naturally attractive people, but they strive to be as personable as they can. For employees, being attractive to others is mostly a matter of caring about others. For sure, Workplace Warriors do nothing to repel them. To whatever extent Workplace Warriors are not isolated by the Bullying Boss, they are free.

7

A GOLD VEIN
A STRATEGIC PLAN

Section One

Hard and Soft

THE PARTY OF LESSER POWER

There are more strategies and tactics available than there are ways to talk about them. Sentences themselves are the product of tactical thinking. The most fundamental differentiation between them is the ancient Chinese one, those that are "hard" and those that are "soft." Yang and yin. As an employee, the person of lesser power, the use of hard strategies is not usually recommended. If an employee politically pushes hard against the front of the institutionally larger Bully, whether man or woman, the Bully will soundly push the employee back and down with his or her greater political force. This is why personal confrontations with Bullies are not generally productive. They certainly won't change the Bully or change the Target's circumstance for the better, but they can result in harm to the Workplace Warrior, while distracting him or her from strategies leading to more winnable goals.

For the weaker party, "hard" frontal assaults are essentially the same thing as political suicide attacks. Because they are visible and challenging, they serve best when used as a ruse. Predictably, they can draw a Bullying Boss's attention away from whom the Warrior is actually working with, and from where the Warrior plans a real action to occur. Although hard strategies are disfavored, hard tactics can sometimes be useful. They can be used to prod a Bully into exposing his or her deviations from the employer's mission whether it's a bullying deviation or some other under the employer's rules. Being hypersensitive and reactive, and generally limited to single mindedness, Bullies are remarkably easy to steer towards irrelevance. To the Bully, "I can't talk now. I'm already late for my appointment with HR" -- when the appointment was about nothing. HR becomes the Bully's focus.

It would be a "hard" tactic to lay hard charges against the Bullying Boss, such alleging he or she padded his or her expense account or mistreated a customer or employee. Being "hard," they are fairly accurately remembered and repeated by listeners to others. Eventually, they may very well find their way to the Bullying Boss, bouncing back politically to hit the Target even harder. Having institutional authority, Bullies play the "charging" game better than most any Target. Instead of using "hard" tactics when having very little institutional power to back them up, Workplace Warriors are wise to curtail how often they discuss their Bullying Boss with coworkers and, as mentioned, softly limit themselves to disgruntled yet vague statements indicating optimism when they do. Laying charges brings out the worse in Targets, and others have the least interest in. Trading charges with a Bullying Boss isn't the point anyway. For the Workplace Warrior, the heartfelt, collective concerns and support of his or her coworkers is. That's where a Workplace Warrior's power and protection lies.

BE INDIRECT

In a variety of ways simultaneously, where "hard" tactics would have employees charge forward, "soft" strategies guide them around, under, over, and through obstacles, while making as small a presence as possible. Their most basic maneuvers are *flanking, cover,* and *camouflage*. Where the "hard" relies upon the use force and directness, "soft" relies on grace and cunning. Where "hard" is exposed and brittle, the "soft" is opaque, largely unformed with no edges to define it and no visible center for a Bullying Boss to strike back at. Where the "hard" is impersonal and aimed directly at a perhaps isolated Target, the "soft" finds and nourishes the Warrior's supporters and allies. On its own, "soft" can lack sufficient definition to be practical and can also be of questionable endurance but with a thoughtful plan that includes obtainable goals, the Workplace Warrior will have sufficient focus to use whatever combinations of "hard" and "soft" strategies and tactics are most productive.

HARD & SOFT

Direct & Indirect

Activity & Stillness

Firm & Flexible

Exposed & Stealth

Forceful & Cunning

Stuck & Fluid

Isolated & In Concert

Proud & Humble

Bullying Boss Janise approached Target Crystal's desk with hostile intentions. A negative incident ensued. It was comparatively mild and ended quickly. Yet, Crystal's work area felt somehow soiled by Janise's noise and self-righteous indignation. The threat of a return visit hung in the air. Crystal's Bullying Boss had violated her space and boundaries. She'd marked Crystal's office in much the same way a dog marks its territory. Air freshener wasn't going to be enough.

In this case, as in most for employees, the "hard" options were extremely limited. A "hard" tactic would be for this bullied employee to burst into her Bullying Boss's office screaming about how she couldn't take it any more and maybe tossing something to the floor while she's at it. That employee would have overreached, put herself in an exposed and brittle position, and would soon find herself not only in retreat but also in a full-bore rout. Not recommended.

Another "hard" tactic might stem from a naïve temptation to reach out and try to reason directly with that Bullying Boss as a matter of social habit and as a showing of mutual respect, if nothing else. Workplace Warriors, by definition, are over that. They're the former Targets who have taken charge in some measure. They think in bigger terms than what's merely going on with the Bully as it affects only themselves. They're patient having confidence in their power to choose the types of strategies and tactics they'll use and when.

HARD & SOFT

Leading & Following	Initiating & Responding
Offensive & Not	Advances & Retreats
Battling & Surrendering	Flurries & Calms
Loudly & Quietly	Constructing & Deconstructing
Fighting a Wound & Healing	

Crystal tried a soft tactic. The next morning she showed up in her office with a modest bouquet of flowers for her desk. Not large and not roses. She needed to leave some room for further growth later, if need be. Of course, Bullying Boss Janice knew that Crystal's bringing in flowers was "all about her" (Janice) but then what wasn't? With her flowers, Crystal clearly communicated to everyone, including Janice, Janice had not succeeded in getting her down. Crystal had known she'd get no pity in a defeat and defeat would only invite a follow up attack so she had made a strong plan and she stuck to it. She'd refresh the vase regularly, trying different types of flowers and new vases from time-to-time. Her bouquet would not sit there like a one-shot statement and a passing thing; it'd be a work-in-progress. They not only announced Crystal's continuing inner strength and served a cleansing purpose for her office, but sitting to the front of her desk, they served as a soft barrier between her and her Bullying Boss; like armor except with bursts of color, beauty and love. Her work area once again became tolerable.

A fresh bouquet of flowers for one's desk is just one type of soft tactic that does everything a Warrior would want from a hard one, except more competently. If Crystal had instead written an angry memo, her Bullying Boss would have found something in that hard-edged thing to strike back at but she could not very well strike out against flowers or the employees who brighten the office with them at their own expense. For just six to ten bucks, Workplace Warriors can actually buy a small victory, a thing of beauty and some measure of joy.

BE OPAQUE

Soft strategies tend to be opaque, sometimes to the point of being invisible and often times creating an illusion of largeness when there's actually very little going on. That can be good or bad. Being opaque is the secret behind how the Warrior can survive the hardest of blows with grace. That's not done the "hard" way by taking the hits stoically, but by taking solace through identification with the larger view of things, then letting the local swings just pass through. Simultaneously and on other fronts, the Warrior is maneuvering quietly and circuitously into the corners and seats of workplace power, discovering supporters while being unnoticed in the midst of Bullying Boss's noise. When it comes to what's "soft," Bullies can be a bit blind.

If Warriors circulate among co-employees seeking out their concerns in an obvious and "in-your-face" sort of way, that'd be "hard." If instead Workplace Warriors are stealthy, barely visible at all, then their visits with the others might not be noteworthy even to the people they talk to. That would be successfully soft. It's soft to use empathy to hear and understand the impressions and concerns of others, then find ways to work with them. It would be a hard thing to try to make their thoughts conform to the Workplace Warrior's personally and politically important goals. It's soft to rally co-employees together around any given issue of their mutual concern, rather than the Warrior's own.

These soft techniques are more effective than standing hard, alone and firm, perhaps shouting politically hollow insults at or about the abuser, such as calling him or her a "Bullying Boss" when the Warrior had not yet educated his or her listeners to understand what that means. It's "soft" to let coworkers figure out for themselves that the "Bullying Boss" described in the literature, the literature the Warrior carefully and covertly left in the coffee room, is their very own supervisor rather than lecturing at them. (More on that.)

In addition to fighting battles, an employee has an actual job to do while, in contrast, battling is the only daily activity Bullies care about and probably the main thing they do generally. They call it supervising when it's actually gratuitous and costly infighting. If they want to play hardball, they can. They have what it takes institutionally to back it up. It's only natural for Targets to want to get their "pay back" in that same "hard" way, Bullies clearly deserve it. But predictably if the Target attempts that, the less powerful Target will loose. To proceed consciously by way of the "soft" is not to put the self below the Bully, but tactically to locate the self apart from the onslaught and strategically above-it-all.

Section Two

"The Story"

Strategic planning is not about the past, but that's where we start. It's not about future either, it's about presently appearing possibilities and potentialities. Defensive actions are aided by planning but offensive ones require it. Planning includes developing a vision that facilitates the discipline needed to get along a positive course of action. Planning does not include becoming struck by something originally thought helpful. Targets who aimlessly repeat their "The Story" with only negative results are stuck in exactly the negative incidents they seek to escape.

Targets want to be heard. That need is central to the Bullying Boss experience. Melissa's Bullying Boss, Laura, came at her out of nowhere while she was sitting in the coffee room on break. Laura's rage was reserved but the political threat she posed to Melissa was unmistakable. This was their second negative encounter in a month. In the first, Laura launched at Melissa about how she supposedly failed to follow recording procedures while winning a truly excellent contract. She just would not let it go. It was a horrible experience, one among many and emotional damaging.

Bullying Boss Laura was wrong in every respect, and Melissa vowed that she absolutely would not allow for a repeat. Melissa didn't officially report the exchange. She thought it was a fluke but she did give a blow-by-blow description to her best work buddy, Doris, complete with her outrage at every point. She repeated her The Story to a couple of other workmates and her partner at home. The smoke slowly dissipated but her resentments still lingered.

Every Target develops his or her own "The Story" and while it may be a great attempt at explaining a bullying dilemma, for structural reasons rather than personal, "The Story" is always counterproductive politically. Repeating it to others at work is a hard strategy that goes nowhere good. Yet, a Target's The Story has other values. Identifying and separating out the elements found in it is the first step in workplace planning. But, as scripted, the problems with The Story are many. It can be converted into some other more productive form but it can't be fixed. The first problem is that it tries to describe Bullying Boss activities that are difficult for people to believe. As already stated, when people try to communicate something inherently unbelievable, they are not believed. The Story itself begins life as the description of a single awful Bullying experience, and then becomes increasingly complicated as it's augmented with each new, negative experience.

WHAT WOULD ANNA DO?

Anna would never repeat her "The Story" in the workplace again. She'd break it down into its parts, putting them on note cards. With her partner and therapist, the cards would become her props.

Melissa barely relaxed for a month from her first bullying experience before it happened again. The second bullying incident had essentially the same structure. It came out of nowhere, was done in the presence of others, and was emotionally threatening. But the second was both on a different topic, a client taking his business somewhere cheaper, and in a different location, the copying room. The words Laura used were different, but the theme remained essentially the same. Despite Melissa's reputation as an excellent employee, Laura accused her of being careless, and had overstepped her authority by trying to renegotiate the departing contract. Melissa hated being called stupid, particularly by someone clearly her intellectual inferior. As before, the attack fell well short of yelling but was made all the more powerfully undercutting by its veiled restraint. Melissa hurt as before, but this time the hurt lasted longer. She didn't understand any of it. As with all her contracts, Melissa had done a stellar job. Again, she went to Doris seeking solace and support and got them again, but the second time there was a small, inexplicable distance between them that wasn't there on the first.

The big difference in reporting the second attack, Melissa was telling two stories at the same time. In their telling, and because of their many commonalities, the two stories and their facts got jumbled up as one. After the second altercation she ended up at least twice as hurt, and she held twice the damning facts against her Bullying Boss but she made much less sense to anyone, including to herself.

A week later, Laura came after Melissa for a third time. This one had the same structure as the other two—differing only in the details. In telling her greatly expanded The Story this third time, Melissa was no longer describing discrete events, but laying out a multi-layered saga of ongoing oppression. The facts of all three incidents were interconnected and, in their telling, interwoven. Instead of The Story being heard as all the more damning of her Bullying Boss, Doris could only shake her head in bewilderment. The intimacy they once shared had lessened. Melissa's credibility had been compromised not just by the incidents themselves, but also by the telling of her The Story.

Melissa was carrying a heavy load. She was beleaguered and besieged, increasingly alone. Some people at work had begun to keep their distance. Doris, family and friends were still listening but they just weren't getting the import of the experiences she was describing. She wasn't being understood. With three attacks in that many months, Melissa was finding it increasingly difficult to trust and connect with people generally. She began to entertain doubts about herself. Maybe she really had overstepped her authority. With her reputation tainted, she was concerned she'd never be able to get another job anywhere. All of these things further compromised her story-telling capability and ability to win support, but didn't stop her from repeating her The Story. She'd become someone different than the Melissa everyone had known. Her thoughts turned to revenge but that was a poor substitute for the justice that was society's and her due.

Because Targets' The Story is not recorded firmly on paper but only loosely recalled from memory, it's just naturally disorganized with some parts coming up chronologically, others topically and, as events unfold, most of it not being organized at all. From the beginning, The Story is too complicated, confusing, and self-contradictory for others to understand. Worse, it's unduly long. As it develops in an organic way, the Target remains honest but what he or she actually conveys stops being true. Its snippets of fact get stuck in time and so are not sufficiently pliable to be fashioned into a more coherent and accurate account relevant to a present conversation. All anyone can hear of the plight from The Story is that the Target is having an interpersonal dispute with the Bullying Boss and, according to even her, she just keeps on losing.

TO EXCLUDE

No matter how much patience people may have, The Story will never make sense to them by itself. They'll stand or sit politely as they watch and listen, but what they see are not moving images of the events as they unfolded before the Target but rather, hear a tangle of confusion of words instead. Typically, with their The Story, Targets repel coworkers and loose workplace political capital. As the Bullying Bosses first cast it and Targets unwittingly cement it with each person they tell The Story to; they confirm the illusion that what's going on is a garden-variety "personality conflict" at work – between no one beside the two parties – certainly not something that involves the bystander listener.

The Story has a negative emotional quality that also repels listeners and thus potential supporters. By its very nature, The Story is melodramatic. Before Targets utter their first word, they're already in a state of emotional distress. Knowing from experience that communicating their plight is difficult, they may amp it up with additional emotion in an attempt to compensate for these deficiencies. That's natural. But no one has ever been positively impressed with a melodrama or with someone stuck in his or her pain. No matter how justified the cause, or how much compassion someone might have, no one wants to hear the awful sounds of oppression with its howling and whining. As a purely practical matter, at work nobody wants to go down to the sounds of a sinking ship. In that mess, it's automatic for the listener to assume that The Story is at least biased, maybe false, or possibly even delusional.

With all this going on and there being no apparent goal to the conversation, the listener can easily become annoyed. They can feel "put upon," and wonder how Targets can reasonably expect someone else to fix the Target's problem for them when it's theirs and no one else's. As Targets build the intensity of The Story, they'll probably also end up sounding pious to the listener. The listener may not appreciate the Target's asserting their moral superiority over the Bullying Boss, a judgment most people will only make for themselves.

Indeed, The Story can't do the single thing any good narrative must do; it can't involve the listener. Again, for a speaker, communication is all about the listener. The Story describing bullying is just the opposite. It's self-oriented, when those around the Target are mostly oriented towards themselves. If a listener were to be a full party to the conversation and, if he or she's to truly understand what's going on, he or she needs to know what his or her role is. Does the Target have a goal and does it involve or affect the listener? Is there something specific the Target wants the listener to do? At its end, does the Target want the listener to submit a certain piece of paper, or talk to the Bullying Boss or someone else for the Target? Thus The Story, when standing alone, should be reserved for loved ones, lawyers, and therapists, but even they should be spared its repetitions.

In effect, The Story is the Bullying Boss him or herself made manifest inside a Target's mind, and then projected outwardly by the Target for others to see. It's no wonder people don't like being exposed to it. But there's a good chance a therapist would want to develop those experiences fully, complete with details that Targets didn't consider before, but this kind of discussion is inappropriate at work. It might seem as though it is—after all it's about work—but it should not ever be repeated there again. In that place, it has a great many negatives, and no gainful purpose. There are better, more strategic ways to go with the facts. By deconstructing The Story of the past into its elements, then rearranging them analytically, patterns will emerge to create a strategic plan and a more predictable future.

Section Three
Making "The Story" Make Sense

TO BE ABSTRACT

The Story is so hot and close to Targets, it cannot be willed away. No matter what, they are injured and still need to be heard but, so far, they could only watch as people's eyes glazed over. They were obviously not listening. By taking advantage of the physicality and flexibility of note cards used as props, Workplace Warriors can finally be understood because the delivery of information becomes structured and can be not only heard but also seen. When story telling on its own hasn't been working, it's time for Warriors to upgrade their approach. There are too many elements, emotions, and rationalities for any of it to make sense for as long as all of its pieces are spinning around in the air as abstractions. It's frustrating to be in chronic pain and not be understood but it doesn't have to remain that way.

Sometimes, oftentimes, Targets are called, "paranoid." That's an undeniable signal it's time to change their approach. There are plenty of other problems too big and too dynamic for story telling, and a bullying battle is one of them. Scientists develop treatises. Lawyers write briefs. Artists paint canvas. Workplace Warriors make note cards. As with the others, by getting physical, they make The Story real.

TO BE PHYSICAL

The Warrior can readily grab a handful of note cards or a pad of small paper sheets. The only difficult part of this exercise is the act of starting. After picking up just one card, this process takes off on its own, increasing Workplace Warriors' energy and that of their listeners with each card laid on the kitchen table. In the middle of one card, in bold letters, Warriors write their own name. On other cards, they do the same for the Bullying Boss and each person, if any, who personally witnessed the last negative encounter.

These cards will, as will be seen, have several more important and strategic uses later, but this first use is to make visual and real what happened the last time the Bullying Boss jumped the Target. A table is used as if it represented the floor plan of where the last incident occurred, probably meaning the office, or shop floor. Chopsticks work well to symbolize walls. The few cards that were just made are placed on the table in the positions best representing where the Target, the Bullying Boss, and the main witnesses were just before the encounter started. Those are their starting positions. The Bullying Boss's card might be placed somewhere down the hall and out of sight, and it might only be a best guess, while a coworker's might be next to the Target's.

A STEP-BY-STEP CHRONOLOGY DOCUMENTING THIS INCIDENT

On Monday at 10:30 on July 12, I was sitting at my desk reading a report that Witness Janis wanted me to look over for her. Bullying Boss Martha entered the office from the far door looking exasperated. I knew there was going to be trouble. She stomped over to my desk.

Witness Janice retrieved her report from me, backed away from the noise but didn't leave. She stood nearby and watched.

Bullying Boss unfairly and harshly criticized me for supposedly being slow and not careful in my work. She said she knew I had a new lover and blamed my poor work on that. I denied all of it except having new lover. That seemed to be the real reason she was angry.

She walked over to Witness Janice, grabbed the report she was holding, and then threw it down on my desk making a loud noise. She left the same way she came in.

The Workplace Warrior slides the cards along to replicate the paths that each individual took while describing the events at every step. The Story is this time disciplined by the facts as they occurred linearly, and is understood separately from other incidents. It's heard in digestible bites. The table and what gets placed on it serve as simple visual aids. These images won't be quite television quality, but they'll communicate better than the airy confusion that had previously proved unworkable. As with the actual conflict being described, The Story takes on a physical form so there's no need to flail one's arms about the room using emotion, intensity, and commitment to justice. The cards do the work.

For the first time, the Workplace Warrior has successfully described an inherently emotional and difficult harassment event. Getting what happened out of what once was the Targets' spinning head and on the table makes it clearer even to them. They feel much better. Having been heard, they can once again feel like a part of the Social Fabric that their Bullying Boss can never be. Very importantly, they are now ready to convert their The Story into something infinitely more powerful, the beginning of their strategic plan.

story: account or recital of an event or a series of events, either true or fictitious... A usually fictional prose or verse narrative intended to interest or amuse; ... a tale...

strategy: ...The science and art of... overall planning and conduct of large-scale combat operations 1. A plan of action resulting from strategy or intended to accomplish a specific goal. 2. The art or skill of Using stratagems in endeavors such as politics and business...

—*Dictionary.com (2005)*

Section Four

Playing with the Elements

TO PLAN A PATHWAY

When politicians, generals, or litigators construct a strategy, they ideally start with a clean slate. They identify their goal, survey the facts as elements, and then maneuver the relevant elements around until they form coherent plans, all before taking their first defined action leading to their goal. Generals, for example, have used long rakes to push and position miniature tanks and soldiers, which are "elements," around on a large tabletop map or move them on video display equivalents. In contrast, Workplace Warrior employees begin their strategy making with the battles already in progress, the war having been initiated by their Bullying Bosses a good while before, and for reasons all their own.

STRATEGIC DEVELOPMENT

The General Procedure	The Warrior's Procedure
Ambitions/Goals	Multiple Hostile Incidents
⊍	⊍
Strategic Plan	The Story Evolves in Jumps; Tangled
⊍	⊍
Tactical Plans	The Story Deconstructed (by elements)
⊍	⊍
Actions/Non Actions	Strategic Plan Constructed (with elements)
⊍	⊍
Goals Achieved (modified)	Tactics Devised (Actions/Non Actions) *And Consciously Executed*
	⊍
	Goals Achieved (modified)

Strategy making for Workplace Warriors begins by their breaking their The Story down into its elements. In hand, they already have note cards representing a few of the people involved. As they think about the people at work and how the work sets up, they'll then think of additional cards they'll want to include to representing more people and other forces as well. All of these are workplace elements. Like the general's toy tanks, these cards are maneuvered into both graphic and analytical formations to discover actual and potential relationships, the sources of power as well as the probable trajectories of individuals and other political forces. Although probably not exactly on purpose, these cards will eventually appear as stepping stones leading to the Workplace Warrior's goals, possibly including actual relief.

ANNA'S TIPS FOR TARGETS

» Elements are pieces or sets of information you identify and sort into analytical frameworks and operational plans.

» People, aspects of people, and groups of people are elements.

» Products, services, problems, and possibilities are elements.

» So are economic, political, and cultural matters.

» Focus on the objective and operative effect of each, rather than just their presumed moral postures.

The workplace is not multiple sets of paired individuals having a series of bilateral, interpersonal relationships, as it might seem when Targets are stuck in the Ring of Fire with Bullying Bosses. It's a political organism that has a character of its own. Functionally, a workplace is a hive that includes a multiplicity of events and interrelationships too complicated to render linearly. It's the hive's *buzz* that matters more than most any particular individual or other element. As with the written word generally, the cards allow for a greater complexity of thinking. When the elements are eventually rendered as a whole, they illustrate that buzz and that's more informative than mere line thinking, speaking, or planning can ever have.

GIVING STORY CARDS DEPTH

It's not necessary to have cards representing every individual involved, or try to figure out who should be included. Warriors will think of people to include as the process moves along. Eventually, there will probably be ones for each significant contact point at work.

ON HER CARDS, WHAT NOTES MIGHT ANNA INCLUDE?

Name.	Victor, Neutral or Victim Nature.
Official Title.	Animal Archetype (lion, mouse...).
Political Role (e.g. peacemaker).	Hot-button Issues.
Role for Warrior (ally, supporter...).	Special Strengths & Weaknesses.
Other People Connected To.	Expert? Witness? Complainant?
Ambitions & Career Objectives.	Editorial Comments.

If anyone represented has a special and relevant feature to consider, it can be included on their card to give it depth of character and the Warrior breathe of understanding. It might be a certain attribute like an attitude, ambition, pending grievance, or work relationship. Warriors might note the relationship of an individual to them (e.g. supporter), a particular and relevant demographic factor (sex, race, age), their functional role in the case or campaign ("witness to…"), and their warrior propensity (victor, neutral, victim). This is a good place to note the name of the animal species that best represents their personality and role in the workplace. These are the character elements. As the card analysis is worked manually, the elements with greater weight drift to the center of the table and the others away.

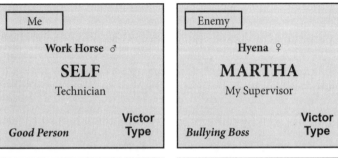

Me	Enemy
Work Horse ♂ **SELF** Technician *Good Person* — **Victor Type**	**Hyena** ♀ **MARTHA** My Supervisor *Bullying Boss* — **Victor Type**

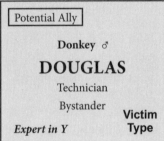

Ally	Potential Ally
Eagle ♀ **MARY** Technician Watcher *Wittnessed X* — **Neutral Type**	**Donkey** ♂ **DOUGLAS** Technician Bystander *Expert in Y* — **Victim Type**

A TACTICAL PLAN

Even before manipulating the cards, Anna knew she had a particularly insightful witness to her last Bullying Boss attack. Eagle Mary. She wondered if, after work, Mary would write a witness statement documenting the event but she knew, from experience, that Mary was not dependable in a confrontation, preferring to stay clear of controversy. Adjacent to Mary's card, Anna placed another card representing an expert in operational matters and possibly an expert witness, Donkey Douglas. Douglas tended to be slow moving but he also had a mean kick (anger). He didn't witness the last confrontation but Anna wanted to secure a witness statement from him to validate her work skills. Like Mary, Douglas preferred to stay clear of uncomfortable situations but he was also clearly a supporter of hers. Anna intended to spend time to learn each of their viewpoints and concerns, maybe later to groom them into active supporters, if possible.

On the other hand, Hyena Bullying Boss Martha was a fighter of a particularly low down and unrelenting sort. She was not a good person. In fact, she was the enemy of a good person, the Workhorse Anna. In all candor with herself, Anna might also have reason to doubt her own fighting capacity but she ultimately found, with planning, that she had what it took to do the battling that needed to be done. Of course, her first instinct had been to make peace but, then again, a fight is a fight.

Non-character elements also got rendered on note cards, possibly in a different color than the character elements. These were political forces to be considered, including the relevant cultural, economic, political, and legal forces at work in the workplace. The most important of these cards was the employer's mission generally. No matter what Anna's objective and plans might ultimately be, she wanted to be most attentive to the employer's objectives and plans. Separately and for focus, near the center of the table, she put a card with just a couple or three words describing what her best contribution to the fulfillment of the employer's mission could be.

WHAT WOULD ANNA DO?

For each *relevant factor* affecting the workplace, she'd identify:

The Employer's Mission	Economic & Financial Factors
Relevant Cultures & Roles	Political & Legal Factors

The noted cards are parts of a machine powerful enough to create a future reality. Just as only a chess genius can plot a chess game in her mind with no help from a physical chessboard, most employees' minds can't realistically plot out a workplace strategy in the abstract. A strategic plan with productive actions will emerge from what was chaos – but there's no telling in advance what that plan will be. Just as each chaos is different, so are the plans that emerge from each. Trial and error on a tabletop, discovering and exercising strategic and tactical options, just has to be a very good idea before a Target ventures out into hostile territory as a Warrior. Out there, regular people get regularly hurt. The Bully plays for keeps. Now, so does the employee.

> "You can't *think* your way to right action.
> You can only *act* your way to right action."
>   —David Milch, Writer, Producer

Section Five
Power Cards

THE FORMAL ORGANIZATION CHART

A good, solid starting point for analyzing any workplace is to make visible its official organizational structure. Workplace Warriors move the cards around to match just that portion of their employer's organizational chart, relevant to them. This demonstrates visually the formal chain of command as well as lateral relations. Previously, the official chart may have seemed irrelevant, out of date, and mostly wishful thinking on someone's part, but if Warriors are going to understand the flow of power around them, then they've first got to take a good look at how things are at least supposed to work from the management team's point of view. Warriors probably don't have the actual flow chart, although there might be one hanging on a wall somewhere or printed on the inside, back cover of the employer's internal phone book. In an alphabetized list format, the same information can be found inside as well. All of these tend to be out-of-date but corrections can be made as progress moves along.

ORGANIZATIONAL CHART

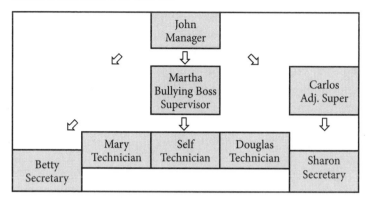

In this formal arrangement, the cards are organized into a pyramid shape. The Warrior has constructed "The Busy Person's Organizational Chart." In it, all official power flows downwardly from the top manager to everyone else below. Warriors can see graphically exactly what their standing is in the larger matrix. That's an organizational/political position that gives them not only a position to defend against the Bully, but also a platform from which to fight. Whatever their responsibilities in their position might be, each duty attendant to it holds potential for influencing others through good work efforts and the contacts made. It's good to take a long look the arrangement as a whole, to commit it to memory as an image.

ACTUAL POWER RELATIONS CHART

By now, Workplace Warriors have shifted from the one-dimensionality of verbal descriptions of how things work to the two-dimensionality of cards, but that's not enough. Any one thing or idea can enter the picture from any direction, at any time. The flatness of the chart can lure Warriors into simplistic thinking. The actual workplace is fully dimensional. "Sh_t runs downhill," not just along a flat plane. Most importantly, power is not static. It's always flowing and always changing directions. Never ending change is good news for Targets who don't like the way things presently are. The trick is to know its flow, and flow with it. It surprises many employees to explicitly recognize from this next chart what they've long known implicitly—power flows not only down the chain of command, but up it as well.

ADJUSTED FOR POWER

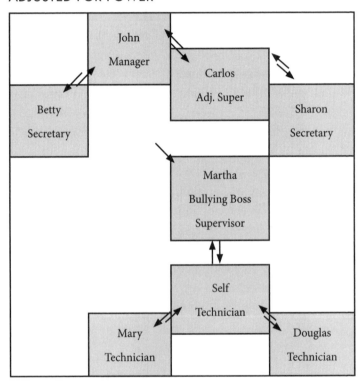

The cards can be moved around to reflect the real power relationships as they become known to Warriors, as they talk to the people at work. When considering real power, it has many possible sources potentially affecting outcomes, including power elements such as position, personality, connections, turf, seniority, age (young or old), relevant skills/talents and, level of motivation or the ambition. In this configuration, the card for the active and productive supervisor in the department next door, Carlos, will rise to near Manager John's and so will the ones for both of their secretaries, Betty and Sharon. Carlos is the power behind John's throne, as is Betty in a very different way. Indeed, her card will skyrocket from quite lowly to near the top. Actual power in the forms of information, contacts, ideas and production flow up from the two of them to John. John uses their power and his own to further his version of the employer's mission.

If Bullying Bosses are intent on exercising their official power to dismiss a Target, then the Warrior can look around the actual power chart to see whose influence the Bully will probably go after to support that drastic action. Working along the Target's level, the Bullying Boss will seek the support or at least the neutrality of co-employees by making negative comments about the Target on a regular bases. Working on higher levels and at the same time, he or she will seek support from the managers and co-supervisors. It will be through a combination of both actual and official power that he or she will make the big move against the Target.

Section Six

Stepping Stone Cards

A PATHWAY CRAFTED IN STEPS

Jeri's overriding goal, of course, was to get free from Martha, her Bullying Boss. One way out from under would be a transfer or, even better, a promotion. Her preferred goal was to get involved in, and maybe even direct, a new and exciting project that had just been approved. That would not only get her free of Martha, it would also put her on the same political plain, a much safer position to fight from, if still need be. It would also mean an increase in salary and doing work she loved to do, while giving her experience invaluable to her career.

It's been said that when possible, "The best defense is an offense." As noted, offenses require planning. In her fourth usage of the cards, Jeri moved them into various political and geographic, stepping-stone formations to make a pathway from hers to Manager John's card. Her planned-for path would be uniquely her own, but the manner in which she created it is pertinent for all Warriors. Jeri started with the goal of securing Manager John's support in her difficulties with her Bullying Boss, Martha. She believed that John was the true decision maker. Legally and morally, he was certainly the responsible party.

With her cards in power chart formation, she could see a direct path to Manager John. She could simply walk into his office and tell her tale but she, as the weaker party, knew better than to do that. He would probably not believe her reports of maltreatment—practically nobody had. Although he might not say it at the time, he'd probably object to not only her bothering him, but also take offense at her going over her supervisor's head in the process. As the weaker party, she needed a path both more circumspect and that held greater authority.

She saw two indirect pathways to that same end. Her eyes locked onto Betty's card. She was Manager John's secretary but going through her would be almost as direct and maybe more counter-productive an approach than going to Manager John personally. Apart from access, Betty offered little authority. Her eyes shifted to the cards on the right for Supervisor Carlos and Sharon, his secretary and occasional lunch mate of hers.

From the arrangement of the cards on the power chart, she visually appreciated that Carlos was politically tight with Manager John, whereas her Bullying Boss was not. Yet, she remembered that on the formal organizational chart, Carlos and Bullying Boss Martha were officially on the same level. The contradiction between card arrangements told her that there was an objective basis to assume there was, or would eventually be, a rub between the two. Substantively, Carlos was widely respected for his product expertise while Martha didn't really bring anything of special value to the employer. Carlos was personable and she was anything but. The additional contractions between work roles and personality types as marked on the cards told her there was a subjective basis for a rub as well.

Although she had no evidence of an actual problem between them, the cards demonstrated that her nasty Bullying Boss and the powerful Carlos were both natural rivals and organizational competitors as well. She then knew to look for that evidence. In a row between her and her Bullying Boss, Carlos might prove to be helpful or at least stay out of the way. *The enemy of my enemy is my friend.* She didn't know Carlos personally, but Sharon, his secretary, obviously did. Jeri could see that she needed to set up with Sharon their next lunch date for as soon as possible.

A STRATEGIC PLAN

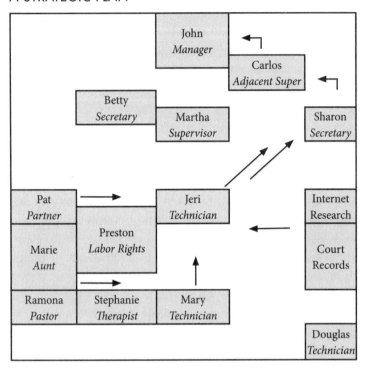

Although not then known to Jeri, Carlos was already onto her Bullying Boss Martha's tricks. Just a couple of week before, he had his own little run in with her. It was a small thing, but a significant warning sign to him nonetheless. Manager John and Carlos were sitting next to each other in the conference room when Martha came in with a distribution problem. She didn't show Carlos the same respect she did Manager John when it was Carlos who was the responsible party for her issue. As an event, it was nothing. But that differential in treatment between the men, based solely on status rather than substance, was all it took to set Carlos thinking about her strategically.

A week after that, and also unknown to Jeri while she was developing her strategy, Bullying Boss Martha had visited Carlos' office. Within Sharon's earshot, Martha ran Jeri down with a list of both alleged work-related and personal faults. Martha gave Sharon (and a lot of other people) the creeps anyway. The third time with Carlos, Martha was as charming as she could possibly be, pretending they weren't rivals, but suddenly best buddies. She'd obviously figured out along the way that Carlos had Manager John's ear. To Carlos, it was obvious she was playing him, going to great lengths to lay negative foundation against Jeri, but had nothing real to say. That's why she was reduced to using the list approach.

Carlos was a great deal sharper in these matters than most people. This is why, when it came to dealing with the trickier political issues similar to the one the Bullying Boss presented, Manager John relied on his input. That and Carlos' production expertise were the reasons behind his influence with Manager John generally. Jeri didn't know any of these things while she was crafting her plan, but apparently she knew enough. Her good instincts were made possible by, by then, a deep informational foundation supporting them. While her Bullying Boss was running down Jeri to Carlos, his secretary Sharon was shocked by what she heard. Knowing Jeri, she knew her boss was being fed a pack of lies and she told him so afterward, and then left to have a lunch with Jeri that they'd already planned.

At lunch, Jeri could tell that something was up with Sharon but understood that Sharon would never betray her boss's confidences. Sharon eventually acknowledged that there was a problem and displayed strongly negative feelings clearly aimed towards the Bullying Boss, Martha, but said nothing specific. When Sharon returned to work, she didn't say anything to Carlos about the Bullying Boss's lies. But she did make a large point about how great it was to have lunch with someone as intelligent and insightful as Jeri. But out of his deference to Martha's authority—supervisors virtually always share administrative solidarity—Carlos politely opted to stay out of it. He was also biding his time for his own reasons.

A week later, Jeri and Sharon had lunch again. Sharon didn't know the details but she knew Carlos was watching the Bullying Boss carefully and took that as an encouraging sign. While still protecting her boss's confidences, Sharon and Jeri decided that Carlos needed to be better briefed about Martha without implicating him in the Bullying Boss's nightmare. His approach would undoubtedly come from another direction. With the right materials, he could decide on his course of action better informed. When Sharon returned from lunch, she was upright and clear. She walked into her boss's, Carlos' office, looked him in the eye then repeated verbatim her comments from a week before, "It was great to have lunch with someone as intelligent and insightful as Jeri." Her words were generic but with their purposeful repetition, their import was made clear to Carlos. In the broadest of terms, Carlos commented that Jeri seemed to be on the right track – seemingly meaning both being a good employee and maybe on his side in potential conflict with Bullying Boss Martha. He commented, "I don't believe I've seen anything of hers before." He very casually let it be known that if he happened to see something informative from Jeri, maybe about Bullying Boss Martha, he wouldn't throw it away.

A file with copies of Jeri's written and collected documents somehow found its way to Sharon, and then somehow ended up on Carlos' desk together with a great many other papers. Sharon was Jeri's strongest ally. As it turned out, Carlos didn't give Jeri's materials to Manager John. It didn't seem like a smart play for him to make, at least not right then. But by reading them, he was better informed, down into the details, about how his opponent thought and worked, what her hot-button issues were and, for future use, exactly how businesslike Jeri turned out to be.

As Jeri learned, the Story probably can't be successfully suppressed no matter how important it might be to do that. However, it is often possible to sublimate it under a fresh and more powerful force, a strategic plan. The Story will still be hanging around, but it will no longer matter as much as it once did, not when Warriors are marching forward with the strength of objective understandings. They rest better and are calmer throughout their day, thus being more attractive for the people at work to talk to.

Jeri received no immediate relief but was not discouraged. By flanking around Bullying Boss Martha through Carlos' office, Jeri had taken some risk but not a lot. She had not offended anyone by going over Martha's head yet had successfully made favorable contact with powerful player, Carlos. Jeri didn't know it at the time, but when it came time to staff that special project, the one she'd been anticipating, Carlos would be the supervisor responsible for deciding who got selected to work on it. He wouldn't be forgetting Jeri. Her analysis and strategic plan had become more profound than she planned for or imagined possible, because it was rooted in the facts that she had already worked objectively. It's said that a battle is already won or lost before it begins. This is that.

Section Seven

Good Timing

TIME IS SEEN FROM ITS CONTEXT

There is no political rule definitively instructing a Workplace Warrior when to act or not but good timing is not an entirely mysterious phenomenon. If nothing else, in retrospect, good timing feels good and bad feels anything but. From there, Warriors learn by trial and error, but good timing can be seen more directly than that. Just as people can see the power and character of a wind by the way it affects the leaves on the trees around them, they can see good and bad timing in the way it affects them and their surroundings. When Warriors examine the power flows at work, they'll probably notice that timing is the mechanism by which all of the connections between elements come together and apart, creating order and disorder through a continuing process of change. By being attuned to time, Warriors fit themselves more perfectly to that flow.

> It's not about understanding the world,
> *It's about learning to dance with it.*
> —*Playwright Richard Foreman*

Ultimately, the best way to discover good timings, as with most political things, is to look away from one's agenda and to the context. The main way to do that is to ask those involved casually presented, oblique questions to test the timing waters. A phone call or two will say when it's the safest to travel beyond a Warrior's immediate work area, to canvass for information, to make contacts, or possibly to discover potential allies. When scouting a coworker for a potential witness statement, the witness's immediate fear or resolve can be tested with a few preliminary questions. Immediate fears are subject to change. When Ricky wanted to move from one workstation near his Bullying Boss to another soon-to-be-vacant one farther away. He had no idea when it would be available or, more importantly, when would be the best moment to show his interest in it. Instead of launching forward with a request without regard to timing, he made gentle inquires at the other end. His timing would be perfect.

With the documents on hand and those Warriors create, they can take into account the relevant patterns of people's mood swings; break and meal times; vacation and production schedules as well as the seasons, weather, and times of day. They pay good attention to project timings with their onsets and completions. They match what they do with the visits from suppliers, customers, regulators, and the brass from headquarters. When any of these show up, workplace timings shift to accommodate them, and so should the Workplace Warrior.

On a smaller but just as important scale, the rhythms of people and events are a subtle but actually visible indicator of temporality. At a meeting, each person speaks with their own cadence that may match the rhythm of the others, or not. There's also a rhythm to the ordering of speakers and, if any, the dead air spaces between them. Linguists with enough funding, time, and equipment calculate these things with precision by observing them through one-way mirrors, but a Warrior need only relax and feel them. When their timing feels right to a meeting, the Warrior will speak up on the beat to advance and not against it to be shut down.

A sense for good timing will guide Workplace Warriors in differentiating between when it's time to exhibit their loyalty to the employer by being its "Best Worker," such as when their Bullying Boss is comfortably gone or distracted by other priorities, or cloak their offerings from attack by their Bullying Boss, such as when he or she is actively stalking them. As a matter of survival, good timing will pull Warriors out of fights with their Bullying Boss in the exactly right moment, after the point when leaving would be insulting and increase hostilities, but before he or she's gone off the deep end. Instead of looking at a clock for good timing, Warriors watch for when the veins on their neck start to bulge, their sentences become disjunctive, or their eyes turn from fire to ice.

When any employee is absent from their workplace, such as when on sick, bereavement, or extended leave, the events and their various timings don't go on hold. It's wise to remain aware of developments at work even when away. The Warrior can check in with co-employees by phone to stay abreast of events and the timings they occur in. They listen not just to the works, but for the rhythm, tone and texture found in their voices. With these small efforts, they can know when and how it's best to return to work, then step into the ongoing flow flawlessly. They'll have maximized the chances of finding warm welcomes as their timing matches theirs, rather than being shocked by cold shoulders indicating a disconnect. The Warrior will have kept in touch with the workplace pulse all along.

MOVE WITH TIME

The greater Workplace Warriors' understanding and comfort with their complex political environment, the sharper their instincts will be. It won't be magic that they "just know" when to act, they will have incorporated into their understandings all the data they need, then relaxed into it. From that place of integration, and likely without noticing it, they rather simply "become one" with their work environment. If Warriors want to test their instincts and are good at these things, they can tell a joke. If the joke is both meaningful and "in the moment," it will work. If it's contrived in either respect, it will fall flat.

Good timing is a product of being both mentally and emotionally present in the present time and environment Warriors are actually in, and not drifting off to some other. Although haunted with injustice and degradation, the past can never be anything more than memory reflections activated in the present tense. Memories can carry useful lessons or, just as easily, burden Targets with hurt feelings and bad attitudes that are counter-productive in a great many ways. The future can never be anything more than a set of projections a Target manufactures in that same present tense. The future may seem like an excellent place to visit for planning, and is excellent for dreaming, but it's an unhelpful place to take up residence. Even for visions, only the present is real.

For Warriors and everyone else, living in the present is to be living with reality even if it's uncomfortable. That's exactly where they want to be because that's the only place events, remedial or otherwise, unfold. If the joke mentioned earlier falls flat, that's a good indication that the Warrior has wandered away from the present and more daring, political moves are ill advised. For one to push against timing, instead of swimming with it, is to go to political doom. With relaxed good timing, a Warrior will move towards his or her goals, largely unimpeded and with style, flexibility, and fluidity.

When timing is bad, it'll often be because the Warriors have become unproductively self-centered. They'll have attempted advancement when things, including the Warrior, are actually quite stuck, still, and stifled. Too often people move when their impatience or despair prompts them, finding disastrous results. When timing is good, those same things the Warrior might have done in bad timing, will have actual power and positive effects. Even waiting for good timing is "future tripping" just the same. It creates the illusion that good timing is a limiting factor, something historically and currently in the way of progress, when it's actually never ending, cyclical blessings. To have good timing is be on track with the cycle, regardless.

When others at work watch the Workplace Warrior accomplish a minor feat, it may appear to them that it was the Workplace Warrior's sense of confidence that created his or her success but that view is far shy of the full truth. It'll be the Warrior's instincts for good timing that created both the confidence and the results.

Section Eight
Measuring and Balancing a Plan

DO THE POSSIBLE

It's been said, "Politics is the art of the possible." That doesn't mean Workplace Warriors compromise their own vision in any degree because of what then seems possible; instead, it means they won't allow others or unfavorable circumstances compromise it. If a Bullying Boss is standing solidly between a Warrior and a promotion that frees him or her from bullying activities, the vision of that promotion remains in tact for however long is necessary.

By now Workplace Warriors may have completed the heroic act of devising their first version of their strategic plan but are naturally uncertain about its effectiveness in reaching their goal. Before stepping into battle, how can a Warrior tell whether it's any good or not? Sure, once they're in motion the truth of it, good or ill, will be known, but in what ways can it be tested and improved before then? It's tested by very casually sharing it aspects of it with others—at work and outside as well. Is the plan balanced? Is it reasonable? Will others find what's said and done believable? Keeping one's life partner fully briefed and involved can be a frightening prospect but can also be enlightening in practice when their comments and criticisms are solicited. With co-employees, Warriors have to be considerably more circumspect in their queries; but they're the ones with a best feel for their workplace's dynamics.

An important point for evaluation is to look at the plan's costs, multiplied by risk factors, and compared against what might be gained. In every political stratagem, there are degrees of nourishment and exhaustion to be considered for each individual involved. To be successful, a plan must ultimately provide nourishment for each relevant supporter (profit) beyond any exhaustion there might be (loss). As noted, group gripe sessions, just as with calls for workplace justice, will exhaust employees to no productive end. If drained, the Warrior and his or her allies are not very likely to make it all the way to the goal or even have enough energy to escape the field of battle if need be. If instead they're nourished through the experience of joinder and maybe successes, there will be plenty of fuel to carry employee forces all the way home.

DO THE BELIEVABLE

"Believability" is enhanced as a positive element if the underlying act being described is "reasonable," but that's not enough. Ultimately, both believability and reasonability are only abstractions and so have a loose quality about them. They require questioning in light of each hard fact, and that includes input from others. Does the plan's success depend upon the credibility of the Workplace Warrior? If so, there may be a problem. The credibility of Targets is normally compromised from the effects of bullying long before they know to move forward as Warriors. Is there someone with greater credibility who can be incorporated into the plan? If respected colleagues present a Warrior's facts and points, they will tend to be believed more readily. Is there a publication with inherent credibility, such as a professional article, that can shift current beliefs forward without regard to the Warrior's credibility?

Will the Warrior's credibility be stronger in one political context, such as with supporters, than if played out in another, such as at a general meeting? Can the location of events be shifted to accommodate concerns for credibility, such as shifting away from the conference room, over to a restaurant? Any given audience is also more likely to find an act or assertion credible if there's a well-known history or proof supporting it. These are items to think about including. If the proof is not patently obvious, and requires the listener to make any kind of effort, it may not be useful. If there is any question for debate, then the element of a "debate" itself cuts against believability, regardless of the underlying strength of the argument or assertion. For sure, bald proclamations of truth won't do it, good planning will.

DO THE REASONABLE

Strategies and tactics are less dangerous and more productive when relevant others see them as being reasonable. That means being both logically constituted and not excessive. Excess repels potential supporters and attracts hostiles. The first requirement of reasonability, being logically, internally consistent, seems like it should be an easy enough criteria to meet. But logic is itself a slippery thing, not just for other individuals but for Warriors as well. When left abstract and unfettered by evidence, logic can be used and misused to prove most anything. It can sell snake oil to snakes. In arithmetic, logic alone is the underpinning of all equations. The correct answer is truth. In science as in the world generally, what's merely logical and seemingly reasonable is actually nothing more than a hypothesis. To be regarded as true, it must first be successfully tested against the physical realm through the trial and error processes of experimentation. Workplace Warriors do exactly that by talking to their co-employees.

The second requirement of reasonability is that the plan and action not be excessive. That depends on the myriad cultural norms of the people involved, and not on any particular individual's perspective, including the Warrior's. Again, in all communications, it's the members of the audience, their values and their languages that matter. Older people tend to view the young as being too strident and radical. Young people can become insulted by what they perceive to be unreasonable limits on their adult selves. Each group tends to see the other as being excessive on a regular, if not nonstop, basis. Beyond age, the members of each general and occupational culture also have their special perspectives determining what is and is not excessive.

Winston was a very well kept, young, African-American man obviously headed for success and likely to get there. His public sector job required a great deal of travel and that necessitated his making innumerable travel expense reports. On a handful of them, his employer found some discrepancies and so withdrew its approval for reimbursement. It also decided Winston's errors were purposeful so imposed a two-week disciplinary suspension on him. Winston was both personally offended and professionally compromised. From his point of view, his reports were reasonable, logical, and not excessive, as was the offense he took when his promising career was marred. After all, they were only talking about a few discrepancies in a large number of routine reports.

At a civil service hearing, Winston lost his appeal from the suspension. He took the matter to the court. On the morning of his court hearing, he had to wait until the criminal calendar was cleared before he could be heard on his civil appeal. From the back of the courtroom, he watched 25 men of about his age and race (but without his prospects) being sentenced to prison terms, one after the other, on an assembly line basis. In this unfamiliar, but instructive, place, his understanding of reasonability shifted dramatically. While he was sitting there dressed in a designer suit, he watched guys in orange jump suits being sent away, some for stealing less than what was disputed in his expense claims. All of a sudden, a two-week suspension from his job looked less excessive and more reasonable.

GENERAL CULTURES DETERMINE REASONABILITY

Men and women, different races, ethnicities, and nationalities have differing cultural constructs leading to different perspectives as to what's excessive and moral or not. An American visiting a traditional culture may find it entirely reasonable to put her tired feet up on a stool when talking to her host. Her host may see an entirely different event. He may see the bottom of her feet pointed at him, to be an insult. Her conduct was appropriate to her but excessive by a different standard. There is no amalgam of values to determine what is "reasonable." One must pay attention to each relevant culture – and not just to one's own.

In our mostly English based legal tradition, for a long time we've applied a mediaeval concept and law of Nature, "the reasonable man" standard to determine reasonability in court. A jury would be tasked to see the events from the perspective of what a "reasonable man" would have perceived or done under the circumstances in dispute. In recent times, that standard morphed into "the reasonable person" standard. Would a reasonable person find Mr. Gray's conduct to be reasonable or excessive? With the advent of employment laws specially protecting women, minorities, and other protected groups, it became evident that each protected group had special notions of "reasonability," particularly as applied to them, and that it was appropriate to apply that group's standards to the facts, rather than those of their opposites or attempting for global ones. Kerry Ellison alleged she had been sexually harassed. The anti-discrimination laws were designed to protect her from exactly that type of negative activity, so the standard applied had to be a "reasonable woman's standard." Women are disproportionately the victims of rape and sexual assault, so they tend to be more concerned about sexually oriented, negative behaviors. The perspective of women is the better one for judging what is the harassment of a woman.

IRS employee Sterling Gray relentlessly pursued co-employee Ms. Ellison despite her attempts to dissuade him. Imagining they had some sort of "relationship," he pestered her at work, repeatedly invited her out for drinks and lunches, chased her demanding personal conversations and eventually left messages she later described as weird and getting even "weirder." The last ones "shocked and frightened her." [24] Would a hypothetical reasonable woman find Mr. Gray's conduct to be sexual harassment or merely tasteless and stupid? It's always been obvious that men and women have different views and communicate them in different ways.[25] In modern times, we've made it official. In the workplace, not only must the values and perspectives of both genders be considered, but all the permeations emanating from them as well.

The same holds true in racial harassment cases where we now also have "the reasonable African-American standard" among others. An African-American lineman, George McGinest, claimed that he was subjected to a racially hostile work environment in a large number of incidents over a 15-year period. They included his being assigned to work in dangerous conditions, denied bonus pay, forced to endure racial taunts and insults, was subjected to racist graffiti in work restrooms, and denied a promotion. An uninvolved, hypothetical Caucasian construction worker might see an African-American, like George, working dangerous jobs and made to operate faulty equipment and think nothing of it. That hypothetical Caucasian might also see racist graffiti on the wall, yet be unaffected. He might hear an African-American coworker being referred to as a drug dealer yet hear no racism in the comment. He might interpret these events as being, at most, pranks. Yet, both George, as an individual, as well as a hypothetical reasonable African-American representing a separate history and very different set of life experiences, might react in the opposite way, seeing racism in each of them.[26] Our own lives are extremely instructive as to who we are, but not necessarily as to who any other person might be.

OCCUPATIONAL CULTURES ALSO DETERMINE REASONABILITY

Different occupational cultures also have widely divergent notions about what's reasonable and what's not, depending on what its employees do with their minds and bodies. It's productive to define explicitly, in a list format, the relevant occupations together with several occupational attributes so they can be consciously worked to the best advantage at each step. For example, construction is often a rough activity, whether it's banging something together or banging it apart. It's coarse, loud, painful, and dangerous. Its organizational form creates, and is dependent upon, a strong work ethic. Behavior that elsewhere would be regarded as bullying might be regarded in construction as part of a normal day's work, and certainly the other way around as well. Medically based cultures are, in some ways, just the opposite. The culture of registered nurses derives from their work that is both scientific and compassionate. Their daily duties require close attention to how others are feeling, then precision in care giving. Any strategy in that arena that compromises "patient care" is doomed while one that fosters patient care is strong.

Nurses demand and, depending on the circumstances, receive respect as professionals. Enhancing the respect this occupational group receives are the economics associated with their scarcity. Their employers have recruitment and retention problems, making nurses valuable assets in the medical community. As valued employees, nurses can, more strongly than most other occupational cultures, hold to their cultural norms with relatively little compromise. Each of these elements is inseparable from the values of the occupational culture.

A card representing carpenters' cultural values, such as meeting construction deadlines regardless, might bounce off one for nurses, representing patience. The attributes indicating strong work ethics shared by both might coincide.

An employer's overall culture depends not only the occupational ones within its operations but also the employer's institutional culture. Is the management structure a traditional one with a formal hierarchical structure? If so, whatever actions and plans the Warrior devises can either respect that chain of command or circumvent it. To be in accord with a management culture is the generally safer approach, while circumstances decide which is the more productive.

An employment culture may be rooted in liberalism, meaning that it still has a hierarchal structure but it's hidden below a façade of toleration and affability. In that unusually comfortable mix, informal avenues to secure relief from a Bullying Boss may be encouraged and, in a natural way, protected. It might also be that the liberalism makes managers worthless in conflict situations. Whatever a Warrior does, it's prudent to remain mindful that lying just below that soft surface is a command hierarchy reality. For sure, somewhere in there, somebody's in charge.

When strategy making, it's important to define, out loud so that use can be made of it, the managerial culture that rings most true for the circumstances: traditional, formal, liberal, alternative, ruthless, fair, or some other?

A FEW GENERAL AND OCCUPATIONAL CULTURES

Public sector & private
Service, business, manufacturing, construction
Female or male dominated or mixed
Uniform sexual preference or mixed
Uniform race or ethnicity or mixed
Uniform age or mixed
Union & non-union

There are a great many elements that can affect a workplace. Workplace strategists take account of each of these. For ease and accuracy, note cards representing each and spread intelligently around a table do, somehow automatically create clarity without there necessarily being a whole lot of thinking involved. When made physical, the matches, conflicts and potential paths to pursue tend to be obvious.

PERSONAL DOCTRINES TEND TO BE UNREASONABLE

No matter what a person's race, the narrowness of a racist working near them on an everyday basis is oppressive. Sexists, racists, homophobic people, and those whose thinking patterns are structured narrowly and linearly create their own artificially small world. It's all figured out in neat little boxes. From watching them, the boxes themselves appear to be more important than what might be inside.

Whatever people feel through their senses or emotions is, for structural reasons, necessarily at variance with the abstract truth found in their preexisting dogmas (the boxes). That differential has long generated conflict. The experiential side of those variances offend the dogmatists as if each were yet another piece of jetsam hanging in the way of the "pure" thinking or morality they aspire to. If there's an error, blame is placed on the facts. There's generally a book or some other hallowed source involved to define their small reality, to be pulled out when the complexity of the earthly events whirling all around them gets too confusing for people not of an essentially simple, *feeling* kind.

Kelly Carson was an openly gay, 17-year employee of Coxcom Inc. in Phoenix. She was assigned to work for an evangelical Christian supervisor, Evelyn Bodett, who disapproved of her homosexuality. As a subordinate, Ms. Carson was essentially Supervisor Bodett's economic captive; a condition made worse by her concern that she might not be able to make house payments even if her job remained stable. Enhancing her vulnerability, she had just broken up with her partner. She was in "a state of emotional distress" which Ms. Bodett exploited for the purpose of imposing her religious doctrine. Supervisor Bodett repeatedly instructed Ms. Carson that homosexuality was against her religious beliefs. Through criticisms, discussions, and prayer sessions held behind Ms. Bodett's closed door, Ms. Bodett "worked with" Ms. Carson to help her overcome her "sins."

Finally, Ms. Bodett insisted that Ms. Carson attend a Christian woman's conference that was held out of town. Ms. Carson initially agreed to go but ultimately declined because she didn't have the money. Supervisor Bodett bought Ms. Carson the plane ticket and sent her off to the conference.

According to the complaints she made to coworkers at the time, Ms. Carson was not a willing participant. Clearly, her privacy rights and personhood were being violated. When she eventually received a promotion to a position at the home office, she took it. Their higher-level supervisor, Mireille DeBryucker, heard second-hand about Ms. Carson's complaints, and took Ms. Carson to lunch to find out why she was leaving their office. It was to escape Ms. Bodett's homophobic activities. When asked why she didn't say something on her own, she replied, "Bodett was her boss and she could not afford to loose her job." Nobody cared to ask before.

The Human Resources Manager, Sue Hutchinson, had previously authored a change to the company policy concerning unacceptable employee behaviors. As typical and in accord with laws against discrimination, the preexisting policy prohibited harassment but only when it was specifically motivated by someone's race, gender, sexual preferences, and the others. Greatly simplifying and civilizing matters, the amendment Ms. Hutchinson added prohibited all harassing behaviors regardless of motivation, including "verbally or physically harassing, coercing, intimidating, or threatening a coworker, supervisor, or customer." Such conduct would "be cause for immediate discharge."

The employer's investigation determined that Ms. Bodett was harassing Ms. Carson in violation of company policy. Ms. Bodett was terminated and she sued Comcox, taking the matter all the way up into the appellate courts. In her view of her religion, she was required to harass homosexuals into compliance with its doctrine. To deny her that opportunity was to discriminate against her on account of her religion. As a legal matter, court disagreed with her. As a workplace matter, Ms. Bodett had no right to misappropriate her work authority and financing to impose her non-work doctrine on an essentially captive subordinate.[27]

The workplace works best when it defines itself by experiential reality rather than unrelated doctrines. It's about the basics of what works and what gets the job done. Bringing non-work related, outside doctrines into the workplace is to chuck a monkey wrench into that machinery. Bullying Bosses are monkey wrenches. Ms. Bodett was effectively blinded by the hard line limits of her doctrine and acted accordingly without regard to the workplace context. External, theoretical perspectives belong in the workplace only to the extent they further the employer's mission, perhaps adding vision. Otherwise, they're a daily problem.

In a different case, Hewlett-Packard Company went beyond prohibiting aberrant, abusive behaviors. It affirmatively fostered a strong diversity policy, "Diversity is our strength." In its Boise office, it distributed a series of company posters, each heralding the humanity of each traditionally disenfranchised group, including one for gays. In response to the gay poster, an offended, devout Christian employee of 21 years, Richard Peterson, believed he had a "duty to expose evil when confronted with sin." At cross-purposes to the company's program and in public view, he posted a series of large scriptural quotes that he interpreted to ban homosexuality. His supervisor instructed him to take them down, but he refused. A series of meetings with management ensued during which, among other things, he proudly stated that his postings were "intended to be hurtful" to gays to compel their compliance with scripture. Hewlett-Packard eventually fired him.[28]

As stated, while Bullies may boast of their bullying activities and achievements, for purposes of enhancing their status on petty levels, they don't normally admit to their anti-social intentions in formal settings, yet, this sightlessness one did (as did the one at Comcox). Mr. Peterson was aware of, and received personal instruction about, the employer's twin policies of fostering diversity and prohibiting the harming of Hewlett-Packard employees. He confidently counter-posed that he took instructions from a higher policy, "I don't see any way that I can compromise what I am doing that would satisfy both (the employer) and my own conscience," with his conscious requiring him to harm the other employees around him. No one needed to take time to develop a tactical plan to set him up for exposure and ejection, although that could have very easily been done. He did it to himself. As judged against the general, occupational and employer cultures they worked and were amerced in, both Evelyn Bodett and Richard Peterson were excessive in their attitudes and behaviors. They defined *reasonability* and excessiveness by external standards.

If other employers were as principled and protective of their human resources as in these two cases, then employees wouldn't need to go to elaborate lengths to defend their personhoods and livelihoods. Hewlett-Packard took time on several occasions to counsel Mr. Peterson. They explained to him as best they could their diversity program protected his right to be a Christian just as it protected his coworkers' right to be gay. The flip side was that, because of the primacy of everyone's work responsibilities and everyday proximity to each other, no party could impose its views on another. Unfortunately, Hewlett-Packard and Coxcom are rare in their willingness to protect their employees from being abused, and thus compromised as producers, by others they employ to promote production.

ATTEMPTS AT *JUSTICE* TEND TO BE UNREASONABLE

Many if not most, Targets repeatedly verbalize the community-based value and word, "justice" but get no reply in the workplace. Similarly, some others get fixated on protesting the failure of yet others to behave in accord with their own interpersonal standards, ones generally appropriate with family or friends. In both cases, when they espouse their outside values, anger tends to be present also. Functionally, these attitudes and emotions are not unlike those of the prejudiced Evelyn Bodett and Richard Peterson. These employees are still Targets, not yet Workplace Warriors.

While virtually all people see the vengeful attacks of angry people as excessive, angry people too often see them as being entirely reasonable even when confronted by caring others. Being angry, excessive and blind all go hand-in-hand. Even when angry people fully recognize that they've exceeded norms for reasonability, they often do not to take heed of their precarious position. Instead and without thought, the angry regularly determine that the special righteousness of their cause will carry the day despite their methods and postures being excessive by the standards of others. Certain of their cause, they do not have a clue. A failure of inquiry is self-imposed blindness. While entirely confident of their mass support, they construct a consensus of exactly one.

Apart from a select few supporters who share the same values for justice and relationships as the Warrior, it's wise to remember that when at work, very different and businesslike rules of conduct and values are standard operating procedure. No matter how respectable, no foreign ones imported from the community are going to remedy the bullying problem in the workplace, but the already applicable businesslike ones might. Indeed, any outside doctrine that fails to further the employer's mission is best served by staying outside.

For example, a pair of ex-employees, Michelangelo Delfino and Mary Day were on a misguided mission for "justice." They clearly thought themselves clever, not excessive, and thus reasonable when they posted over 13,000 derogatory messages on a Yahoo bulletin board slandering two executives with their former employer,

Varian Associates. Among a great many other things, their messages attacked the executives' professional competence, veracity, and mental health. They implied that the woman's clothes were stained because of giving sexual favors for advancement. A lawsuit was filed to stop them and to collect damages but that didn't slow them down. Their confidence in their special notions of reasonability was not so easily compromised. They actually increased the fervor of their message making. In stark contrast and ultimately, the jury also thought it was being reasonable when it made a whopping $775,000 liable award against each of them.[29]

Reasonability is clearly in the eye of the beholder. Just a clearly, it's not wise to let one's own anger define what's excessive or not. How do Workplace Warriors calculate which is which in a political environment? On their own, they can't. As with everything political, they have to ask around. Each person to be talked to represents not only a set of different cultural influences, but also their individual self. Nothing can be assumed. Everyone is entitled to an opinion and, when prompted, will generally share it. If one happens to be angry, they should do a lot of asking.

In the process of asking others for their perspectives, a Workplace Warrior is simultaneously building support for whatever they end up doing. With each person involved and talked to, the Warrior shows respect by creating for them an opportunity to share their perspectives, as people tend to do. As co-employees working in the Warrior's midst, they may very well be affected by his or her actions and that potential affect will go a long ways in determining what they ultimately regard to be reasonable or excessive. Perhaps they have a moral right to be included. Once included and once the action starts, they might see themselves in what's being done because their judgments, in some way, will be visible to them in the Warrior's actions. These are the people who might be considered likely supporters or, maybe even, allies.

ANNA'S STEPS TOWARDS CRAFTING HER STRATEGIC PLAN:

Gather information for consideration as elements.

» Canvass other employees for their views, opinions and agendas.

» Document events by their elements in standardized formats.

» Collect work documents on herself and her workplace.

» Research her industry, employer and bully (e.g. online)

On note cards, record each element relevant to her plan for action:

» From "The Story" she's been telling.

» From the documents she'd collected and made.

» About herself and her Bully.

» About other employees (e.g. allies, potential allies, opponents).

» About cultural, business, economic, political and legal factors.

» About relevant individuals and factors outside the workplace.

Physically work the note cards.

» Give each note card depth and character (e.g. personality information).

» Arrange note cards in analytical formations (e.g. power relations).

» Manipulate note cards to discover patterns and advantages.

» Use note cards to craft an indirect path to goal: *"The Strategic Plan."*

CHAPTER

8

GOLD PLATING
DEFENSIVE ACTIONS

AS BETWEEN SWORDS AND SHIELDS,
DEFENSES ARE SHIELDS.

Section One
Workplace Defenses

THE IMMEDIATE WORK AREA

Employees mostly try to stay completely away from Bullying Bosses, but that can sometimes be impossible if they work in close proximity. If Bullies notice that someone's ducking them, they will not see an employee's sensible avoidance, but will see cowering behavior. Targets are subject to entrapment by Bullies at any moment. Whether a particular Bullying Boss bullies subtly or crudely, there are some areas where a Target is more vulnerable than others. Some Targets, particularly women, sometimes feel the most at risk in isolated areas or at odd times where and when Bullies can "have at" them without witnesses. That certainly happens.

More likely, though, Targets are at the greatest at risk when among co-employees and Bullying Bosses have an audience to show off their powerfulness. For Bullying Bosses, that's the main point of the show. The safer spots are areas with other supervisors, known allies, and particularly upright co-employees. Even safer are areas with customers or other outsiders who have importance to the employer. It's amazing how a basically out-of-control Bully can find self-control and even become polite when necessary. If employees have identified a particularly safe area before the next incident, they'll more likely move themselves there, perhaps coaxing their Bullying Boss to come along with them. If they actually take a quiet moment to stand in that safer spot in advance then even if their brain happens to freeze up when challenged, their body might walk them to safety.

Sometimes it's just a matter of shifting a Bullying Boss's attention slightly away from themselves, and over to something, someone or someplace else. The use of props, particularly items that represent an authority, can be helpful as a diversionary tactic. Warriors can pick up almost anything physical—so long as it's not physically threatening—such as a critical file that requires the Bully's attention, a note with an important phone number that needs to be called.

Being physical, they can sometimes also be useful in coaxing another person's physical movement, perhaps easing their Bully towards one of the safer havens without being confrontational, defiant, or disrespectful. In this way, they "work" their Bully by pointing at something or someone in that safer place that production requires they show the Bully for no real purpose other than to change their focus of attention, or maybe, in steps, to move the Bully and themselves to the next spot that the Warrior would prefer the two of them to be in. It's just like tossing a ball to distract or move a dog, except both more difficult and important.

Some Bullying Bosses may make it a point of spontaneously walking by a Target's desk to check up on them once and a while, and the Targets can't know when. That puts a full-time tension in the air. Bullies are already certain that the employee is up to no good, so the outcome can only be negative. It may be difficult to predict when they are most inclined to trespass on the Target but there will be patterns. It might occur most often in the mornings on the pretence of making sure work has begun or, and this is a favorite, at 5:00 on Friday afternoons.

Warriors can try turning the sequence of events around. They can pop in on the Bullies from time-to-time to make pointed and preemptive contacts in their own timing and on issues of their choice, instead of those the Bully artificially generates. With the contact recently made, the Bully has a diminished interest in making his or her own in the near term. If done to the extreme of becoming an annoyance, the Bully may actually become the one to avoid contact.

DON'T HOLD TURF

A critical mistake many people make, particularly those who have private offices but including those that have workstations as well, is to hold their ground while under attack. One-on-one, a Bullying Boss is a superior institutional fighting force to the Target. Bruce was typical. Bullying Boss Norman regularly charged into his office. The challenges were different each time but the result was always the same. Emotionally, Bruce felt like he was being pinned to the back wall of his small windowless office. It seemed like there was nothing Bruce could do, apart from asking his superior to leave. So he did, and it didn't work. It didn't occur to Bruce to leave himself.

The places employees work in are not their property. There exists no reason for employees to defend territory that's simply not theirs. Too often employees hold their turf and disaster follows. They say afterwards: "But he wouldn't leave my office," as if the Bullying Boss's departure upon their request were mandatory—the same as it would be from their personally owned property, their home. It's extremely difficult to compel any person to do anything they don't want to do, but it's easy for the moving parties to do something for themselves.

Being control-conscious, Bullying Bosses, like dogs, jealously guard their turf – both physical and political. The importance of "turf conscious" can't be overstated. Many if not most supervisors regard employees' work areas, together with each of their employees as being *their turf*. Turf is external and it's externality they use to define their existence. When Bullying Bosses challenge Warriors in their own work area, the employees should leave as soon as it's practical and relatively gracious to do so. In the moment of their departure, Bullies are deprived of a confrontation, which was the whole point of their being there in the first place. Just seconds later, Warriors can return. Bully smoke and fire will have blown over.

RESTROOM RETREATS, DON'T LEAVE GROUNDS

Employees' departure, when under fire, shouldn't include leaving the building or grounds altogether if reasonably possible. Technically, they might be regarded as having "constructively resigned." Leaving the grounds converts what could have been an intelligent retreat into a political rout, thus pleasing Bullying Bosses greatly while alienating employees' allies and potential allies with a display of weakness.

Employees may instead excuse themselves to go to the restroom. The timing of their announcement has to be excellent, they don't make a big deal about it, and certainly don't beat a hasty retreat. They don't cower or leave themselves open for insubordination; and they don't actually enter the restroom if being pursued. They proceed in a businesslike fashion as if there were no dispute going on.

IN CONFRONTATIONS,
MAINTAIN PERSONAL BOUNDARIES

During aggravated confrontations, there really isn't any such thing as good response, but the first line of defense is not becoming entangled in the Bullies' anti-social behaviors or gamesmanship. That includes avoiding not just escalation, but also cowering and insubordination. If Targets engage Bullies on their level and in their manner, Targets will only be exposing additional parts of themselves to challenge (intelligence, dedication, vulnerabilities, etc.) to Bullying Boss manipulations and political compromise. Workplace Warriors are separate and strong people. To protect their personhood, their emotional boundaries must remain firmly intact even when under direct challenge by an organizationally superior, bullying force.

It's generally best to just let the bullying run its course, if possible and appropriate. Warriors can fall silent while maintaining an upright posture, relaxing their body in a way that's visibly noticeable, and maintaining eye contact as appropriate to situation. Warriors stand softly, still and firm; solid like a mountain. Non-engagement is not a concession of strength or honor. Any emotional or other response Warriors might make tends to add their new energy to the Bully's, as they send it back to the Bully, creating a feedback loop for additional, escalating cycles. There's no point to it anyway. Any words that Warriors might offer would necessarily be different in some way from the Bully's. Bullies too easily perceive even a tiny differential as a challenge requiring escalation, or pretend they do.

Frequently, the bullying dynamic compels Warriors to participate or respond directly to aggravated Bullies in some way. Like a mountain's echo, they can provide feedback to Bullies using just their keywords, maybe together with a few general listening noises, but adding nothing new. On the return, the Bullies' keywords inform them that the employee is not only listening, but also understanding what's being said. They have no additional reason or excuse to increase the volume. On the contrary, the Bullies will hopefully feel the respect they so desperately demand, while probably not being entirely aware they are expending themselves without the satisfaction of engagement.

WHAT WOULD ANNA DO
WHEN BEING ACTIVELY BULLIED BY WAYNE?

» Keep her emotional weight outside the workplace.

» Identify, remain in and return to safe areas when possible.

» Maintain personal boundaries but not hold external turf.

» Observe her Bullying Boss left Earth. Let him go out there alone.

» Feed just his keywords back to him, out there.

» Not engage him. Avoid tethering him back to her.

» Maintain good, relaxed posture and eye contact with the Bully.

» When on challenged "how" she did X, advocate the work goal.

» Avoid insubordination traps. "Obey now, grieve later."

» If need be, define the "abuse" or "bullying" out loud for all to hear.

Paul was ordered to report to the Bullying Boss's office at 2:00. He knew he was in trouble and that there might be a quarrel. While his particular Bullying Boss was normally passive aggressive rather than directly confrontational, he doubted he could stand up to him when he was in serious trouble. His boss was very good at getting under Paul's skin, so Paul took advantage of his own poor eyesight that required him to normally wear Coke-bottle-thick glasses.

By putting them in his pocket, he became partly blind, creating emotional distance between the two of them. As Paul expected, his Bullying Boss dressed him down sternly with no yelling, but great intensity just the same. Unable to see his Bully, Paul was not reactive to what he knew had to be condescending and maybe intimidating facial expressions. The encounter took on a depersonalized and artificial quality, making it feel less threatening and thus more manageable. Paul's emotional boundaries were protected by a blurry wall that limited what he could see and what he was affected by.

WOULD ANNA RETURN HIS STARE?

She'd certainly be attentive, not competitive or defiant.

No stare: Merely maintaining eye contact.

Solid stare: Unflinching, straight back into his stare.

Deep stare: Focusing past his eyes to the back of his skull.

Nose stare: Focusing between his eyes, on the bridge of his nose.

Fuzzy stare: Removing glasses prior to encounter.

It's when employees are being challenged or charged, that they are most vulnerable to becoming reactive and insubordinate. A touchy trap for some employees, usually hourly employees, is signing for the receipt of a document they don't agree with and know has damaging implications. Salaried face the same dilemma with other documents, like being made to sign a report they don't want responsibility for. Joey was a young man with a strong sense of dignity resting, in part, on his strongly held convictions for honesty. His supervisor presented him with a performance report on which, even at a glance, he could see had checks in all the wrong places. He knew he was being unfairly set up for dismissal and refused to be a party to his own execution.

When his Bullying Boss ordered him to sign it, he refused. It was the employer's standard operating procedure to ask an employee to acknowledge receipt of a performance report with a signature. He was not being asked to agree with its contents, but there was no way Paul was going to sign a blatantly dishonest document. His principles would not allow for that; neither would his pride. He was fired on the spot. While his performance could have been debatable as good or bad, there could be no debate about his refusing an order.

He could have signed it with a simple note under his signature, such as "under protest," but he didn't know he had that option. Actually, he didn't even need to do that. Under the signature line, their standard form read, "Acknowledging Receipt Only." When faced with an offensive order and the prospect of insubordination, the well-established rule is to "obey now and grieve later" except where there's an imminent and serious threat to health or safety, or when being ordered to violate a law of significance. By obeying the order, employees keep their jobs as well as buy time to rethink, regroup, and build support.

WARRIORS WRAP THEMSELVES IN THE EMPLOYER'S MISSION

When Targets are being made to suffer a lose-lose argument, the Bullies are probably challenging how they did something instead of the accomplishment itself. As discussed, the "how's" make for great bullying arguments because "how" something is done is potentially subject to Bully supervision, and that means it's an opportunity to exercise control. The "how's" generally also lack definition, thus precluding a definable defense. To the extent Warriors speak at all, they can try to smooth the Bully over and onto a more productive topic, just as they would smooth the two of them into a safer work area. The better topics for Best Worker Warriors are those that are result-oriented and concretely defined, such as the employer's immediate service or production goals, the Warrior's actual results or, although less well-defined, the "big picture" goal of the employer's mission.

In politics, there is a tactic of being extra patriotic called "wrapping yourself in the flag." What it suggests is that no matter how well or badly things are going for politicians, if conditions are right and they fervently demonstrate patriotism, then their political position will improve. Others who, in contrast, fail to "wrap themselves in the flag" become suspect. When employees wrap themselves in their management's mission, both generally and in difficult moments specifically, things will usually improve.

To use a prop to help distract Bullies or to change a topic, employees' might hold up a memo representing the current goal of that work group. With a prop in hand and evangelical zeal clearly directed at a neutral item, employees can advocate for their employer's mission as if they were the ones who cared most and were inviting the Bully to join them in caring. In the process, they are effectively challenging the Bully to join them in loyalty to their common employer. By using Bullies' uncommonly competitive edge against them, employees direct the discussion away from themselves.

DEFINE IT AS "ABUSE" OR "BULLYING" FOR ALL

When employees are made to suffer active harassment, the act of creating a written record immediately after the fact should be automatic, but there is more that they can do to memorialize the events. During or shortly after the event occurs, Warriors can also make a social record by talking to their coworkers about key specifics, preemptively defining it in employee terms. No two memories of an incident are likely to be the same, not with each other and not with a Warriors' either. With some leadership, the Warrior can guide the memory processes of the group by recounting a couple of the details of what happened out loud for the witnesses to hear and absorb. If someone sees it differently, they should and probably will speak. If the event is seriously negative and still in progress, Warriors can define it out loud and for all to hear, with exactly the word that fits best, "This is harassment," or "bullying" or "abusive." If the event includes a critical fact for onlookers to remember, it gets stated out loud and more than once.

Under all circumstances, Workplace Warriors are the most likely to garnish political support when they are inclusive. In a confrontation, the Warrior can accomplish that by defining the dispute as common to the group rather than personal to the Warrior. If the bullying comes in the form of a criticism or charge, Warriors define it in group terms for the listeners, by speaking in the third person, and saying out loud, "It's not the employees' fault."

Section Two

Be Mindfully Detached

EMOTIONAL AND PHYSICAL CONTACTS LIMITED

A workplace defined by bullying abuse prompts employees to wisely minimize their exposure by holding back portions of both their personal selves and work efforts. Except for handshakes, physical contact with other people should be avoided together with any personal intimacy. Intense forms of personal connection have little or no interpersonal foundation to sustain them in the workplace. It is, by design, a business environment where production goals and impersonal interactions predominate. When the work world and various self-interests inevitably shift just a bit, two "friends" will each find themselves not only in new positions relative to each other, but having a new form of relationship. As discussed, friendships are not particularly compatible with the work structure, but equally intense ally relationships are.

Handshakes are the one great way to make physical, thus more intimate, contact with others than conversation alone can do and without any interpersonal confusion. Handshakes are formal rituals. If done with emotional presence and a sincere grip, they convey both connection and respect. They are businesslike. They are safe and effective. Any other attempt at intimacy or touching is problematic, particularly if it involves members of the opposite sex. Any other touching losses the safety of ritual and interposes the specter of emotional and occupational chaos. They're confusing. A hand on someone's shoulder might signify to that person the Warrior wants to be a good friend or maybe has a romantic attraction, when all that may be intended is a friendly gesture.

For people who've had particularly difficult family, friend and intimate relationships or who have suffered trauma events associated with other physical contacts, this is very serious business. A Workplace Warrior can't tell who suffers these plights and who doesn't merely by looking. In that business environment, and particularly if there's a Bullying Boss on the prowl, people may choose to keep to themselves, avoiding anything that resembles over-familiarity and the vulnerabilities it creates. Or, instead, it could be that they're fine inside themselves, but just don't like the person approaching them. A Warrior isn't likely to know.

WHAT'S PERSONAL STAYS PERSONAL

In any workplace, but particularly in Bullying Boss territory, it's not wise, long-term, to talk about dating, romantic, or marital matters at work. The same is true about sex talk or sex jokes, not even with the co-employee who currently plays the role of "best friend." If a romantic detail absolutely has to be shared with someone, it's best to call an outside friend on break from a cell phone. Interpersonal confusions with acquaintances outside work usually go nowhere and generally do no damage. At work everyone's job is on the line.

Innocent flirting in the workplace is a fiction, and frequently a manipulation. Even if earnest, either party will end up rejecting the other at some point in time. Bitterness often ensues. Jobs are often lost or they become working nightmares. "Hell has no fury like a woman's (or man's) scorn." Proximity, over time, may change the appearance and nature of a relationship, but not the person. They remain who they were on the first day they were met. It's wise to look back to that day, to remember who and what they saw then.

A hypothetical Jill found a hypothetical Jim attractive. Another coworker reminded Jill that Jim looked like a former crush of hers, Jack, and that relationship lasted exactly seven weeks. Was Jill willing to put a job of seven years on the line for, maybe not exactly a person, but to pursue what might be an echo of Jack? And where was Jack right then? She didn't know and was actually glad he was too far away for her to know. But she already knew where Jim would be when they inevitably broke it off. They'd be right next to each other at work, probably with one or both harboring very bad attitudes about the other.

Under the best of circumstances, both friendships and romantic relationships known at work are entanglements that make both parties, and the connections between them, vulnerable to a Bullying Boss challenge in ways so numerous they must make bullying mouths water. Bullying Bosses regularly perceive intrigue where there is none, and are likely to imagine that Targets are at least friends with, and possibility involved with, most anyone they see the Target talking to. Bullies tend to be limited to what they can see superficially. That makes them dangerous. If they had a significant capacity for empathy, they could easily discern that the substantive nature of most any relationship is not a threat to them. Discretion is advised. Ultimately, if there is a romantic element anywhere in the mix, employees can anticipate, and prepare for, Bullying Boss intervention and possibly fury. Bullies not only don't "do the personal," most don't tolerate it in others either.

Warriors may be very good at protecting their information from disclosure, but their emotions can sometimes give them away. No matter what the Bully prods, Workplace Warriors can't let their antagonists get a first-hand view of their spiritual and emotional insides. For them, that's the bullying bull's eye but, being limited, they can't make it out with definition unless the Target exposes him or herself. But if employees can put up a great front, and take advantage of the Bully's naturally narrow viewing range of people, he or she will see the mask and not the actual person behind it. It's in that blindness that Warriors will find the greatest safety, but only if they keep their insides dark to the Bully world. It's best to share our personhoods only with invitees, and not ever those intending harm.

There is an ancient-to-contemporary theater genre devoted to masks. If a Warrior thinks the bold thought of trying on an actual mask, maybe when no one's looking, it's guaranteed to be hugely informative. It doesn't seem like it should be a big deal, but it is. People discover there's a distinctive and powerful feeling that comes from wearing one, a feeling that's memorable. The mask is simultaneously both protective and proactive. It gives Warriors a significant sense of distance from events, protecting them from the more intrusive incidents. With that protection, it's far easier for a Workplace Warrior to do the abnormal and critical thing of strategic thinking, pulling pieces apart and putting them back together, objectively. Once the mask is personally experienced, that experience, sans mask, is readily and comfortably taken into the workplace.

Harold was a young man who took a job in a nearby city where he was not known. On his first day, as he was scrubbing his assigned desk clean, a senior employee whom he had not met before (Katherine) came into his office. She was a woman on a mission. During the short course of uncomfortable small talk, she trapped him behind his desk. Her come-on was not subtle, but he deflected it gracefully. His new boss, Keith, popped in from around the corner. He had obviously overheard the exchange. He remarked, "Better you than me." Katherine immediately put out the word that Harold must be gay. Harold said nothing to the contrary. He had no interest in any romantic involvement with anyone in that awful job, and didn't expect to remain in town for long. He went home for weekends, and that somehow confirmed people's convictions that he was gay. Over the next 16 months that he worked there, he was never bothered again. And he was straight.

With people losing community and devoting themselves entirely to their jobs, work is where people are meeting each other including for friendships and romantic relationships. This may be the most important reason for Warriors to keep their emotional and social weight outside of the workplace. It's wise to find friends, and one's true love in a place of beauty and excitement rather than one charged with money and power––and run by Bullying Bosses. This isn't merely about exercising discipline or restraint in potential social and romantic endeavors at work. It's about Warriors generally holding themselves at a certain distance from what goes on around them. It's as if they adopt the role and attitude of watcher, sitting slightly above on a perch from where they can objectively observe people and forces and develop a plan accordingly. That perch and perspective will go a long way toward sheltering Workplace Warriors, former Targets, from harm.

Section Three

Control the Flow of Information

CREATE AN INFORMATIONAL VOID

Controlling what information flows from Warriors to Bullying Bosses is not only a "must" activity, it's also a full-time devotion. Information is power. Management teams are generally very good at keeping information close to the vest while keeping their employees in the dark, supposedly to render them less able to question management's decisions and more pliable to their will. However, employers sometimes may, rightfully or wrongly, compel employees to share sensitive information with their supervisor Bullying Bosses. The default flow of information begins with employees and works up to supervisors, almost never the other way around.

Being required to share private information with Bullies is particularly unfortunate given that, as noted, Bullying Boss already press to "to get inside the heads" of Warriors, where emotional vulnerabilities can be found. Conversely, Warriors strive to evict Bullies and otherwise keep them as uninformed as possible. No Warriors should allow Bullies access to information about their personal lives and their sense of personhood. Given the close proximity of Bullies to Warriors, and the relentless nature of bullying, this is not always easy.

MINIMIZE THE FLOW OF INFORMATION TO BULLYING BOSS

Family Matters	Good/Bad Things in Life
Activities	Finances
Achievements	Purchases
Health Issues	Trips

Bullying Bosses are known for invading employees' privacy, peppering them with questions about love and family lives. Yet, it's understood that nothing about one's own private life is the business of anyone connected to work. It's protected information about a protected part of life, but Bullying Bosses exploit the employer's authority, and the radical power imbalances between supervisor and employee, in order to trespass. An outright refusal to answer these disallowed questions—a hard tactic—might later be considered insubordination, although probably not of an actionable type.

The employee may feel compelled to say something when their Bullying Bosses successfully puts them in an inquisition's checkmate. The Bullies revel in gamesmanship with the advantage of authority, so they also have to expect self-protective, game-like diversions as countermeasures, and that's what they frequently get. That means employing soft and indirect tactics such as *flanking, cover,* and *camouflage.* These can be done artfully so as to avoid hard tactics such as insubordination.

WHAT WOULD ANNA DO?

Trespassing as always, Anna's Bullying Boss prodded her about what she and her family did over the long weekend.

Anna fondly remembered, they cut the grass then took the boat up to the lake. The kids loved it.

She answered: "We cut the grass then spent the rest of the time watching it grow. The kids hated it."

When there are Bullying Bosses in the house, some employees will talk incessantly while others clam up. In stark contrast to self-protective managers and Bullying Bosses, employees who feel victimized too frequently also feel compelled to spread their information far and wide, hoping its power will be so compelling to others that, once unleashed, it will bring them relief when things don't actually work that way. Being social but remaining reserved is a good and healthful instinct to follow.

FILL THAT INFORMATIONAL VOID

Warriors ought not try to guess what makes Bullying Bosses think like they do, and not to figure what information is safe to share with them, but silence alone is not good enough. It allows for a workplace void into which Bullies will, consciously or subconsciously, fill with their malice. It's better for the employee to fill that space with carefully chosen information. Most people accomplish that with empty chatter meaning very little. Wonderful conversations can had about interests the Warrior hasn't pursued in years. For most Bullying Bosses, that's about as close to substantive as they can understand anyway, so it's good enough. Personal privacy will be protected, Bullies' feelings will be spared and retributions made fewer.

On the political side, Workplace Warriors distribute pieces of information of use to coworkers. His or her comparison charts will generate more than a few. The problem for most Warriors, at least in the beginning, is that victimhood tends to predominate their emotional disposition. Long-term, circulating information of that off-putting sort works to their social and political detriments. The information being shared is about the self, and none of it looks good. Workplace Warriors, instead, make contact with people in soft, stealthily ways – mostly by just being their authentic selves, seeking out the authenticity in others. Being a victim and being an authentic person are mutually exclusive. It's about being sincerely "present" when talking to others. As Workplace Warriors circulate around the workplace, they fluidly circulate true but highly selective information about the workplace, workmates, and themselves and, to a far lesser extent, about their Bullying Bosses.

EMAILS AND MEMOS CONSTRAINED

To collect and keep organized the emails, memos, reports, and correspondence of others as well as one's own, is to accumulate wealth. To pass them out is to distribute wealth to allies and supporters, but they can also create vulnerabilities. Emails and memos are a particularly big problem for Warriors working under fire. In crisis, they offer a quick but ill-advised way to relieve stress and anger. Through them, big pieces of negativity that had been held inside are sent away with aplomb. But, they tend to back fire, and sometimes in a big way. Under all circumstances, the less paper Warriors put out there, the smaller the targeting profile they offer the enemy.

Emails in particular, with the lightening speed with which they get written and sent, are dangerous even if withheld. To the astonishment of many employees, seemingly confidential materials written on the employer's computer are generally subject to employer review. Even those intended to be private can, and frequently are read by employers. If a Warrior is already under Bullying Boss fire, there's a good chance the Bully, as a supervisor, has arranged for their review.

Trading paper shots back and forth is never a good idea, except when done dispassionately, altogether expertly, and only then to prompt Bullying Bosses to expose themselves. More generally, whatever papers Warriors throw at their Bullies in the heat of battle will not only create vulnerabilities as openings, pieces of them can also become the Bully's ammo to be fired back against the Warrior. If the Bully has caused the Warrior pain with a particular assault, endless replays of it in an argumentative "boxing match," serves only to multiply that pain.

Regina just came away from a particularly difficult altercation with her Bullying Boss, Elaine. The temptation for her to shoot off a hot email seemed irresistible. Even though the verbal shots from the battle had been quieted by then, Regina still felt torn up inside. She couldn't comfortably sit there at her desk steaming, doing nothing. But being an experienced Workplace Warrior, she understood that her powerful need to fire an email at her Bully was also an equally powerful, bright red light telling her not to. She had to cool off. It helped to write up a powerful reply by hand, an activity made safe because she would keep it in her pocket until at least the next day. On that next day, she ultimately decided that the best thing to do was to put it in her "Bullying" file at home. But that did not mean she was going to forget the incident. It meant only that Regina would save that set of information for future use when it could actually be effective in reaching a goal.

ANNA'S TIPS TO TARGETS:

» Don't send out paper unless absolutely required by external circumstances.

» For hot issues, first share your paper with someone you respect, and then do as they tell you.

» For very hot issues, first share your paper with someone you love then file it safely away.

Of course, exercising restraint in the heat of battle is a tough thing to do. A seemingly great retort naturally feels compelling, but that doesn't necessarily translate it into something of interest to others. As always, when Warriors make a move, whether orally or in writing, they need to focus on their audience if they are going to be effective in accomplishing anything. Hot emails and memos are virtually always about the sender, addressee, and never the audience. They are not inclusive of constituents, which is the heart of bad politics. Hot emails are not only costly to Warriors, they don't communicating much of anything that matters down the road anyway.

SOME INFORMATION MUST BE SHARED

There are times that employees must disclose information, preferably to someone in authority other than Bullying Bosses. If employees file a lawsuit, a court may later reduce the award of money if they failed to take advantage of an employer-procedure for resolving matters in-house. The questions in a judge's mind, and not that of reasonably thinking employees, is whether or not that procedure was reasonably protective of employees from reprisals and effective in resolving complaints. It's called the "avoidable consequences rule."[30] It's difficult to imagine that, in a place that protects Bullying Bosses, there would be a complaint procedure safe from Bullying Boss reprisal, but it's easy to imagine a court would later think there was.

Also, if an employee puts a work-related medical condition at issue, such as a workers' compensation claim, or a request for reasonable accommodation for a disability under the Americans with Disabilities Act, the employee may have a duty to present certain medical evidence,[31] while some of it, possibly a lot of it, remains confidential.

Some employers, like Household Automotive Finance Corporation, have rules requiring supervisory employees to disclose when they're having an intimate relationship with subordinate employees. A few employers prohibit all off-duty "fraternization" between employees, typically meaning intimate relationships. As typical for work romances, Robert Barbee's and Melanie Tomita's workplace affair was conspiratorial in nature. He was a national sales manager for Household Finance. These romances start as two-person conspiracies of love, and then grow as other people inevitably become aware of them. Love is wonderfully delusional and can easily create the impression of invincibility. When Barbee did not tell his superiors what was going on, he was violating an important employer rule.

As it frequently happens, he and Ms. Tomita tried to keep their relationship secret, while at the same time sending proud little hints of it around the workplace. Barbee got canned and the appellate court found that while employees have a reasonable expectation of privacy in general, they do not necessarily have one when it comes to intimate relations with subordinates, and possibly with other employees as well. There is a reason for this. Workplace affairs frequently end with the employer as a defendant in litigation so employers have a so-called "legitimate business reason" to know when they occur. Courts also have an interest in avoiding another employment lawsuit when yet another workplace romance sours.[32] If a particular romance is truly important, important enough to keep, it seems always advisable for one or the other romantic partner to get a new job. That protects both of their careers and their relationship as well.

Section Four

The Truth
and Its Consequences

BULLIES GET THE BENEFIT OF THE DOUBT

Bullying Bosses lie with impunity, and it can be frustrating when they repeatedly get away with it. Targets pour their hearts out, to no avail, and Bullies can say anything they want and be believed. Being disbelieved may be the most painful aspect of being a Target. It's certainly the most disorienting, but there is no "personal" aspect to it. Structurally, Bullying Bosses are supervisors, and supervisors are given the benefit of the doubt over employees, particularly over supposed "problem employees." That bias is even applied by some outsiders (like arbitrators) when it's hard for them to tell who is telling the truth in a workplace dispute. It's unfair, but Bullying Bosses are a part of management. Management owns the store.

With significant freedom of movement in the workplace, Bullying Bosses can be liars in ways that are consciously protected. Much as a crooked salesperson might prevent his lies from bumping into pieces of truth by staying on the move, Bullying Bosses accomplish the same thing by compartmentalizing their contacts. The managers have no idea what's going on with their staff other than what the Bullies tell them, and they don't really care so long as their production or service numbers are good. Given this general lack of oversight, Bullying Bosses can take on the role of traveling storytellers. They can tell very different stories to various people, each tailored to each particular listener's interests or hot-button issues, but all will cast the Target as antagonist. Each story will be told in conspiratorial terms and in the utmost confidence, maybe even in whispers. The Bully's confidences will almost certainly be honored. That story will not be shared or crosschecked with anyone, particularly not with the Target. And by being included "in the loop," listeners are prompted to feel good about themselves, just as they feel increasingly uncomfortable with the Target.

It is generally believed that a pathological liar can pass a lie detector test with impunity. For them, there really isn't any such thing as a truth or a lie, so there's nothing to register on the machine or in life. For them, life's all one long con anyway. Bullying Bosses seem to work in that same way. Not being of the social fabric, they simply can't feel the person they're talking to so they can't really do the back and forth of a genuine personal exchange that might otherwise expose them. As external substitutes, they have their agendas.

Being agenda-based, it's not generally their practice to engage in directionless conversation. Watch for it.

CROSSCHECK INFORMATION

If Bullying Bosses say something that matters, Workplace Warriors would be wise either to crosscheck it or to ignore everything that was said. Bullying Bosses are masters of manipulation. For most, included in their every serious conversation will be enough misinformation to make the listener better off not having heard any of it in the first place. Utterly disregarding what people say can be difficult, particularly given our innate need to find fellowship with others.

Making it all the harder, when Bullying Bosses talk with purpose, they'll typically toss in hot little nuggets of insider intrigue and maybe a few confidences they've gathered or fabricated. But their words will have zero or negative intrinsic value. As in other bullying contexts, those nuggets work much like a magician's hands to misdirect attention away from where it belongs. Lacking truth, the point of their speech will be found by focusing on their intended effect. With an eye towards cause and effect, employees can ask themselves, "If I accepted my Bully's representations, how would things be different than I now intend for them to be?" Bully meaningfulness will be found in the intended operative effects, not in the spiel.

Bullying Bosses' lies are frequently the most damaging tool in their arsenal, but they also present opportunities if the Workplace Warrior examines them with businesslike detachment. Nothing is gained from taking offense from a Bully's lies. They expose rather precisely their biggest points of concern and vulnerability. After calculating the objective of a lie, make a couple of notes. What particular fear or ambition prompted it? Who was it directed towards and why? Were any of the Bully's particular points emphasized by a body or facial movement, or change in language or voice, and what were those points? After breaking down these elements and others, the employee is well served by consciously honoring, exploiting, or ducking each element as appropriate. A lot can be learned from lies by remaining a good long step back from them, to examine them as a part of the larger weave.

Beyond the Bullying Bosses, Workplace Warriors objectively observe, and take notes about others who lie in their midst, whom they lie to and what subjects they lie about. The answers to these questions can provide the best information there is about coworkers' true points of concern and vulnerabilities, inadvertent self-disclosures that are useful in working with them whether positively or negatively. If patterns can be found, the behaviors of others become more predictable and perhaps can be influenced. There's no need "to call them on it," exposing an observation for no purpose. Instead, Warriors just pay attention.

One can listen in the same objective way to people who have close contact with their Bullying Bosses, such as their known allies and support staff. These people are not just close to them, they are also positioned in between them and the rest of the world. They tend to know, at least know better than most people, where Bullies are headed. They can sometimes be prompted, in support of the Bullies, to say so when the Bullies are not present to speak for themselves. From them, an attentive listener can oftentimes hear the Bullying Boss's words, verbatim, slipping out the mouths of these interme-diaries – sometimes actually falling into Bullying Bosses' voice and cadence. While the speakers may or may not be earnest, they com-municate Bullying messages that are anything but.

"Spins" are lies with political pretensions. Their structure is essentially the same as the others, albeit on a larger scale. Bullying Bosses are in spin mode all the time. Directly or indirectly, spins will be intended for a larger audience than just an individual. The true meaning of spins can't always with accuracy be found just by looking to the intended effect on a particular person. Instead, it's sometimes also informative to try to identify the Bullies' larger strategic objective from the elements surrounding them. It might take watching a couple of repeat performances under somewhat differing circumstances to triangulate on their true objective. It will be found hidden somewhere inside their weave of deceptions and misdirections.

It might be that an office manager, Bullying Boss suddenly puts a large negative spin on the currently rented office, making a big hullabaloo about the carpets, windows, and the like, with no apparent intention behind the display. He was just plain disgusted. Just to start, Warriors' basic feelings might tell them, that the Bully's demonstrations were artifices covering real but still unknown intentions. A quick look around might disclose that the office was as it had always been, and the carpets and windows were fine. By asking the right person a question or two, the Workplace Warrior might discover that the lease is almost up. Simple observation might indicate that the Bully's office is not the biggest, best located, and thus does not have the highest prestige. Objectively, the Warrior could note that certain employees senior to the Bully, and with specialized credentials but no authority over the office, had been long-settled into their spaces.

When looking to identify what would be different if people accepted the Bully's negative representations about the current office, a move to a new, maybe more upscale office would logically follow. Of course, as office manager, the Bully would be the one to make the fresh assignments of space. All of his chatter about carpets was manipulative nonsense, leading to the bullied employer paying for the whole and expensive deal.

EXAMINE LIES IN THEIR CONTEXT

When it comes to interpreting acts of lying, as with all aspects of strategy making, context, and oftentimes that means cultural considerations, determine just about everything. Anyone who has had significant exposure to other cultures has noticed that lying occurs in every one, with the differences being between what's a culturally appropriate lie and one that's not. These are more often differences of type rather than degree. In the United States, it's acceptable to lie to a police officer when pulled over and to fudge one's resume. But it's not acceptable to lie during a business transaction or under oath, although both are certainly, and perhaps regularly done. Traditional cultures have their own and different constructs. In them, during marketplace dickering it might be acceptable for the seller to overstate a value or fail to disclose a defect. But if they're a people who believe in a literal and personal God, lying under oath is lying to God. That's not acceptable and much less often done.

In a workplace context, the truth can be dangerous precisely because of its enormous power. It can be hard edged and easily seem rude if it's ability to affect people and events is not respected with sensitivity. People who tell only those so-called "little lies" designed to smooth social interactions, are not really lying at all. They are putting personal courtesy and respect for another person ahead of discourteously projecting one's own truths onto them.

But on substantive matters, the consequences of employees lying are evident. If an issue of particular importance to someone else is involved, and employees lie about it, then that relationship is at least damaged and perhaps gone. If word gets around that Targets are liars, their complaints about their Bullying Boss will be doubly disregarded.

Workplace Warriors really have no choice but to be on, and remain on, the high road even as Bullying Bosses attempt to pull them down to their low. This isn't just about morality. Having no hierarchy to hold them up, the high ground of integrity is the only functional ground available to Workplace Warriors. Securing supporters and allies is at all times primary. That means earning the trust of others by balancing between speaking candidly and judiciously, while coming through for them when need be.

TRUTHFULNESS IS STRENGTH

Workplace Warriors do best when they stick to the truth, to the extent reasonably possible. To be trusted, a person has to trust others. To eventually be believed against a Bullying Boss, they first have to be believed generally. The truth can often be backed up, has minimal internal contradictions and is least likely to be refuted by any facts unexpectedly coming into play. It's easy to remember cleanly and clearly. Employees make horrible liars anyway.

For employees, who have no control over the official flows of information, there are plenty of feedback facts and actions surrounding them that can serve as contrary proofs. There are not only Bullies, but also coworkers and paper trails all over the place that can expose a lie. And there are many good and legitimate reasons for at least some people to challenge employees' veracity, even if they don't do so out loud. Challenging the Bullies' veracity is pretty much a nonstop activity in many workplaces, one having no impact or meaning. Bullies are a part of management, and managing information is central to their duties, thus they can mostly spare themselves from facing proofs. Even when "caught," there is rarely a consequence for the Bully.

Integrity is more than just refraining from lying. Workplace Warriors admit their mistakes. They get more for their candor with their coworkers than they could get from any lie to them or management, no matter how important or persuasive it might be. That means they also share the heat sometimes, but they have the good graces not to place blame on any coworker unless absolutely required. Bullying Bosses do enough of that for everyone. When displayed, disingenuousness is weakness for the Warriors exposed, just as it is for the Bullies.

For some people, to cut corners with a lie or two is extremely tempting and maybe even a well-developed habit. Some of these believe themselves to be very good at it for the same practical reason people trust their other personal observations to be accurate. It's because perceptions and deceptions are almost never challenged. In the course of a day someone can make literally thousands of observations without the benefit of being challenged by people or contrary facts. From that daily experience, people get the impression that their observations are accurate except for once or twice in several thousands, when that's not even close to true. As noted, when someone, for the first time, gets an opportunity to interview several witnesses to the same event, they are amazed at how little commonality there can be between different peoples' observations and remembrances. This experience can be humbling for interviewers when considering the accuracy of their own observations. When an employee is taking measure of their observations, including alleged abilities to deceive people, it would be wise to assume that same humility.

People can lie to ten merchants in a row, get away with it unchallenged each time and come away thinking they're a very good liar when they're not. The other parties didn't know them, and probably weren't paying much attention anyway. Even if a merchant happened to recognize a lie, there's no profit for him or her in challenging it. People can walk away from a series of these experiences believing they are good liars when what they really are is under informed. Armed with baseless confidence rather than humility, persons of the lying sort who are being prepared to give testimony virtually always "know" that they are one of the few people who can do it well and will benefit from it but, unless they are a professional actor or sociopath, they are almost certainly wrong. On the witness stand, as in the workplace, there are plenty of contrary proofs compromising even the slickest delivery.

WORK THE POWER OF TRUTH CAREFULLY

In general, managers "know" that employees lie, or at least they conveniently assume so. For employers, that's gospel. Employees lie about why they're late to work and why they didn't finish their assignment on time. It doesn't matter to managers that in our general culture, these very specific fabrications are acceptable as ways to soften the too frequently oppressive employer-employee relationship. In a different way, one having to do with hierarchy, these "sub-truths" function much like the "little lies" noted above. They are not really about integrity but our struggle for dignity and survival. Nevertheless, while looking downwardly, employers generalize about employees, people they rarely know personally, without having occasion to remember their own misrepresentations and spins to governmental agencies, their consumers, and the public. These are not among those authorized in our general culture.

> "Honesty is closely associated with freedom."
> —*Mister (Fred) Rogers, Two-Time Winner of a*
> *George Foster Peabody Award.*

For a number of good reasons, when information passes from employees to Bullying Bosses, telling the truth should always be the first choice, as noted, but Bullying Bosses can make telling the truth difficult, frequently counter-productive, and even politically dangerous. It might be that a certain occurrence with a client needs to be communicated, or that rarity, a fact about one's personal life needs to be accommodated. The starting point is that Bullying

Bosses may believe there is such a thing as "truth," after all they believe themselves to be the exclusive holders of it, but they don't believe anyone actually tells it. They don't and, it's certain to them, neither do their Targets.

Truth as told by employees is nowhere near sinister enough to be considered credible by them. If employees simply put the truth out there in the normal fashion, Bullies will probably not only disbelieve it, the truth will thereafter become the very last thing they will believe. Again, to communicate one must address the members of the audience, speak in their language while being attentive to their values. To be credible to Bullying Bosses, "underhandedness" (as an element) has to be present in a message. Bullying Bosses expect to find it in the message itself, as a lie, but a Workplace Warrior can instead protect their honor and their information by strategically including that element in the manner the message is conveyed. If a Workplace Warrior arranges a communication so that it appears to Bullying Bosses that they secured the information by underhanded means, the element of "underhandedness" will be consciously or unconsciously identified by the Bullies. They can move forward to interpret the actual message.

If Bullying Bosses tend to stay at work alone after everyone has gone, it's predictable that they will search at least the Warrior's trashcan for intelligence gathering purposes. Knowing this in advance, Warriors seeking to communicate to Bullies, or even to just plant an idea in their minds, can drop what appears to be an early draft of a private note containing pertinent information into the trash at their desk or in the copy room. Truth is thus conveyed to Bullying Bosses, and because it was secured by what the Bullies believe to be underhanded means, the Bully will more likely accept it as believable. Alternatively, the truth can be spoken into a dead telephone just as employees hear Bullying Bosses coming his or her way but act oblivious to the Bully's approach. Later, when the Warrior officially shares the same information directly with the Bully, a foundation for its acceptance will have already been established. In each case, the delivery is completed and the Bullies walk away pleased with their clever (underhanded) selves.

A mythical but heroic Louise had a difficult problem. The Australian wing of her family was making an impromptu visit with the American wing, which was organizing a large family reunion to receive them. Louise needed for her Bullying Boss, Gerald, to approve a week's vacation on short notice. It would probably be the last family gathering while her grandparents were still alive. One week was all she needed, but it had to be a specific week. She could have done the direct thing of walking up to Gerald and just asking him but, of the dozen other ways she could have told, the straightforward approach would not have been the most effective. Being a Bullying Boss, he would have assumed she was being underhanded, certainly lying.

Begun well before these events, Louise had an always-changing chart of her Bullying Boss's positive and negative personality traits and personal responses to various stimuli. His personal needs included both controlling other people and having opportunities to demonstrate it to others. She saw that he responded favorably to getting attention from anyone and to winning prestige for himself. He was at his most charming when either kissing up to the higher bosses or chairing a meeting. As for those traits negative for her, Gerald was easily incited to feel his shame, particularly when exposed to information about others having personal relationships, thus seemingly enhancing their status at the expense of his own. Nothing bugged him more than underlings feigning "love" as a status symbol—with family, lover or otherwise—when, obviously, there is no such thing. In several places in her notes and charts, she read that he couldn't tolerate criticism. She didn't need notes to tell her that the past conversations Louise and he had alone in his office, produced negative and sometimes awful results every time. The plan she made played with each of these elements.

LOUISE: HER BULLYING BOSS'S FIVE PERSONALITY TRAITS:

» Seeks attention and prestige.

» Seeks to demonstrate control over others.

» Charming with higher bosses or when chairing a meeting.

» Feels his shame when exposed to peoples' so called "love" or other status symbols.

» Feels his anger when faced with criticism.

As planned and to set a foundation, she shared family memorabilia, mostly photographs with her coworkers, Grace and Hazel. The photos made her family visual, with looks, styles and even personalities. They were made more *real* than what the abstraction of mere words could convey. She also showed them a printout from a website listing the available flights making the trip *real* as well. But as she told them, she was concerned their Bullying Boss's general bad attitude about her might get in the way of her family life. She was concerned that the timing on a specific project might become problematic for getting her vacation approved. It hadn't yet been assigned to her, but with the Bullying Boss anything negative was possible. She told her mates the truth and they understood.

Louise made it their plan to make their move at the upcoming staff meeting where Gerald would be vulnerable to his foibles, his need for attention and control as well as his avoidance of criticism. She knew the potentially vacation-blocking project would come up. It had to. Her tactical goal was to convert the project discussion into a vacation discussion. As planned and developed, instead of going directly to Gerald, she passed her issue over to Grace and Hazel and thus around to him, to come at him from another direction (*flanking*). In the moment the project came up and Gerald glanced Louise's way, Grace and Hazel legitimately volunteered to take care of that little bit of work (*cover*). For good measure, they added a bit of flurry about the importance of family gatherings (*camouflage*). In that flurry about families and not wanting to feel excluded, the Bullying Boss Gerald's obsession about perceived status markers briefly washed away. Vaguely understanding that he had been set up, the element of underhandedness had also been included and was respected by Gerald. Ironically, it lent credibility to what transpired.

Probably without thought, but to avoid public criticism, shame and an apparent loss of control, Gerald spoke up demonstrating his authority to everyone present. He suddenly reversed a course he had planned, but never quite got started on. He became Louise's biggest supporter. To an outsider, he would have sounded like he was actually sending Louise to see her family.

Section Five

On Guard With Management

It doesn't seem reasonable at first that an employee should have to be on the defensive with their management team. It normally seems to Targets that because management is responsible for Bullies' misconduct and Targets' cause is utterly compelling, which it probably is, they should only need to approach management with a complaint and justice would prevail. In a more perfect world and with more enlightened managements, it would; but in the management world, with its complicated set of self-interests quite apart from justice, it probably will not.

Going to management directly is a high-risk, possibly high-cost move with a generally predictable zero yield. This fact of life first becomes apparent to Workplace Warriors only after being repeatedly rebuffed. This understanding deepens as Warriors slowly develop their networks and databases providing them with a broad view of how workplaces actually work, and don't work. It's always possible, with the right approach, to find a receptive manager but the odds are strongly against this occurring. Until Warriors have developed a powerful base of information and found their political footing, they're wise to hold a defensive posture relative to management.

MANAGEMENT'S FAMILY AND FRIENDS

Part of the disconnect between employees and managers is one of class difference, real or imagined. Class blinders are a function of social divisions running deeper than any single employer's hierarchy. Think of Cathy, the CEO's niece. She's smooth, smartly dressed, and smiles just exactly the right smile. Her teeth are perfect. She's never been soiled by labor and never sullied through direct contact with working people. She just seems so "right" and progressive. She's a feminist, so one can assume that she is against workplace harassment. Isn't she? Maybe the Warrior will consider going to her for advice and perhaps support? After all, she's a strong, seemingly approachable woman and the big boss's niece as well. That can't hurt.

Targets are advised to stay away. If she's anything like most, every cell in her body informs her that employees are the bad guys. For her, like others on high, it's "us vs. them" and the employee Target is one of them "them." When she hears about a sexual-harassment complaint, all her little synapses fire against the employee. Management is the true victim. She knows that whatever an employee says is beyond misguided; it's fabricated for financial gain in litigation. After all, it's in the nature of those that "do not have," to steal from those that do. She's the very embodiment of entitlement-based values, and she is one of the people "entitled." If successful in getting her attention, Targets will be giving her information that can and probably will be gamed back against them later. Actually, it's worse than that. What will be played against Targets will be a different, tortured, and entirely negative rendition of what they actually said.

While Cathy's perceptions make some sense given her background, coworkers sharing that same "above-the-workers outlook" baffle most everyone. Most employees assume that as the classic underdogs, as in the movies, most people are rather automatically sympathetic to their cause. After all, they are the oppressed workers but that's often not the case. It is then surprising, even incomprehensible to most employees, that a great many people in their midst, including coworkers, hold to the exact opposite perspective. These others just as automatically challenge a supposedly oppressed worker's perceptions as faulty, the worker's values as underdeveloped and the worker's complaints as baseless. After all, they might say, there is another side to the story that they're not hearing; one their life experiences tell them is more likely accurate. It's not wise to assume *anything* with people of different backgrounds, class, or otherwise. Indeed, it's wise to never assume anything about anyone. Inquiry is required.

HUMAN RESOURCES AND EEO

Some of the leading figures against Bully bossing come from the human resources field, including author and international HR expert, Andrea W. Needham and the United Kingdom's "*Personnel Today*." But there's almost no chance Targets' HR departments in the United States will be like these. More likely, their employer's HR will be hostile but not necessarily in a way that's visible. The typical HR department can be the chilliest place any employee can visit, and also dangerous. Ultimately, they will almost certainly oppose any plea Targets might put forth.

The more Targets are able to convince HR of their complaint, the more attention HR will put into destroying it and them. For HR, Targets exist strictly as threats to their employer. Many have no feelings about who is right and wrong or about what they do. As they listen to Targets, they coldly calculate the best defense strategy to protect their employer and, in Targets' cases, that means defending the employer's Bullying Boss. If Targets' employers have an internal Equal Employment Opportunity (EEO) office, they should know that it's not the same thing as the United States Equal Employment Opportunities Commission (EEOC). Indeed, the in-house EEO office will probably function in the same way as HR but their approach may be considerably warmer. It is more likely to invite Targets in and encourage them to disclose what they know and what their concerns are—but also to no good end.

If Targets harbor any illusions about HR's bias, they can visualize the HR person most likely to defend them standing ready for battle and facing their Bullying Boss. Taking that HR person's point of view, would it be smarter for him or her to side with their management which is mistakenly siding with the Bullying Boss; or go to war for the Targets' rights—when their own job would also be on the line? No matter how well meaning these exceptional HR people might be, they'll choose their jobs. But they might, in confidential terms, inform Targets that they've had other complaints about the same Bully and none of them went anywhere. There's nothing they can do.

If their employer has an internal complaint resolution procedure, Targets will most likely find it at HR and EEO. As noted elsewhere, if Targets intend for their cases to go to court, they may have to exhaust those procedures. Consult counsel.

MANAGEMENT'S ATTORNEYS

Managers pay enormous sums to the attorneys they hire in employment cases, making the competition for business between them fierce. Managers tend to select the ones most demonstratively ferocious. Managers rather obviously want them that way, apparently thinking their self-interests are better served by an attack posture than good sense. The chances of a management attorney reporting the presence of a Bullying Boss back to his or her client, management, are slim to none. But there's an excellent chance, if fierce enough, they'll get the next employment case generated by that same Bully.

HR people may or may not feel the wrongness of their actions but these attorneys revel in it. At no point in Targets' wildest imaginations should they let their guards down with these guys. No lay employee can beat them by outsmarting them or being clever. There's just too much to know and too much going on that's outside a layperson's range of view. If they get even indirectly involved, probably through HR, Targets must enlist the support of someone that has the same information and skill sets as they do, and that means getting get their own lawyer or union rep ASAP. Yes, attorneys cost money but these bad guys are guaranteed to tear employees to shreds otherwise and that costs much bigger money. If Targets think that's not fair, then that's the only thing they and management's attorneys will agree on.

9

GOLDEN THREADS
CORE ADVANCES

AS BETWEEN SWORDS AND SHIELDS,
ADVANCES ARE SWORDS.

Section One

Toxins to Gold: Documenting

CAPTURE OWNERSHIP OF EVENTS

Throughout Bullying Boss dramas, their *modus operandi* is the intentional infliction of emotional distress on Targets and it hurts. Although not every Workplace Warrior will document these events, most know that they're supposed to in some fashion or another. Many never will, anticipating that in the process of writing, they'll be uncomfortably reliving and re-exposing themselves to the incident and trauma caused. But, what actually happens is, some measure of personal and political empowerment, as well as healing and peace. Through the writing process, however brief it might be, they shift some measure of the damage done to them from their pained emotional memories onto neutral paper.

In the process of re-framing the incident, Warriors replace the Bully's structure and definition for the adverse event with their own. Workplace Warriors recapture their original power, while at the same time shaking off some of their Bully's. It's been said, "He who names a thing, owns it." To document a Bullying Boss's activities may not give employees "ownership" of the Boss but it does reconfirm their "ownership" of themselves and, in significant measure, control over future events, as they are about to happen.

Documenting events is not an elaborate undertaking; it takes very little effort. In the lexicon of the field, there's a somewhat insulting but powerfully important directive to follow here, "KISS, Keep It Simple Stupid." With each incident, the Workplace Warrior merely jots down just a few key words describing it without the bother of writing a narrative. These key words are compared against those from other incidents. There's power found in precise dates, times, places, people and quotes. When arranged together intelligently, these pieces of information form a cohesive whole not previously known or fully appreciated.

BE PROFESSIONAL: WRITE IT DOWN

The starting point for describing most any bullying incident is sharing The Story verbally so that a full measure of outraged indignation can be communicated. Besides, there is sometimes the illusion that it's more of a hassle to take pen to paper than simply talk, of course hoping that the listener will do the work of writing for them. But the written word and spoken word one are not the same and cannot be equated. With the written, Warriors convert their concerns and complaints into official documents. Their reports, concerns, and complaints become matters of substance and permanence. Their stories are made responsible by being made physical. The individual a Workplace Warrior eventually seeks to communicate with can actually touch the paper the facts are written on then pass it and them on to others. Physicality makes a big difference. It gives their presentation edge beyond the abstraction of data alone. It has authority.

Although bullying is not uncommon—many people can't comprehend it, and that includes people who have witnessed it or even experienced it first hand. To people in authority, anything besides the written word does inevitably sound like empty whining to be distanced from, and disregarded as quickly as possible, so that they can return to more serious undertakings. Without the formality and precision of documentation to back Warriors up with substance, their verbal descriptions will come across to others as a personal opinion or even grudge rather than a statement of facts. With the written word, Workplace Warriors create documentation that can be shared not only with a select few at work, but also with outside supporters, governmental agencies, unions, activists, attorneys, mediators, and maybe just the right manager, maybe on the last day they walk out the door.

Employers understand the power of the written word. Before managers do much of anything, they write a detailed business plan. Management creates strategies with organizational charts, budgets, flow charts, and organizational plans. Keeping operations standardized and on an even keel, they create manuals, protocols, rules, and regularized reporting schedules. There may be shareholder reports, tax analyses, and environmental impact statements directed to stakeholders, the government, and the public. Employers take seriously only those who also communicate seriously. When Workplace Warriors collect information in a disciplined way, they create an attitude of professionalism. A victim's attitude matures into a Warrior's.

THE LARGER PERSPECTIVE

It especially bears repeating here that workplace politics is not optional, but playing it well is. Working the papers is the centerpiece of playing it well. For Warriors to merely survive much less thrive in their workplace requires that they make a plan that's both accurate and effective. That includes making objective, comprehensive self-evaluations and comparison charts. When Warriors get their facts documented straight both on paper and thus also in their heads, they are no longer weak. Their Bullying Boss no longer sees them that way. Warriors may not end up on top of their Bully, but they can end up on top of the situation. That is a much better feeling to have and the only difficult part is getting started. Once the first notation is made, this project takes off on its own steam. There's a whole lot of energy stored up in those scraps of memories and ideas bouncing around inside of a Warrior's brain. Every single person who has put pen to paper in this way, shifted from a state of confusion and de-moralization to one of enthusiasm and engagement. Everyone.

Jerry was a beaten man. He'd become true victim. Bullying had changed the very nature of his personality. Locked into his victimhood, he spared no effort in demanding justice as if it were an actual thing that could be handed over to him. But he made no practical effort to save himself. Booting his computer to email friends and family was automatic. Imputing data only about work made no sense. He was on his own time. His goal had become less about securing relief from the bullying, and more about pursing a higher calling, one dictated by a sense of morality he demanded that others adopt. And he was not going to let the immorality of others cause him to do, or not do, anything he didn't already want to. On this point, he would not bend.

But if he was going to get management's attention focused on his Bullying Boss, he had to generate his own power to influence them. Morality isn't worth much without the juice to fuel it. Poor Jerry didn't work that way. Jerry was not a practical man. For him, the issue was one of right v. wrong. It was a matter of dignity. He was a stubborn man pretending to stick to his principles, but was actually stuck in his victimhood.

ANNA'S DOCUMENTATION OF FACTS

> » Incident Reports
>
> » Hot-button Issues
>
> » Personal Inventory
>
> » Healthful Calendar
>
> » Note Cards
>
> » Witness Statements

INCIDENT REPORTS

The general rule for Workplace Warriors requires they keep notes on a small pad at work, and then transfer them into a journal with further comments at home. They make their journal entries on the same day events occurred while the details are still leaping out at them. They need names, times, dates, events, and salient quotes on their note pad if they're going to have the basic facts of the matter to put into their journal.

Incident reports are shorter and more powerful than journals. Journals, being long narratives, can be tedious and overwrought. They take over whole evenings and weekends. Usually they end up including information that the employee later wished wasn't included and maybe compromise sharing otherwise valuable materials. Instead, Workplace Warriors can write up short incident reports on large cards or small but uniform-sized pieces of paper – one for each incident. Being separate, each is readily included or excluded as things develop.

Being uniform, particulars are easily found even when the data pile inevitably becomes deep. They're small so they can be maneuvered physically to compare details from one to another. They can be moved in combination with the Warrior's note cards for elements into strategic formations. When they're compiled, they form a coherent whole that can be flipped through much like picture cards. Patterns will appear visually that could never have been thought up. If a narrative is included, it's limited by space to just a few words.

ANNA'S (fifth) INCIDENT REPORT (sample)			
DEVIATIONS FROM THE EMPLOYER'S MISSION			
www.bullyingbosses.com			
Date:	2-May	**If a Bullying Deviation:**	
Time:	Noon	Isolating Act ☑	Subtle ☐
Location:	My Desk	Official Act ☐	Abusive ☑
Deviant's Name:	Wayne	Twisting Act ☐	
The Deviation:	*Bullying*	Type of Act:	*Degrading*
		Attitude:	*Furious*
Rule # violated:	Policy 22.4 (e)	Voice:	*Loud*
Rule Title:	"Treat with Dignity"	Threat level (1-10):	*Level 6*
PERSONS:		**Witness Statement Secured?**	
Participant A:	Boss Wayne		
Participant B:	Self		
Witness 1:	Harriet	Yes.	
Witness 2:	George		
Narrative:		**Key Words (quotes)**	
		Stupid, Careless	
		Overstepped Authority	

Blank forms that can be filled out online, printed and/or emailed are available at www.bullyingbosses.com

These incident reports record each type of Bullying Boss deviation from the employer's mission, whether it's bullying or some other. If a Bullying Boss does anything that impedes production or compromises relations with a client, the Workplace Warrior documents the incident using the same, standardized format. Managers are not at all interested in hearing about alleged and vague stories of supposed wrongfulness or unprovable claims that there's a decrease in morale. Employers are generally interested in protecting their mission. When there are deviations from it, they need behavioral data that's precisely defined and matched against established standards.

The reference numbers for violations of the rules are included. In the workplace, numbers have power. They're particularly impressed with measurable costs to their operation and whether or not an alleged deviation can be proved repetitive.

Because Workplace Warriors take time to review their employer's rules, protocols, and manuals, they're able to spot violations with precision. If a Bullying Boss violates governmental regulations or laws, Warriors can document those also. It is through these quick entries that they can later demonstrate there exists a pattern and practice of deviation from the employer's interests, including bullying, and precisely what it consists of. Otherwise, complaints about individual incidents might seem random, as if they were interpersonal disputes gone awry, and likely to be dismissed. Except when finally making one's case in a formal setting, incident reports are never mentioned or shared at work but the informational power in them probably will be.

ANNA'S TIPS TO TARGETS:

» Privately "Keep Book."

» Document each Bullying Boss deviation from your employer's mission.

» Never mention it to anyone at work.

» Never use the words, "Keeping Book."

HOT-BUTTON ISSUES

Comparison charts function differently but are equally cryptic, and thus quick to initiate and then revise. The charts record factors to consider rather than incidents or elements. They are living documents functioning in an ongoing way for however long the bullying lasts. Basically, they are reality checks for the Warriors, and possibly coworkers and eventually management as well. It's said, "That which can be measured gets done." It's recommended that Workplace Warriors take objective measure of themselves, their Bullying Bosses, and maybe a few others as well. The inventories Workplace Warriors create for others can serve as rough guides to help protect themselves from adverse elements as well as help them develop common cause. The inventory Warriors take for themselves can and should be accurate with unblinking clarity. This is probably where one's life partner can be of the greatest help, however scary that might be.

For clarity, efficiency and safety, it has repeatedly proven helpful to list a Bullying Bosses main hot-button issues, list the Warrior's own separately, followed by lists for relevant others. That's not very exciting so far, but as these sheets of paper sit out in plain view at home, Warriors will cross off some and add many more. Each time a Bullying Boss blows up over nothing that could have been guessed in advance, another hot-button issue gets added. Like a windowless submarine navigating intelligently through a three-dimensional mine field, with this list of vulnerabilities and potential triggers, Workplace Warriors can adopt strategies and tactics consciously tailored to avoid or exploit each as appropriate.

ANNA'S INITIAL LISTS OF HOT-BUTTON ISSUES:

Self's	Bullying Boss's
Challenges to Family Time	Outside Lives (any)
Degradations, Insinuations	Our Talking to Managers
Bully's Sexist Thinking	Wednesday Deadlines
Micromanagement/Control	Spelling Errors
Inappropriate Assignments	Brown Shoes
Not Being "Heard"	Employee Travel

DOLLARS AND SENSE

Warriors' continued employment is placed at risk by Bullying Bosses. Their income, benefits, assets, and health are likely to take a beating. All of these are critical elements for Warriors to consider when designing their advances, defenses, and retreats. If a Warrior is to "be real," each must be identified and analyzed, even if some seem too obvious to worry about or too threatening to consider. There can be no room for Workplace Warrior guessing or self-deluding. Are they truly prepared to stay, and for how long? Are they prepared to do the work required so they can stay? No one can know the answers to these strategic questions without taking an inventory, and that includes numbers. As discussed elsewhere, the greater Workplace Warriors' recognized resources and options for leaving, the greater their power to protect themselves and to assert themselves, and thus stay where they are.

What exactly are Bullying Bosses putting at stake for Warriors? How do Warriors' current pay and benefits package compare to the market for the work they do—or could do—if they left? If they suddenly had to, how quickly and favorably could they fit into their employment market? Do they have health insurance and, if so, is it dependent upon their employer? If their insurance is work-related and they lose their job, could they afford continuing their insurance under COBRA, stay with the same insurer, or get new insurance? Exactly how much would COBRA coverage cost with their employer, and would it be prohibitively expensive, as it often turns out to be? Does the employee or dependents have a pre-existing healthcare issue that could make securing or paying for independent insurance difficult or impossible?

Finances are critically important. To be objective, these elements must be listed with number values on a sheet of paper as positives and negatives. This is the Warrior's version of a business balance sheet. Financial positives include income from other sources, savings, liquid assets, 401(k), both institutional and personal borrowing capabilities, and home equity. Do they already have a functioning budget and do they, in practice, generally stay within it? How naturally frugal are they? Are they good with finances? Do they have economic buffers that might help them if need be, like a supportive relative? Could they qualify for unemployment insurance or disability benefits of some sort? *When You Work For A Bully*, Susan Futterman, details each of these considerations and more.[33]

Financial negatives include responsibilities for supporting themselves and others, including all their various costs of living such as food, clothing, shelter, health care, and transportation. What debts do they carry? What assets could they liquidate? Are there other economic limitations or liabilities that must be accommodated in any plan they make, such as a bad credit rating?

A PERSONAL INVENTORY

Beyond financial considerations, it's also helpful for employees to chart what might be their own personal positives and negatives, and chart them also for their Bullying Bosses and maybe a couple other people involved. No one can take someone else's inventory with perfect accuracy. It can sometimes be particularly difficult for embattled employees to avoid insulting an adverse party when evaluating them, but if they do they risk misleading themselves.

WHAT MIGHT ANNA LIST
AS POSITIVES AND NEGATIVES FOR HER
AND OTHERS?

(+)	(-)
Empathy & Compassion	Emotional Blindness
Youthful Passion	Passionless
Elder Wisdom	Immaturity
Personal Boundaries	Personal Boundaries Weak
Hard Worker & Creative	Beaten & Blocked
Intelligent & Logical	Confused & Scattered
Appropriately Emotional	Emotionally Unstable
Trusting & Trustworthy	Not Authentic & Dishonest
Stimulated by Challenge	Bored & Frustrated
Counts Her Blessings	Voices Her Curses
Excellent Production Record	Bully Boss Might Discharge
Innovative	Job Market Tight
Integrity Established	Skill Set Narrow
Excellent Heath (but stressed)	Angry (sometimes raging)
Exercises Regularly	Bullying Boss Attacks Health
Family Unit Tight	Bullying Boss Harms Family Life
Therapist Solid	
Physician Solid	
Partner's Earnings: $___.00	Mortgage, Large: $___.00
Home Equity Worth $___.00	Restaurant Eating: $___.00
Savings Substantial: $___.00	College Tuition $___.00
Stocks Worth: $___.00	Health Problem(s): _____
All New Home Stuff	Need New Car, Cost: $___.00
Aunt Marie good for: $___.00	Bad with Money
1 Employee Ally Solid	Talked To Only 2 Coworkers So Far
1 Former Supervisor Listening	Papers Not Yet Collected
1 Customer Quietly Loyal	No Chronology Yet

This is not an academic exercise, but rather a critically important, practical and ongoing analysis. With the data collected with accuracy, then organized sensibly, priorities will emerge in places where maybe there had been none before. There will be items to add, to delete, and to modify but not just on paper, but with the benefit of disciplined analysis, in one's actual life. Warriors' personal, political and economic profile will change as their thinking about these critical matters moves from merely casual, avoided to the extent possible, to fully conscious.

A HEALTHFUL CALENDAR

Keeping track of their health issues is critical for Targets and Warriors, and it should start at the inception of battle, well before their health is almost inevitably compromised over time. It's helpful for them to keep notes on a monthly calendar used for just that purpose. A retailer may offer a free one. Whatever the health issues, it's best to record numbers reflecting their status if possible. Certainly they should jot down specifically what ailed an employee on each particular day, as well as when they felt better. If sleeping is a problem, the employee records the hours that they could or couldn't sleep. If blood pressure is an issue, these numbers can also be recorded. If employees are experiencing either physical or emotional pain, they can use a 1–10 scale for measuring it. If they are taking medications due to workplace stress on an "as needed" basis, they should record the days they needed them, and the dosages.

Rather than on their calendar, it's better for employees to put their detailed descriptions of health problems on incident report cards. To facilitate finding patterns in the employee's medical history, and to minimize what might someday be shared with management in litigation, it's best if all notations are accurate but kept minimalist. The physician's file will record many of those same medical facts.

There's no need to duplicate them, possibly creating confusion and discrepancies, but sharing this calendar with the physician might be helpful to him or her.

Section Two

Gold Mining Information

EXHIBIT A: ORGANIZING A DOCUMENTS FILE

No one, not an outsider and not even a Workplace Warrior, can understand a case or campaign in a full and balanced way without knowing the particulars recorded in the paperwork. That includes the employer's papers as well as the Warrior's. Collecting them is definitely worth the effort. The company's policy manual is practically indispensable, but can be difficult to secure. If there's a union in the workplace, and even if the employee is not a member of it, a copy of the collective-bargaining agreement is extremely valuable. Although it may be tempting to just take other people's word for what's in these, no Warrior can afford to. Even if the rumors about their contents turn out to be true, which is very unlikely, each affected employee must read the text for themselves with their own particular circumstances in mind.

Performance reports and disciplinary papers are critically important to secure. These documents can give helpful outsiders their only opportunity to hear the Bullying Boss's "voice" and get a feel for his or her attitude. It's also important to collect grievances, complaints, compliments and commendations, together with any other formal and personnel-related papers, including those to and from state and federal agencies. These can sometimes be secured from the agency. It's always helpful to collect any individual employment contracts and pay schedules. If there exists a piece of paper that the employee can get that's not employer confidential, and it relates to work, it should be included in the Warrior's collection.

Ideally, all employees would collect their documents throughout their employment so that they already have them on hand, but this is very unlikely. Beyond that, a trusted coworker may have some of the general documents missing from the Warrior's collection. Human Resources will certainly have many, if not all, of them. Generally, employees have a right to review their personnel files, and that's not limited to just the papers already placed in a single folder with their name at HR. That right includes reviewing all personnel documents related to them, wherever they might be. Personnel files mostly make for boring reading with all the minutia documenting various personnel transactions that employees have long forgotten, but they also contain things that will surprise and frequently even shock them. The employer knows what's in it–after all they're the ones keeping it. The Workplace Warrior might as well know also.

Often, employees are reluctant to visit HR because they tend to be inhospitable and, rightly or wrongly, employees are concerned about exposing themselves to the enemy. HR could wonder, why would someone want to see his or her personnel file unless there's trouble? Actually, there are other reasons and most of them are routine. For sure, no one is going to stomp around HR making demands about legal rights and files just because they've had a bad day.

But Workplace Warriors are persistent if they have to be. Warriors can use a benign reason to see their file, such as resolving a healthcare provider issue. Maybe they need to see the employer's policy binder to clarify their dental coverage. The red flag a Warrior may think he or she raises by visiting HR may or may not be real and may not matter. In any case, it should be routine for employees to review their personnel file anytime after their employer takes either positive or negative action. Sometimes, the only way to resolve confusion about an even minor action is to check.

When employees ask to see their file, they are generally not allowed to see it right away. HR may tell them they need time to find it or put it together, which may be true, but they'll also want time to take out what they don't think truly belongs there. That's all right, particularly if they are cleansing the file of papers adverse to the Warrior. If possible, it's ideal to get HR to make a copy of the whole file to be picked up at the convenience of both parties. The pages will either already be consecutively numbered or the Workplace Warrior will number them before leaving, while standing at their counter so there's no confusion later about what was and what was not included. That original set is kept untouched. To protect it, the Workplace Warrior makes a working copy.

The Warrior arranges the documents in chronological, or reverse chronological order to create their comprehensive documents file. But when sharing papers with others, the Warrior picks out only the pages he or she anticipates others will need to understand his or her circumstances, and no more. Depending on circumstances, it may be helpful to the intended reader to include, in a separate file, copies of research done on the employer, the Bully Boss and bully bossing in general. Without fail, if any document is about to leave the employee's custody, it's a copy that goes out the door. In the moment of loaning it, going to a copy machine, perhaps driving to one, can seem like a hassle but that's easy compared to the alternative. Many an employee has regretted not making a copy of a document.

WHAT WOULD ANNA COLLECT?

General Documents

Personnel File Records
Original Resume, DV, or Job App
First & Last Job Descriptions
First & Last Duty Statements

Individual & Union Contracts
Rules, Policies & Procedures
Manuals & Protocols

Articles by Occupational Experts
Articles by Bullying Experts

Organizational Chart
Employer Phone Lists & Addresses
Private Phone Numbers & Addresses

Online Research Discoveries
Public Records Research Discoveries
Library Research Discoveries

Internal Job Listings (fresh)
External Job Listings (fresh)

Personal Documents

Incident Reports
Statements by Witnesses
Statements by Experts
Compliments & Commendations
Emails, Memos, Correspondence File

Grievances, Complaints & Legal
Filings with Organizations &
    Agencies

Performance Reports
Investigation Reports
Disciplinary Papers
Police Reports

Physical & Mental Health Documents

Pay Stubs (to corroborate)
Phone Logs (to corroborate)
Calendars (to corroborate)
Telephone Bills (to corroborate)
Credit Card Bills (to corroborate)

EXHIBIT B: BUILDING A CHRONOLOGY

There frequently comes a time when Workplace Warriors are poised to seek formal help from attorneys, interest groups, unions, coworker allies, and maybe a selected management representative. To make possible the communication of inevitably complicated circumstances, the Warriors write a chronological "statement of facts" initially based on their documents file. Listeners pay more attention to, and better understand disciplined presentations and the combination of documents and chronology accomplish that. The statement of facts is a series of very short paragraphs presenting a simple history of the dispute.

Drafting a chronology is a rather mechanical, repetitious exercise. As employees flip through the documents, parsing out significant events, they should jot down two or three quick and succinct sentences to describe each event. The point is merely to state that certain events occurred in a certain order, rather than interpret them. The ordering itself should to that. Each short paragraph opens with the same, parallel structure. "On October 22, 2005, John Smith (did something)..." When done on a computer or on 3 x 5 cards, there is the flexibility needed to feed in and take out information as it develops or becomes relevant. Workplace Warriors state only the facts, including zero argument or hyperbole. Amping it up with emotionality may seem to make it more powerful with a demonstration of damages and commitment but, in real life, most people are not impressed by drama. Professionals sometimes zone out when faced with yet more. As Jack Webb insisted, "Gimme just the facts, ma'am."

As a preliminary draft, it shouldn't be longer than five or six pages. Indeed, except for chronologies, any document longer than a page or two is ill advised. A non-party reader's commitment and interest is probably limited to reading one hundred or just a few more words, so it's better for the Warrior to be the one who chooses which particular words will ultimately be read.

For the participant witnesses to events, such as Warriors, the events seem quite simple, but they're not simple for someone was not involved and didn't watch them, actually unfold singularly and sequentially. When urged to write it up, participants often say,

"There's no reason to, it's very simple. Let me explain." What emerges is the same confusion that the Warrior has already seen when he or she used to tell their "The Story" at work. The participant can't understand why, and may not even notice, but the listener almost immediately becomes perplexed – assuming they're listening at all. Even if he or she is attentive, if he or she is required to take dictation due to a lack of employee preparation, what would have been thoughtful discussion is overwhelmed by busy work. For the Workplace Warrior, the interested party, there's nothing to be gained by forcing the outsider and not-yet-interested party to do the work of discovering and separating out the facts from a perhaps passionate but difficult narrative.

On April 14, 1996, I began my employment with ABC Corporation. Rosa Gomez was my supervisor. We had an excellent relationship.

On October 22, 2005, John Smith replaced Ms. Gomez as my supervisor.

On November 30, 2005, Supervisor Smith gave me my first ever negative performance report.

On December 31, 2006, Supervisor Smith came to my desk and yelled at me about my supposedly being too slow and not careful enough. His voice was tense. Under his breath, he called me "a stupid woman."

At the same time on December 28, 2006, John Doe and Jane Johnson were less than six feet away and witnessed the entire event. They both heard him call me "a stupid woman." Jane was shocked into silence.

Later on December 28, 2006, I called my physician and made an emergency appointment for a stress sensitive disorder of mine. I left work for the doctor's office with severe asthma symptoms. I lost five hours work that day that I was not paid for.

If the chronology is for an attorney, it might include in large letters "Attorney-Client Privileged Document." This chronology can be thought of as their lawsuit's first draft. A civil complaint filed in a court is essentially a chronological statement of facts starting out much like the one above. When employees show up in an attorney's or public interest group's office, they'll already be speaking the listeners' professional language. Otherwise, a great deal gets lost in translations. It's a businesslike approach. This presentation will greatly and favorably contrast the employee against his or her competitors who are also looking for help from the same people precisely because, unlike them, the employee will not be telling yet another pathetic tale of woe. Professionals, no matter how sensitive or committed, have had enough of that already.

After lining up the facts as a sequence of events organized on paper, Warriors also become clearer in their own minds about the events and their timings. The assembly process allows them to see and resolve errors, contradictions, and confusions they'd never notice with the imprecision of story telling. It additionally gives them a chance to feed in any elements that had been missing from their speeches such as the names, dates and the like. Even their verbal presentations become more rational, make more sense and are better believed by others.

This hard-edged, linear rendition of events includes a hidden blessing – Warriors' peace of mind and spirit. As briefly noted, as long as "The Story" was allowed to race around painfully in the neuropathways that it carved in their brains, they remained miserable. With bullying, there's a lot information and emotionality to keep track of, too much for any brain to handle competently. Getting the data from the brain's version of RAM memory, lining it up, and then saving it down onto a computer's hard disk or on note cards, is both putting it away and protecting it for later manipulation and analysis.

DISCOVER WHO THE EMPLOYER REALLY IS

Management teams do not normally share significant information with their employees, not even with their supervisors. Information is power and it's at its most powerful if veiled—veiled even when being wielded. Most management teams, implicitly or explicitly, regard their employees as an oppositional force rather than among the team players. Unless there's the threat of a layoff they can use to "motivate" employees, they won't generally share if the employer is having serious difficulties with a patron, the government, or its bottom line. Beyond that, Bullying Bosses are not going to share tales about their history of abuse at work or in the home. Instead of being genuinely informed, employees tend to rely on what they are given, mostly rumors.

In a bullying environment, there's an excellent chance that at least some of those rumors were started or changed by the Bullying Boss. By sounding important, particularly if they're repeated, rumors too frequently take on an air of authority, even when they are invalid. Like rules, even when rumors are technically accurate, which is rare, they tend to mislead rather than enlighten. All of these create an atmosphere of workplace mystery. Employees are working blind and in the dark both. Any occasion that a Workplace Warrior takes to "pierce the corporate veil" of secrecy takes some of the oppositions' mystery away from them.

With a few easy research efforts, employees can gather pertinent information. It will be different from the information that the Bullying Boss has, because of the difference in perspectives between inside player and outsider evaluators. From the perspective of outside, and often authoritative sources, the information the Warrior gathers could be broader and deeper than the Bully's. More important than any particular datum is the Warrior's newfound feeling for the whole. That can put Warriors in sync with their employment environment, and that's the basis for having good instincts.

WHERE WOULD ANNA GO DIGGING?

Among Co-Employees & Superiors
google.com & yahoo.com
bn.com & amazon.com
Library Search Engine for Articles
LexusNexus
County Court Clerk's Office
County Recorder's Office

Obvious information sources for information about the employer include astute coworkers and colleagues, the supervisor who will occasionally talk candidly, former employees, online search engines, online newspaper archives, libraries, county court's clerk offices, and country recorder's offices. Research is an inherently creative and, when motivated by workplace tension, exciting process.

The easiest and most productive place to start is with online search engines. Keywords include the name of the employer, its CEO or director, its industry and, of course, the Bullying Boss. It takes only seconds. There's gold to be mined on the web. Each nugget inspires searching for yet more. Making it particularly interesting, and as in other contexts, once a significant base of data is collected, researchers will be able to see how the various nuggets interconnect with each other one to make an employment whole.

WHAT KEYWORDS WOULD ANNA WORK?

Her Industry
Her Employer
Her CEO or Director
A Key Manager or Two
A Key Customer or Client or Several
Her Bullying Boss

What condition are the employer and its industry in? It makes a difference if that industry is growing, dying, or farming out the labor to overseas markets. Are there newsworthy controversies affecting that industry and employer? Is there major legislation or litigation having an effect on the employer? If tariffs, subsidies, or grants are protecting employees' jobs, are they holding strong in the current political climate? If foreign tariffs are holding the employer back, are they getting worse or abating? Is the employer dominant or respected in its field and likely to stay that way, or in some lesser position with less punch? Each of these is a golden nugget, and when combined, they create a new and enormous reality that has the effect of dwarfing Bullying Bosses.

Having information of this sort makes Workplace Warriors better able to position themselves politically. If even one employee is about to get laid off, a moribund mood overcomes workplaces. Tempers can get edgy, including possibly that of the Bullying Boss's. If big and positive things are headed the employer's way, then opportunities are coming also. There might be a bit of jostling for position by those who have ambitions, including possibly the Bullying Boss, and possibly even Warriors. There's danger either way. Warriors are best protected and are better able to promote themselves if they have at least some idea in advance where these forces are coming from, what their general impact will be, and what their effect is likely to be for their position and for other positions of interest to them.

If Warriors find and hear nothing controversial about their employer, then employer stability may be the order of the day. If even accidentally, they or the Bully upset that organizational stability, they could find themselves either in a heap of personal upset. This is frequently the case in public employment and with large, traditional employers. Private sector employees may learn that their industry is in a consolidation phase, and it might look like the employer is a willing (or not-so-willing) candidate for a takeover. The employee may find out who those Japanese men were, the ones who were escorted through the workplace last month.

Once this basic research is underway, and as Workplace Warriors canvass co-employees, they'll be able to share bits of their informational wealth, ask more productive questions and come away with more productive answers. As in all strategic inquiry, they'll be looking for patterns and potentialities in the always-growing database. These lead to well-considered actions

---

WHAT WOULD ANNA DIG FOR?

She'll Only Know It, When She Finds It.

Certainly, She'll Find "*The Flavor*" For All.

Maybe, Legal & Political Issues.

Maybe, Business Projections & Plans.

Maybe, Financial Information.

Maybe, Personality Profiles.

Maybe, Dirt.

PUBLICATIONS FOR DEMOCRATIC ACCESS

Public libraries are the bedrock of democracy. Despite contemporary difficulties with public funding, they still have books worth checking out and reading, although they tend to be older with less availability these days. They also have newspaper and journal articles on the shelves, on reserve, and on microfiche. On many library websites, there are windows allowing searches through their catalogue, as well as searches into their database of periodicals, but there's no substitute to actually going inside the building, armed with a pocket full of quarters for the copy machines. When employees are making judgments about spending money for a particular item in order to save their jobs, like making copies, it's instructive to calculate the proposed cost of the item as a percentage of annual earnings. Most any research expense is worth its cost.

If there's any doubt about copying an article, then it's probably worth the expenditure of time and quarters. It's very often a waste of time to try to re-find an article or record later thought useful. It's far easier to make copies of everything relevant as it's found. If an article or document is good enough to scan, it's probably good enough to copy, then keep, read and reread closely at home. A Workplace Warrior may find a special article on the employer, the Bullying Boss, or on Bullying Bosses generally, then decide to share it with a specific coworker. Good articles can give the Warrior currency and credibility. If lucky, the library will have a subscription to LexusNexus, or a good alternative to it. Otherwise, LexusNexus can also be accessed directly through its website for a modest fee for daily use or a charge by the article. For free, it will produce a list of available articles by their headlines that will, even alone, be greatly informative by giving a contemporary overview of the topic area. But LexusNexus is not an exhaustive compilation of periodicals.

The daily newspapers generally have searchable archives on their own websites. Some are free, some charge by the article and others require a subscription that can be short-term and not expensive. The newspaper search engines are uneven in their performance, but they contain a wealth of particularly poignant information. If the employer is small, search efforts should focus on the local papers. If the employer is significant in the local economy, there's a good chance the researcher will find a featured interview of the CEO in the local newspaper, probably in the Sunday paper's business section.

If the employer is regional or national, the big newspapers are rich with information— *The New York Times, The Wall Street Journal, The Chicago Tribune, The Atlanta Journal-Constitution,* and *The Los Angeles Times.* Business magazines tend to present information and analysis from a big picture perspective, *Fortune, Business Week* and *Forbes*. In normal times, it might have seemed extraordinary to dig out and read articles, but under Bullying Boss circumstances, they become indispensable. It's not hard to do.

Finally, it's sometimes helpful to search for the Bullying Boss by name. There's no way to know in advance what will be found, but, by workplace definition, they have anti-social tendencies, and people like that sometimes end up in the news. If he or she is an abuser at work, it might turn out that he or she is also a publicly known abuser at home. Discovering an article pinning a "domestic abuser" label on the Bully would go a long way towards corroborating employees' complaints of abuse at work.

Ralph didn't much care about the news. He was a sports guy, but he spent several hours each week surfing the web just to see what would turn up. But he'd never conducted a search about his employer or his Bullying Boss despite spending hundreds of hours fuming at work and loosing countless hours sleep. Ralph's work buddy, Jason, told him he'd heard there was a recent *Wall Street Journal* article on his employer but didn't know anything more than that. So, Ralph went to that paper's website and did a name search in its archives. It took essentially no time and cost very little money. That particular article, it turned out, was not very helpful. But the paper's search engine automatically turned up other articles about his employer and industry that were. All of a sudden, his employer and its Bullying Boss looked small compared to the global environment they operated in. After that, even Jason's posture came more upright. His exploration was worth it for his peace of mind, if nothing else.

RECORDS FOR DEMOCRATIC ACCESS

A sometimes game-winning source for information about both a Bullying Boss and an employer can be found in local court files, another important institution that furthers democracy. It's the public record. Even if nothing specifically valuable comes up, there's a very good chance the Warrior will come to know his or her employer down into its insides, and it takes very little effort. The easiest and most productive way to read court files is, on a week day, simply to drive to the courthouse on vacation leave. While doing research, a paper trail may be created. It would be unfortunate for that paper trail to bump into perhaps compromising, workplace attendance records.

Ralph had no idea what he was going to find, but when he got to the clerk's office of the local court, he saw five computers along the wall with several other members of the public, no different than him, imputing names. He typed in his Bullying Boss's name as well as his employer's. When he was done at the civil court, he intended to do the same thing later for his Bullying Boss at the criminal court as well. Several case names and numbers popped up that might have been relevant, so he wrote them down on the little cards provided. He handed his cards to the deputy clerk at the counter. It didn't take long for the clerk to produce a pile of files. He flipped through their many pages as quickly as he could, finding huge amounts of mostly irrelevant information but some unexpected stuff as well. He recognized the names of the big shots he'd only seen from a distance. He read their declarations describing how his employer functions and why. His interest was piqued. From these, he learned more about where he worked than he'd picked up over the preceding ten years he'd been their employee.

The case files were particularly interesting to Ralph because attorneys both for and against his employer had written documents about each other as adversaries. They had a lot to say to the court and practically none of it was complementary about the other. It turned out that his employer had been engaged in battles all over the place and that gave him some perspective on the relative unimportance of his case to management. It wasn't personal. From the files, he could also see for himself how much work (that means money) it would cost him to sue his employer. That no longer seemed to be necessarily the easiest and more efficient way to go.

He saw cases brought by three large customers he had once done work for and which had inexplicably disappeared. Sitting in the clerk's office, he learned they were suing his employer, why they were suing and how he could best avoid getting caught up in messes like that in the future—or take advantage of them. Seeing their familiar names felt almost like finding his own name. He was a delighted in his new role as political voyeur. The mystery of the corporate veil lifted appreciably.

Finally, he found an old discrimination lawsuit filed against both his Bullying Boss and employer. That was a *Bingo!* As he read through the first document at the bottom of the file, the complaint, he saw that many of his experiences with the Bully matched the plaintiff's fairly closely. It was good to know that his employer was already aware of his Boss's bullying activities from that earlier case. They would then also know, when told, that those same, possibly expensive activities were continuing against current employees. But there was another, more sobering lesson. Once before, management had backed up the Bully and his wrongfulness all the way into court, and might do so again. He wrote down the former Target's name with intentions of contacting her through her attorney-of-record.

Until then, his personal Bullying Boss had mostly been a mystery with no apparent vulnerabilities. That mystery gave him power. Motorcycle cops do the same thing with extra dark glasses. He went across the street to the county recorder's office where he repeated the same process, this time looking for real estate records. He found nothing about his employer but picked up some general background information on his Bully. It turned out that he owned a condo alone, the date it was purchased, its appraised price, mortgage documents, and a pair of liens that had once been placed against the property. If the Bully's identity had been veiled, then Ralph had just stolen a good long peek inside. Ralph was not the only one with problems or obligations. His Bullying Boss and employer had them too. With their veils lifted even a little bit, Ralph felt stronger and safer from that day forward. He was *in the know*.

LITERATURE DROPS

Bullying Bosses are enigmas. They defy not only understanding, but also even categorization. When, as a matter of self-defense, Warriors attempt to explain the inexplicable to others, they gain no ground and loose credibility. In the workplace, and much like information, credibility is both capital and currency. It would be a hard tactic to approach people directly to advocate "at them" when Warriors do better with soft. It's far more productive to let experts in the Bullying Boss field, through their writings, teach others at work about workplace abuse. Copies of educational articles can be covertly and randomly left in common areas like coffee, copy, waiting and rest rooms. This tactic is productively soft because coworkers educate themselves as they read instead of being told how to think. It's strong because the authors have obvious credibility, sparing Warriors from further compromising their own. It's effective because no one is being asked to take sides as the price for becoming informed.

Colleagues learn from the materials that Bully Bossing is a worldwide phenomenon and come away remembering some of the indicators of Bully Bossing. Whenever confronted by any supervisory individual thereafter, they rather automatically observed them through the lenses of the behavioral profiles for Bullying Bosses. They can also learn about the specific, negative consequences that exposure to the Bullies causes people and institutions, including themselves. They might, after being briefed, feel personally challenged for their tacit complicity in bullying when previously they attempted neutrality. A business magazine article, left where managers will find it, might delineate the financial costs of bullying for the employer.[34] Each manager might individually feel challenged, if only for a self-reflective moment. They might wonder if the articles were planted in the lobby because of them. Thereafter, like the employees, when viewing their colleagues, they rather automatically measure them against what they have read. An international array of publications can be found with these keywords: "workplace abuse," "workplace bullying," "bully bosses," and "bullying boss."

WHAT WOULD ANNA DISCREETLY CIRCULATE?

United States,
> "Fear in the Workplace," by Benedict Carey
> New York Times, June 22, 2004

> Any of several articles by Dawn Sagario,
> The Des Moines Register.

Europe,
> "Office Bullying Increases in Europe" by Fiona Flek
> Special to The Wall Street Journal Europe,
> December 11, 2002

> Any of numerous articles appearing in
> Personnel Today (UK).

Canada,
> "Workplace Bullying" by Sara Hood
> *Canadian Business,* September 13, 2004

> Any of numerous articles by Chris Morris, released by
> *Canadian Press*
> (published in various daily papers.)

New Zealand,
> "How to Beat the Workplace Bully..." by Debbie Swanwick
> *New Zealand Management,* June 1, 2004

> "Bullied by the Boss" by Jannie Ogier
> *New Zealand Herald,* February 25, 2004

Australia,

"Bullying at Work Reports Soaring," by Jim Kelly
Sunday Times, January 25, 2004

"Victims of Bullying are First Concern" by Bronwyn Hurrell
Herald Sun, April 26, 2004

Subject matter searches online excite and build Warrior energy, security, and power. Workplace Warriors are not alone as Targets. There are others all over the world and they have a great deal to share with each other. It would be nice if Warriors could blank out their Bullying Boss at will in order to enjoy their Sunday mornings. For most, that can be difficult to impossible to do when feeling beaten and all alone, just naturally taking the bullying battles personally. No matter what the research venue, to place one's own bullying experience in the larger sea of bullying information and people, is to decrease its personal importance and increase the powers of strategic thinking.

Section Three

Rules and Rulers

RULES: A MANAGEMENT FUNCTION

Management uses its rules to direct workplace efforts, to coordinate employee activities and, if all goes well, to productively fulfill its mission with maximum efficiency and at minimum cost. Bullying Bosses too frequently use the rules to control and subjugate their subordinates for reasons having nothing to do with the employer's mission. In Rings of Fire, it's mostly alleged rule violations that Bullying Bosses hurl at Targets, as if they were political lightening bolts. Each strike is ding that gives Bullying Bosses a little victory, an imaginary upgrade in status. Dings are proof of the Bullying Bosses' dominance and the employee's lowliness in their presence.

Ultimately, employees can only escape Bully rule mongering when either the Bullying Boss or they leave. But by becoming expert in the workplace rules, Warriors acquire defensive shields against bullying while also gaining expertise useful as offensive swords. With them, the Warrior become capable of measuring the irrationally of their Bully's conduct against the clear standards afforded by businesslike rules.

THE EMPLOYER'S MISSION

In the workplace, the ultimate rule is the employer's operating mission. Only in the rarest cases do non-management employees know and understand what it really is. But, if they don't know where the employer ship is headed, it's tough to know how best to position themselves on it. Frequently, management itself is a bit vague about its mission effectively making employees wholly dependent on their supervisors, including Bullying Bosses, to define workplace operations, priorities, and politics for them. But by discovering the employer's actual overall mission, they can learn what the management team is seeking for itself and so what it really wants from the Bullying Boss and themselves. From there they can, with some precision, fashion a mission statement as it directly affects them and the work they do. This creates the possibility of demonstrating to management, if circumstances allow, that the Workplace Warrior is its Best Worker when, otherwise, the Bullying Boss would continue to send the Warrior in other directions.

In those workplaces where a mission statement is posted on the walls, it largely functions as a fluff piece that's generally and rightfully ignored. These can be the product of political compromise among managers but can also be a signal that management doesn't trust their subordinates, maybe including the Bullying Boss, with information as powerful as their actual intentions. Workplace Warriors don't need to be told. They figure things for themselves regardless.

Bullying Bosses, lacking basic capacities for empathy and compassion to connect with others, do not accept anyone else's agendas, like the employer's mission, that compete with their own. Employees have no such blockages and are free to craft a personal, productive version of their employer's mission.

This analysis begins with employees collecting materials written by the employer in-house and about the employer in the media. As just described, new reporters regularly translate employers' press releases and controversies into newspaper articles. Warriors read what's actually said, read between the lines then craft a short statement reflecting management's central, operational goal, as they perceive it. Their draft statement can't be a merely static thing, defining only present objectives, but must be fully dynamic. It counter-poses where the employer thinks it is against where it intends to be. Even if no one at work consciously recognizes it, the mission is a political manifesto, always evolving and being reinterpreted as it represents varying perspectives and competing agendas. As employees' version of management's overall mission becomes sharp, the Bullying Boss looks a lot less so.

With the employer's larger mission in mind, Warriors fashion a modest one that applies particularly to them and those around them. As with other outreach efforts, once Warriors know the general object of the game, they become more in sync with the employer and thus put themselves on the strongest political turf possible. But that doesn't mean they have escaped danger. If Bullying Bosses have the capacity to understand that an employee is making a contribution, they're not going to like it. But they can't exactly attack a Warrior for being productive in the employer's interest, although they very will might attempt to undermine their accomplishments. Certainly, Bullies will retaliate "to teach a lesson," probably on some other issue where the employee is more vulnerable. Although Workplace Warriors are never completely without offensive and defensive capabilities, when it comes to making a productive and sensible contribution to the larger effort, they may just have to take their bullying licks for it like they do with so many others.

When Ellen, a pharmacy employee, was asked what her part of her employer's mission was, she recited the hospital's PR piece about itself: "Hospital X Exists To Serve The Community." Thus her mission must have been to serve the community. The scale of analysis she chose was too large, community-wide, and too ethereal. The generic words, "to serve" didn't matter to her work or probably anyone else's. Asked again for something more specific, she overcompensated, saying the pharmacy staff's mission was to dispense medications efficiently and safely. That was actually a summary of her and her colleagues' job duties as viewed from inside her department, but not of management's mission for the pharmacy. The clue that it was unhelpful was that it didn't have a definable, institutional goal in its formulation.

Somewhere in between those too-enormous and too-small scales was the management team's operational focus as it related specifically to Ellen. For the pharmacy, what was her management really concerned about? Their current focus might have turned out to be only a passing fashion, but whatever it was, it was her responsibility to further it. Instead of trying to make up a management mission statement in the abstract, as part of developing her strategic plan, Ellen reviewed press reports from over the last couple of years making note of the names and institutions that came up. She compared them to the internal blurbs distributed at work. What she was looking for was the most productive focus possible for her job efforts as measured by the larger employment context. It finally came down to this, as she carefully chose each word:

HOSPITAL X: MANAGEMENT'S MISSION

The mission of the management of Hospital X is to increase government funding by reacquiring a certain accreditation it has lost. That accreditation requires, among other things, that it have an operational pharmacy meeting specific, government criteria.

In that moment, she knew exactly what she had to do. She visited the hospital's resource center. She was directed to a report that included the government's criteria for accrediting the hospital's pharmacy for a certain program, and how it had been deficient in the past. This was what management was really concerned about but, being management, hadn't shared explicitly with the employees. Over the months that followed, she adjusted her work to match each of the criteria relevant to her. She was smart, precise, and demonstratively loyal. Her Bullying Boss knew nothing about her research or the criteria she discovered.

GET EXPERT ON THE RULES

One thing an employee can do with surprisingly little effort is become an expert on the rules as found in the company policy manuals, contracts, health and safety brochures and operating procedures. Like most people, Bullying Bosses have probably not done any of that. Although predictably quite confident in their understandings of the rules, they may have been only guessing they had a certain rule right when they last attacked their Target for its breach. The employee may have also been guessing and thus left defenseless.

When most anyone goes to the reference materials, they're generally looking for the answer to a particular problem. They look in the table of contents or index to find its page reference, then read only the one section relevant to that narrow issue. Few people get an overview, and so don't get the overall point of what the employer is looking for. From that small window, it's not possible for either Warriors or their political competitors, the Bullying Bosses, to judge any single rule reasonably.

Manuals make for remarkably fast reading, and even faster skimming. Their descriptive headings are printed in bold and the paragraphs tend to be short and to the point. A quick scan of its various sections converts an employee from being a Target living daily in anticipation of an alleged rule violation, into a rule expert with an understanding balanced in the text and context. He or she can stroll through the workplace less affected by a Bully's ritualistic dinging. When their Bullying Boss makes the mistake of citing a rule, he or she will probably be wrong about at least some part of it and the employee will have the knowledge and confidence to stand strong in the face of a baseless allegation, certainly making a record of the deviation.

Complicating matters, the employer may not necessarily want employees to follow all the rules. Except in government, rules can be instantly adopted, but there aren't many people who wake up in the morning feeling any great need to delete what's become outdated clutter. If everyone followed every rule, production would be compromised. There's a risky and somewhat disreputable labor union strategy called, "work-to-rule" premised on exactly that point. Protesting employees do their jobs intently and exactly as provided for in the rules. There is no actionable insubordination and production slows to a dribble. Using their control over production, the workers make their collective point to the employer while remaining on payroll at the same time. If Workplace Warriors follow rules too strictly, they can give the appearance of hampering production when that's the last thing they want to do.

What makes rules sometimes even trickier is that they may require significant interpretation involving information employees don't have. What they read may not actually be what's currently intended or even binding. A union's collective-bargaining agreement may explicitly say one thing but an arbitrator looking at additional materials may effectively change that meaning to make it comport with the larger whole. For another example, despite what it explicitly says, an individual employment agreement may not be binding on an employee if the employer's language is illegally too one-sided in the employer's favor. If an employee has any questions about his or her individual employment contract being imbalanced, he or she should not assume its meaning from the bare writings and instead take it to an attorney who specializes in these matters.

When interpreting rules, what counts for Workplace Warriors and anyone else is determining what the employer's actual intent was and is. That requires, as always in politics, looking at the context surrounding a rule including, immediate work demands, the rule set as a whole, as well as the employer's overall mission, then reading the rule in question again. Of course, no matter how well and intelligently an employee balances the employer's interests, their Bullying Boss is, by definition, working a different agenda and will have a different and predictably damaging-to-the-Target interpretation of them. Not only violating rules, but also following them can bring a Workplace Warrior dangerously close to insubordination. Here as elsewhere, if directed to follow a course of action the employee disagrees with, he or she must follow their superior's instructions. Their recourse is to document their contrary-to-the-mission instructions and maybe secure a witness to do the same.

Back inside his Ring of Fire, Bullying Boss Wayne fired again at Anna, "You know the rules. Invoices from our own customers get paid on a ten day cycle, everyone else is on a thirty days." Anna waited for a good long moment, "Maybe not, Boss." She pulled out the three-ring procedures manual and without a further word that might prompt him to reply, she pointed to the page dictating thirty days for everyone. She knew right where to find it and he read it for himself. "Of course, I'll do ten days if you want," she said as he stomped off. "Not bad," she said, feeling good about her stronger self. More importantly, the next ding would not likely come at her any time soon.

With a fast scan over the employer's written materials, Warriors grow in professional competence generally but, more importantly, they grow in political strength and understanding beyond the Bullying Boss's. While Bullying Bosses are busy limiting others, Warriors are busy contributing. Where the Bullies deviate, Warriors document.

ANOTHER IMPERSONAL, INDIRECT COMMUNICATION

Not being a part of Nature that our social fabric and its labors are a part of, Bullying Bosses depend on rules to create an order out of what they can't see or figure directly. Being abstract, the rules are external and didactic, two features that the Bully's favor. They create an artificially simple social structure for their environment that, for them, would otherwise an indescribable chaos. The command system itself is a rule system that defines a Bullying Boss's position and power. For them, to protect rules is to protect their identity. Rules are their equivalent of sacrosanct, not people.

Rather than connect with people directly and personally, Bullying Bosses communicate indirectly and impersonally, in this case through the abstraction of rules. Instead of sharing personally with others, they issue citations. From a place separate and arguably above others, they judge people by rules as right and wrong, high and low with regard to just about everything, when others would join in the general social discourse. To enforce their judgments, with great self-righteous aplomb they issue Fatwah's at those they regard, or pretend to regard, as rule offenders. They're confident in their authority to stand as the judge over others based partly on supervisory status conferred on them by management, but mainly by their sense of personal "entitlement," the source of which always remains a mystery.

BULLIES COMMUNICATE

Indirectly and Impersonally

Through Actions	**Through Withholdings**
Dominating	No Empathy
Ranking	No Compassion
Projecting	
Bragging & Trophies	No Connecting
Citing to Rules	No Sharing
Alleging/Charging	No Loyalty
Fatwah's	
Threatening	
Violating Personhood	No Personhood
Conflicting & Malice	No Boundaries
Bullying Acts (other)	No Validations
Bullying for Audience	
Bullying an Audience	

RULES AS WEAPONS

When employees subordinate to Bullying Bosses deviate from a rule, real or imagined, the Bullies will frequently make as big an issue out of that deviation as they can. Some might feign or be prone toward genuine panic that emphases their importance as rule interpreters and enforcers and the negative importance of others, as rule violators. They may express to others great indignation for the alleged violation, indignation they imagine others share. With considerable consternation, he or she might spin around the workplace exclaiming to each person, "Did you see what Anna just did?" When Anna did nothing remarkable but the listeners didn't see anything so they don't know. Making things easy on themselves, bystanders have been seen nodding their heads in agreement when the only thing they care about is being left alone. It seems that Bullying Bosses have no clue exactly how alone in their pursuit they really are. A Bullying Boss is an outlaw vigilante, a pretend posse of one.

There're the extremely rare but illustrative Bullying Bosses who are able to walk through a workplace, essentially nonstop, dinging most every employee in turn with a cascade of chastisements. With each, they put themselves "one-up" and each employee "one-down." It's bullying with assembly line efficiency. And with each ding, they imagine they've won points for themselves while taking points away from others.

It's their formal charges that have the greatest occupational impact. If an employee is reasonably certain their Bullying Boss is about to file formal charges against them, they should consider filing their complaint against them first. The best defense is an offense. If it looks like Bullies' charges are the harbinger of the showdown Warriors have been preparing for, then it's time to give the battle everything they've collected or created that would be helpful as guided by strategic considerations – including their research on bullying and any occupational issues there might be in dispute.

The party who files first defines the issues and places him or herself on top of the dispute. The party who files second gives the appearance of trying to play catch up or to get even. To others it seems that, if the second party had a legitimate charge then he or she would have filed when it was timely not when placed on the defensive by a claim being made against them. If either the charges of Warriors or Bullies are serious, employees should seek counsel.

OPTIONS WHEN CHARGED

Rebuttals

Cross-Charges

Patience/Silence

Otherwise, to the extent possible, it's best to tune the Bullies out. On the floor, when Bullying Bosses charge an employee with breaking a rule, there can be no gainful retort. And, that's exactly their objective. They've done it many times before and already know very well how it works. Bullying Bosses' words may sound like they're about the job but they have nothing to do with furthering its mission. The literal truth of their charges is entirely irrelevant even to them. Bullying Bosses are out to ding the Target regardless and repeatedly. It's best for Warriors to focus on determining what their real, current political objective is, how best to document and possibly thwart it.

MAKE BELIEVE BULLYING BOSS RULES

Then there are Bullying Bosses' solo excursions into their make believe lands of fantastic rules. Not only do they ding Targets with their conveniently negative-to-Targets interpretations of actual employer rules, they also ding them for violating rules that don't exist in the workplace. They might make up a "rule" entirely peculiar to them, or maybe bring in one relevant only to their demographic but, like most private doctrines, in no way relevant once they enter the employer's production-based domain. Being made up, these rules can't be looked up, reviewed or followed, but for them a ding is a ding with the particularities not mattering all that much. The other employees don't get it either but they see the Target being dinged and they are rather glad they're not.

The black and white nature of Bullying Boss rule applications, whether real or make believe, cuts out all life's ambiguities. There are no gradations, textures or paradoxes. Being external, they are simple for externally oriented Bullies to work with. So it's not surprising that under the imaginary rules of the very most extreme Bullies, there is an exactly correct way to dress, to live, to have a conversation with one's mother and an exactly correct time for each of these things. There are also exactly correct consumer and other purchases to make and (*no kidding*) a correct order and frequency to make them, depending upon the Target's Bully-determined entitlement to these things.

With each ding, the Bully enjoys yet another opportunity to demonstrate to surrounding witness their correctness, in opposition to the individual they're making an example of. Taken together, and as offered, these demonstrations are to make clear to everyone the Bully's special sophistication and high standing in society generally. Indeed and as noted, the typical Bully casts him or herself as the defender the social order, an order that, if correctness prevails, includes him or her in control and at its top.

It's generally on the basis of their make believe rules, rather than recognized ones, that Bullying Bosses define their strongly held views about "duty." In listening to them and about them, it's clear that in this one matter, the generally fraudulent Bullies are serious and sincere. They express feeling both burdened, and proud of their own adherence to "duty's" precepts. The Bullies can sometimes be heard expressing annoyance, offense and even anger at those who fail in their compliance with "duties" known only to the Bully, and probably never truly about work.

The Bullies also use their make believe rules and duties, perhaps to compel sex, to trump arguably lesser ones—such as customs, rules and laws protecting privacy and prohibiting sexual harassment. Thus, the Bullies' use a combination of rules and duties special to them, not only to bind subordinates, but also to "authorize" Bully aggression beyond behavioral parameters agreed upon by people of conscience and law. Functionally, while their rules serve to control the home front, their egocentric duties sanction their illicit actions both at home and afar.

This combination of illusionary rules and duties constitutes an altogether practical, political machine. Fueled by malice, it's what daily transforms the Bullies' also imaginary notions of personal "entitlement," into sometimes real, control, power, and status. The Bullies know what they are doing, and they know that it's wrong, but only wrong in less sophisticated circles.

When investigating an allegation of sexual harassment bullying, an investigator does the logical thing of looking to legal and employer standards when evaluating the discovered facts. Logically, as a matter of self-defense, one would expect the Bully to do the same thing, but the guilty frequently don't. Oftentimes obliquely, sometimes self-righteously, some instead focus on the subordinates' having been immoral by violating imaginary duties of social and sexual sorts. For them, the immorality is the overriding issue, yet to their frustration not everyone seems to "to get." The failure of others to understand makes it risky for them to disclose or expose their true thoughts to those in authority, but sometimes they do anyway. Whether implicitly or expressly made, when confronted with allegations of sexual trespass, the breach of a "duty" by another is their fundamental defense.

The employer's rules are usually available for review, can mostly be followed. They have the potential for significant power for those who read or skim through them as a whole. As for Bully's make believe rules and duties, beyond of being aware of them to the extent possible, there's not much that can be done about what's not real to begin with.

Section Four

A Workplace Golden Rule
Loyalty To The Employer

MERE RESPECT

Bullying Bosses respect power in the abstract and for its own sake. They respect their own positively and employees' negatively but, larger than that, they respect the powers above. It's a genuine respect in every way, one that's certainly appreciated by the management team, but it's respect for the positions and power they hold and not for them professionally or personally. It's inherently thin, subject to cracks and fissures.

Loyalty is a deeper thing than respect. Bullying Bosses have no loyalty to the management team or anyone else. To them, loyalty is just a silly concept other people talk about, probably to affect status through its mention. It's in the contradiction between their political demonstrations of respect and their failure of loyalty that, sooner or later, with or without the Workplace Warrior, the Bullying Boss will meet his or her downfall. Bullying Bosses generally try to forestall that inevitability by great shows of esteem for their superiors. They shake their hands with determination. They speak with deference when in their company. Like dogs in the middle of the pack, the smallish Bullying Bosses have no problem falling submissive to their larger managers, just as they show no hesitation in their dominance over those smaller than them. The difference is that dogs are known for their loyalty and Bullying Bosses are not.

Fortunately in the daily lives of Warriors, their Bullying Bosses do not expect their loyalty, only a showing of respect that's artificial, superficial and yet absolute in its presentation. That's only fair and it's also doable even if it's doubtless impossible for a Warrior to muster actual loyalty for a Bully. The Bullies won't know if an employee is faking it and probably wouldn't care anyway.

DEMONSTRATE LOYALTY

Nowhere in management's mission statement does it say anything about protecting an employee's feelings. That's on the Warrior's agenda, but it really isn't something they've thought about. They're focused on the employer's larger priorities and their own jobs. As just noted, they demand loyalty from everyone they pay but respect is mostly what they expect and get. Respect is good as currency in an employment structure but loyalty is the structure itself. It constitutes its core and all its connecting branches. While the Warrior's loyalty to his or her abuser is out of the question, loyalty to the employer is strictly a business arrangement so employees can give theirs honestly. Employees' attention to management's mission as its Best Worker, to the extent possible and even in the union context, is their loyalty made manifest.

Showing loyalty and respect to the management team presents a completely different dilemma for Warriors than it does Bully Bosses. It's a large structural problem making it difficult and maybe impossible for employees to become known to managers much less impress them with their dedication. As employees, many or most simply don't have significant contact with management team members and so can't personally demonstrate their loyalty or competence to them, at least not directly. And Bullying Bosses will predictably undercut them at every turn. Employees are in a pickle. While their Bully is respectful and in their circle but not loyal; employees are loyal but can't get close enough to show them much of anything. Being a logistical issue, this is the type of problem that study and good planning can address with particular competence.

SPEAKING OUT OR NOT

When frustrated by a management team's failure to address their Bullying Boss problem, the first thing many people think of doing is going to the press. "If they don't get rid of that guy, I'm going to '60 Minutes,'" is something said everyday and all across the country. It may be said with great earnestness, but with a profound underestimation of the relative scales involved between their individual plight and the media's scale of operations. Horrible things happen to good people all day long, but that's not the definition of news. News is what newspaper editors think will sell newspapers or enhance the paper's prestige. Newspaper editors are a fickle bunch. The media does not generally regard employees' problems as significant news.

However, to be a whistleblower, in our day and age, approaches being a secular saint. Whistleblowers are receiving increased political attention and are being backed up by stronger laws. But the fact is, in practice, whistleblowers don't do very well. They tend to end up martyrs. When there's a whistleblower, there's always a question about whether their motive is truly in the public interest or they are actually pursuing a private agenda exploiting an alleged public concern. To management and regardless of circumstances, they're traitors and are fiercely targeted with often-disastrous results. In all potential whistleblowing circumstances, Warriors are urged both to seek counsel and the wisdom of whistleblowers that proceed them.

If employees' problems are specifically with their Bullying Boss and they don't have a larger public concern, then they should almost certainly not engage in the "hard" tactic of criticizing their employer in public. Many employees imagine that because they have First Amendment, free speech rights relative to the government in the political sphere outside work, they also have the same ones with their employer as well. They don't. Indeed, depending on the circumstances, even remarks made in the community that are totally appropriate there can get an employee lawfully fired from his or her job. They should consult an attorney.

If employees dare to speak up, there may be some legal protections, but being right about an issue and having rights won't necessarily stop them from getting fired. Stated very loosely, governmental employees retain some measure of their First Amendment rights even at work but courts very frequently enforce vaguely stated "management rights" as being more important.[35] Also stated very loosely, private sector employees simply don't have First Amendment rights in their private property realm.[36] In both cases, there are specific laws that sometimes protect employees against discrimination and reprisals under discrimination and labor laws. In general, what we call "the law" has a pro-management bias that roots in basic property rights with its ancient traditions. On legal binders to this day, one employment topic is still labeled, "Master & Servant."[37] Fortunately it doesn't stop there.

CIRCUMSPECT SPEECH

As weaker parties whose concerns nevertheless deserve to be heard, employees' stealthy options for communication are limited only by their imaginations. As described above, Warriors may have some success making their case by obliquely passing their documentation to just the right person of authority, in a professional way and with perfect timing. Anonymous postings, distributions, or droppings of literature can be effective, particularly if humorous. Simple images, like political cartoons, tend to work best but apropos ones are hard to find or devise. All of these get the Warrior's message to places and people where their voice wouldn't otherwise be heard or believed.

Nicknames can be an extremely powerful tool, sometimes the most powerful, for the powerless on behalf of workplace truth.

They're compact, only one or two words, and thus are potent communicators. They are humorous and so disarm the listener. They travel circuitously and thus fairly safely for the Warrior. A nickname has to be exactly the right fit for a Bullying Boss, or it'll fail to light up even one conversation. And that's the whole trick. It should be akin to nickname that might be given to a difficult family member—one that speaks an important and uncomfortable truth about the Bully while having zero malice in it. It won't spread if it's malicious. It probably also won't spread if it's known to have come from the Warrior, malice being assumed.

If the Warrior or someone else hits on a nickname for the Bullying Boss that strikes people as being rich and right, from that moment on, it'll follow the Bully wherever he or she goes. If it also strikes a cord with management, even they will end up using it as a substitute for the Bully's given name, maybe even using it in his or her presence. That's ideal. So it really shouldn't be a nickname that management might regard as complimentary to his or her supervisory skills, such as "the general," "ramrod" or "barnstormer." The better nicknames will, directly or indirectly, speak to the Bully's workplace behaviors or attitudes of import to the Warrior. *"Can you hear that tap, tap, tap? Damn. Captain Ahab is back."* The Bully's not got the Warrior down; on the contrary.

10

TO SHIFT EMOTIONAL WEIGHT OUTSIDE

Section One

A Full Richness Of Life
Lies Outside Work's Walls

WORKPLACE AND COMMUNITY

With the breakdown in the family and community structures, the workplace has become a "family" and "community" of sorts. It substitutes for both but does neither job well. No matter how many posters employers put up saying employer and employees are "family," they're not. Buddies outside work are real friends, but even good bosses never will be. Neither are coworkers unless the employee chooses to live dangerously and gets lucky with their choice. Filling a void left by family and community, many people tend to immerse themselves in their workplace worlds. Work is now where we live our lives, so it follows that's where our expectations are likely to lie. For personal matters, these misplaced priorities are doomed by a systemic "betrayal." A Yale study found that twenty-four percent of employees were chronically angry at work. Most stated that the cause of their anger was, what they regarded as "basic promises" being broken and what the study found were actually personally generated expectations being dashed.[38] Employees too often have expectations of the workplace that are too high, or too elaborate.

When some employers project the notion of a workplace "family," they generate the illusion of an egalitarian community, sometimes carrying it to the point of giving the title "manager" to almost every employee. They prod them to take "managerial responsibility" and "managerial initiative" when, in truth, as workers they have no influence whatsoever. Coming from the other direction, managers wearing sneakers and sweatshirts are still managers. They have the same responsibilities to their stockholders as any others. They hire, fire, promote, and demote. Whatever the titles or illusions, the command hierarchy is still there. Even if an employer's sweet sentiments are genuinely intended, the illusions they create are not helpful to employees attempting to navigate what is, for most, an environment inherently confusing and presenting dangerous crosscurrents.

If employees are making only $8.50 an hour, then they are certainly not managers. As workers, they're entitled to overtime pay when they provide their employer with their overtime efforts. An appellate court recently upheld an enormous award of $120 million for unpaid overtime to 2,402 claims representatives led by Rose M. Bell. The employer, Farmer's Insurance Exchange, wrongfully claimed the representatives were administrative employees and exempt from overtime laws. The court decided they were instead, "production workers within the meaning of administrative/production worker dichotomy …"[39] There is no such thing as a classless society; and certainly no classless workplaces; but there is real fellowship and community just beyond the workplace walls.

COMMUNITY SUPPORT AND VALUES

Inside the top-down workplace structure, employees are always "one down" so it makes good Workplace Warrior's sense to keep their primary emotional and social focus outside work and into community where they can find their own footing and on their own terms. That's where they'll get their personal bearing in their specially chosen niche and where some significant measure of equalitarianism can be made real. If an employee's feet and heart are firmly planted beyond the Bullying Boss's reach, then the Bully's workplace power to "trip on" employees is greatly lessened. Employees find both social and employment buoyancy outside where contact with Bullies may exist but is only momentary, probably unnoticed, and not mandated by anyone.

Unfortunately, the effects of workplace abuse are not readily left at the workplace door. As noted in a differing context, Bullying Bosses are, ultimately, isolated creatures who, when successful, convert normally social employees into isolated creatures such as they are – but not like them in any other respect. It's the disease model functioning within the labor-management context. On the other hand, when a Workplace Warrior's friends are waiting outside of work to take a walk or see a movie together, a Bullying Boss's emotional trickery and attempts to humiliate ring more hollow. Employees' book and church groups, sports team and sports bar, their bridge and chess clubs, their community and political organizations, their tennis club and the folks at the community swimming pool are or can become their actual friends. With determination, during the workday Bullying Bosses strive to stuff Warriors into metaphoric isolation boxes below them. If employees just stay home and watch television, they do it to themselves.

When Warriors are suffering a particularly hot fire at work, these outside friends can provide them with real emotional support. For free, they give Warriors the balance of outside perspectives a person experiencing workplace abuse needs. They're also sources for leads to good attorneys, therapists, physicians and possibly an employee support organization, such as a union. In the community, Warriors might also benefit from their technical expertise concerning their job, employer or industry that they can translate into a better understanding of work, or even secure a statement affirming their particular work skills and practices as excellent. Outside friends may know about a job that's better in every way, than the one Warriors are suffering—and not just better because it frees them from bullying.

ZERO TOLERANCE FOR ABUSE VALUES

Most employees report to work bringing with them community values against abuse, harassment and bullying, but too often find themselves in a place where those protective values don't exist. Indeed, in the name of managerial good sense, those community values are frequently dismissed in the workplace as "ridiculous" — together with the employees who report their breach. Yet, even if seriously flawed in their application, these protective values do exist in the larger society. There are criminal laws against trespass and civil ones prohibiting and sometimes preventing domestic violence perpetrators from getting anywhere near their victims. Many of the same antics Bullying Bosses engage in at workplace could easily get them arrested just outside work on the sidewalk.

Until recently, victims of domestic violence, rape, child abuse and elder abuse were also almost never believed by anyone. There now exists a cadre of professionals and volunteers who know enough to listen and believe human beings who report being abused by the petty tyrants who live and work among us. There are particular therapists, lawyers and clergy who have extensive experience with abuse syndromes and can support abused employees. As long as the phenomena of workplace bullying remains isolated from the community that surrounds it, it will remain isolated from the community's values as well. Workplace Warriors and managers as well, are well advised to learn from people with practical experience in syndromes of abuse.

Whether traditional, extended, or alternative, families can be the strongest antidotes there are to Bully oppression. Taking time to play with the kids centers the Workplace Warrior. Still, children can also seem like a burden in the middle of a Bullying Boss war. Without a paycheck-producing job, a Warrior's economic support for them might be thrown into jeopardy. Bullying Bosses know this. Effectively, they use family members as economic hostages to compel a Warrior's attention and obedience.

A mate, spouse or partner can only become a personal and political asset to Workplace Warriors if fully involved in their dilemmas, starting with Warriors moving past nightly complaints about work abuse, to demonstrating to their partner exactly what's going on, that is, the pattern and practice of an abuser. This can be a difficult if not emotionally dangerous endeavor. But nightly descriptions of singular bullying events tend to confuse matters more than clarify them. As with everyone else, they need to be able to see the whole picture before they can achieve an understanding sufficient to explain the strange facts the Warrior brings home.

Understandings of their Warrior's workplace, work processes, coworkers and the Bullying Boss, decrease the likelihood they will misinterpret what's going on. Otherwise, Warriors may find themselves not only unheard when they tell their "The Story," but also pressed by their partners to shut up when they need to talk and be understood by specifically them. It's definitely helpful for the partner to read about the general phenomenon of Bullying Bosses in the same books, articles and websites the Warrior has already been reading.

It's helpful to channel together the negative energy and information into note cards, incident reports, comparison charts, and reviewing the collected documents. Instead of directing yet another story at partners, partner and Warrior might be willing to stand shoulder-to-shoulder as teammates working those documentary and analytical processes, as they watch the pieces come together. The Warrior may be an expert on the workplace, but the partner is expert on the Warrior.

Ultimately out of concern for the family's support, or simply not believing people like Bullying Bosses exist, partners sometimes urge debilitating caution. More often, in partners' love, loyalty or because of offense taken, they may demand the Warrior take stronger action than the Warrior knows to be possible or productive. At lot is at stake for partner as well as for the Warrior, but only the employee knows how the workplace and the Bullying Boss really work. In this, the Warrior is the responsible party – and no one else.

In an emotionally confusing crisis such as those imposed by Bullying Bosses, Warriors are often wise to join their partner in seeing a marriage therapist, clergy advisor or elder family member regularly. The Workplace Warrior can't fight much less win a two-front war, one facing a Bullying Boss at work and an anxious partner at home. The potential disconnect between partners can create considerable consternation for both. If Bullying Bosses were to hear of that tension, they would be quite pleased and proud. Bullying Bosses can't be allowed the satisfaction of witnessing signs of home disharmony as they may leak into the workplace. Maybe, they will instead find themselves standing by helpless as a florist delivers a wonderful bouquet of flowers. The Workplace Warrior need not be isolated.

"TOUCHING THE MARKET"

Whatever the reasons, Herbert was not ready to quit. He dreaded the humiliating and scary idea of applying for and at least occasionally being rejected from jobs. Moreover, he didn't want to face "a learning curve" with a new employer, with new duties, people and surroundings. It was by no means clear that he could ultimately survive in a new place. Maybe worse of all, looking for work felt like defeat. He'd be giving up the one thing at work bigger than his Bullying Boss, and that was his long lasting job there. But Herbert still had to at least "Touch the Market." The idea wasn't necessarily to look for a job in order to actually take one, but to firm up his connection to the larger field of his occupation beyond his Bullying Boss's reach. From what people said, he thought he had a pretty good idea what was out there, but job markets are quite different for every individual. Whatever Hebert knew, he didn't have a clue about his own fit.

It took only a minute for him to scan the listings for work he'd consider taking and to make some notes. As a result, Herbert's personal strength back at his workplace immediately increased, but that wasn't enough. There's no substitute for personal contact. He phoned an old work contact, Joan, and invited her for lunch. With job listings sitting on their table, they did some serious brainstorming. Sharing lunch with an old workmate or two can't be anything but wonderful.

On the other hand, being interviewed for a job by recruiters or potential employers can feel threatening – but it's not threatening to interview a recruiter about the market *under the guise* of a job interview. What they know about the current job market in a particular area and expertise can be invaluable. By merely "Touching the Market," Workplace Warriors acquire new reserves of power outside work and thus make themselves far more potent inside. Here again, and it may be ironic, but by scoping the market with its range of actual opportunities for specific Warriors, they are better able to stay where they are.

Section Two

Healers and Healing

PHYSICIANS

As a Bullying Boss continues to attack an employee, his or her health will, sooner or later, need medical attention. A doctor's office is probably the first stop a Target makes in defending him or herself against a Bullying Boss. A physician will treat at least the medical symptoms but might also help deal with the employer politically as well. That might mean not only prescribing a calming medication but also providing a doctor's a note certifying that the employee has a medical condition requiring that he or she take a specific number of days off from work.

Although the support of a physician – particularly one who's been treating an employee over time – is invaluable, taking sick time off is not necessarily the best way to make use of it. If Targets medically need to then, by all means, they should take the days. If they don't, then they shouldn't. Targets who demonstrate their health weaknesses for Bullying Bosses' reviewing pleasure tells the Bullies that they have their Target on the run. Yet more pressure will likely be applied. If the employee is faking it, the Bully will take that as an equally good result. Taking sick leave is politically counter-productive.

As already discussed, it's best for employees to share as little about their personal self as possible at work and that includes medical matters most of all. Depending on circumstances, an employee might have enforceable legal rights to medical confidentiality, including those that possibly protect even his or her diagnosis from disclosure at work. Consult an attorney. It's recommended that employees work with their physicians to ensure that the diagnosis they choose is not only medically appropriate, but also appropriate to the employment circumstances. The wrong diagnosis, or one stated too strongly, can result in the employee's medical termination. For Workplace Warriors, protecting their good health is central at least to surviving, if not winning, the fight. Maintaining a sustained relationship with a competent and politically savvy physician is of the utmost importance.

PROTECT GOOD HUMOR

Targets might ask themselves, being entirely truthful with themselves and then bouncing that truth off someone who knows them intimately, are they too wounded, angry or depressed for the job and the fight to keep it? Is their general good humor still in tact? Do they have a regular regimen for exercise, meditation or prayer? If they feel motivated to fight anyone solely by anger or revenge, they should call their therapist. On this, all political thought agrees. In the mythology of martial artists throughout history, the effective warrior is the one with a clear heart – or at least one as clear as possible. Besides, revenge can never be anything more than an ugly illusion. It's simply not possible for a Target "to get even." But it is possible for revenge to sabotage both the prospect of political success and the necessity of good mental health. If the battle between a Workplace Warrior and his or her Bullying Boss becomes an avenging slugfest on both sides, the Bullying Boss will most likely win. To do anything, they must protect their good humor.

Good humor is not about jokes; it's about a good and impenetrable attitude. Humor is about holding onto the larger perspective, staying comfortable with oneself, then being just as comfortable with significant others. A healthy humor is both a Workplace Warrior's very best offensive and defensive weapon. The problem is that it's also the most difficult to maintain in a workplace suddenly defined by malice and hurt. After all of the Targets' beatings, it makes sense there'd be only a bad attitude where their good life used to be. If employees are lucky, they will have co-employee companions who haven't been beaten and still have their great sense of humor. They can be critically helpful in clearing a Target's personal attitude on a particularly bad day and the workplace air as needed. Good humor is a way of being.

As opposed to either the socially repulsive elements of abuse or victimhood, a good humor lights up a room. It's attractive. Warriors' light denies Bullies the pleasure of their torment just as it confounds their plots for control. Bullying Bosses have no wit to delight others, but some are adept at ridicule and cutting sarcasm. These never fail to cast a dark shadow over everything and everyone. They are the opposite of humor. Effectively, Bullies are management-sponsored negativity that takes aim precisely at their Target's good attitude. The Workplace Warrior must be vigilant in its defense.

Employees don't have the employer's authority, so again, soft and indirect tactics are again the most effective ones on the job. With humor, Workplace Warriors work in Bullying Bosses' blind spot. This blindness works a lot like listening to someone speak an unfamiliar language and understand nothing. When faced with belly laughs or even quietly shared smiles, Bullies may understand that something's going on but can't see or understand what it might be. They're left out. Their program to isolate their Target has backfired. To the extent they nevertheless attempt to participate, it can only be awkwardly – spotlighting their social disconnect. Bullying Bosses attempt anti-social control, partly through isolating their targets, but that doesn't work at all when in the company of people feeling their connections very personally. Warriors discover that humor is both a core necessity to themselves as well as a social lubricant facilitating group cohesion.

Through Evelyn's confident display of her positive temperament, her good attitude said to everyone that her Bullying Boss had not gotten her down and that she remained connected to her political constituents, her co-employees. The Bullying Boss couldn't isolate Evelyn. She simply was not built for victimhood. In contrast, like Bullying Bosses, victims can't do humor either. They grumble endlessly about justice, and never get any. Instead of complaining with everything that came up, Evelyn saw the humanity in each and found a soft way to share that humor with others. By staying on the high road with a positive attitude, Evelyn could actually demonstrate her Bullying Boss's intrinsic confinement to the low. In steps, her Bullying Boss became the more isolated party, not Evelyn.

A Workplace Warrior can never go wrong with maintaining a sense of good humor. A Bullying Boss can never go there at all. For humor to work, as with everything political except more so, Warriors have to pay conscious attention to not only their own good and strong attitude, but those of the people around them. When Good Humor works, it's contagious. When it's reciprocated, it has the power to envelop the workplace with soft safety beyond the reach of any Bullying Boss blows.

THERAPISTS AND CLERGY

As discussed, damages to the mental health of employees suffering workplace abuse frequently include symptoms of clinical depression and post-traumatic stress disorder. Targets' interpersonal relationships with the people they care about will almost certainly be compromised to some degree. No matter how "well-adjusted" employees might regard themselves to be emotionally, one's attitudes, emotions, and conduct can always benefit from an upgrade.

Mental and emotional confusion pervades bullying workplaces. Perspective is easily lost. Therapists experienced in abuse syndromes can help interpret both the big and small clues in understanding Targets' emotions, thoughts, and behaviors, as well as possibly those of some of the employees they work with. But time spent attempting to understand the Bully is time wasted, and valuable energy dissipated. In therapists' expertise, they might walk a Target through the steps necessary for dealing with the trauma that the Bullying Boss inflicted upon them. Whether measured in time or money, what these therapists have to offer has value.

Targets might be hesitant to seek the counsel of a therapist. They could be concerned that a therapist might be just another person who will disbelieve them, who has no personal experience in the cold, complicated reality of workplace politics, and who sees their symptoms and workplace difficulties as a function of personal neurosis rather than recognizing abuse and trauma. But chances are, even if they can't find a therapist experienced in workplace bullying, they can find someone with experience working with people abused in other contexts such as with children, women, or elders. For a referral to a specially qualified therapist, people can call an experienced friend or community group.

Some therapists charge on a sliding scale and health insurance sometimes helps pay. A Target's employer may have an Employee Assistance Program (EAP). These programs were originally set up to help employees with drug and alcohol problems, but now they cover just about everything. They do have their limitations, starting with the number of visits they'll pay for. Then, too, there's also the issue of a work-related therapist protecting an employee's confidentiality. Without that security and safety, sharing their problems with anyone connected to work is problematic at best. Employees are at their highest risk of exposure if the EAP therapist or counselor is actually an employee of their employer. They're at practically no risk if their employer has a bulk contract with an outside group and never knows who visits them and who doesn't.

Targets may also be reluctant to seek therapy not wanting to be forced, even metaphorically, to sit "on the couch" next to their

Bullies to "work things out." Bullies are openly hostile to anything that smacks of the personal; proudly unredeemable. For sure, even if help were available for the Bully, the Target is not properly made a party to the Bully's therapy. The relationship shared between employee and supervisor is supposed to be a strictly business one. If the Bully were a brother, friend, or spouse with whom the employee shared a personal relationship and commitment, that would be different. But the Target's contact with the Bullying Boss is involuntary, impersonal, and to be escaped as soon as possible.

Their relationship with the Bully is also potentially dangerous. It is imposed on the Target by a hierarchical structure that's designed to confer all the power on the supervisor and none on the subordinate. In the best of circumstance, there's no proper place for *the personal* within power imbalance inherently radical, one made worse by malice substituting where being "businesslike" or "connection" would routinely be. Bullying Bosses are strangers.

Indeed, precisely what Targets require is a separation from the abuser—with the abusive Bully being the one to leave. There can be no proper occasion for any party to bring them together, even analytically. The gruesome world of military torture and workplace abuse are, substantively, very different. But the emotional self-defense processes for their victims have similarities. It's not surprisingly that Dr. Judith Herman reports that "prisoners of conscience," a group of politically strong, particularly sophisticated, and well-connected individuals reportedly, "...protect themselves only by uncompromising refusal to enter into even the most superficial social relationship with their adversaries."[40] Workplace Targets are very clear that there can be no safe, ordinary human engagement with their Bullying Bosses.

Targets in therapy want and maybe need an explanation for what has so far been, and maybe always will be, psychoanalytically inexplicable. As previously mentioned, if a diagnosis is given, it is virtually always "narcissistic personality disorder." Political commentators have noted the general identity of the behaviors of workplace abusers and narcissists. Observation indicates that Bullying Bosses often engage in behaviors consistent with narcissism, but the workplace is far too complicated to describe that simplistically. When bullying is investigated on-site, some seem to be afflicted, while others do not. Either way, the production of a diagnosis does nothing to stop the abuse.

When a Target complains of workplace abuse, the focus for everyone has to be on the political context that allows and supports it, rather than on the Bully or even the Target. Faraway speculations about the nature of a Bully's psychology are sideshows. In the center ring, Warriors' success will ultimately be had, if it is had at all, in the workplace itself and not inside the Bully's head. The instrument of that change will be a workplace manager or managers motivated to take remedial action because of the well-considered efforts of a focused, determined Workplace Warrior—despite the trauma being endured.

Spiritual approaches serve Workplace Warriors in ways that political ones alone cannot. Everyone needs expert guidance when walking down dark and inherently confusing paths made apparent by introspection. If Warriors have pastors or other spiritual mentors in their lives, or are able to find one, they might consider seeking one out. Ultimately, and as stated, for both Warriors and Bullying Bosses, bullying presents a spiritual crisis.

Workplace Warriors' pursuits of spiritual and psychological healing and hope, function on a contrasting, but parallel, track to those afforded by political analysis and action. There's no contradiction between looking inwardly to the core self to heal existing trauma and focusing outwardly to put an end to the source of trauma as soon as possible. Both jobs need to be done.

11

THE GOLDEN ROAD

MINDS, MONEY AND MUSCLE

Section One

Agencies

If the import of any given thing were measured by the number of government agencies regulating it, then work would arguably the most important of society's activities. Very different laws, regulations, and administrative agencies scrutinize and regulate virtually every aspect of work. Very often employees are required to go to one of these agencies, within certain time constraints, in order "to exhaust their administrative remedies" before they are allowed to file a lawsuit. Federal agencies include, among a great many more, the Equal Employment Opportunity Commission (EEOC), the National Labor Relations Board (NLRB), the Occupational Health and Safety Agency (OSHA), and the Department of Labor (DOL). In many states, there are corresponding state agencies as well as corresponding private activist organizations. Adding to the confusion, state and federal governments frequently duplicate each other's work while applying similar but differing standards and procedures. It's advisable to consult with an attorney before approaching an agency for help. They'll know where a Workplace Warrior might best file a complaint and what to say.

Going to a governmental agency and getting it involved on Targets' behalves is virtually never enough. Employers do not shake in their boots when an employee threatens to call the local newspaper or when the Equal Employment Opportunities Commission calls them. Instead, they calmly call their attorneys. For everyone involved, what really matters is the quality and quantity of documentation that has been collected and written. But, in the end, there can be no substitute for securing political support at work.

Section Two

Securing an Attorney

Lawsuits are initially a function of the marketplace. A Target can have great, easily provable facts and significant damages combined with favorable law, but other lawsuits proposed to an attorney may be even better, or maybe just more convenient for a particular attorney to work on. The more a potential client puts into his or her presentation, the greater his or her market value. Targets should avoid claiming it's the principle they care about and not the money. A comment of that type will not be well received.

Targets may call several attorneys, but with no success. They may be under attack at work and then get the brush off from the very professionals who are supposed to help them. It can feel like everyone has turned on them when, in fact, they haven't. For Targets, the starting point is to make sure they're calling the right attorneys.

They will need an employment attorney or a labor one, although other types of attorneys may be relevant to their case. The phone book is not recommended. Ideally, they may have a friend or family member who has had good luck with an attorney. He or she may not do employment cases but might make the right referral. For suggestions, employees can also call one or more activist organizations or a state-regulated "attorney referral service."

Just because securing the services of an attorney can be difficult, it doesn't mean that a Target has to accept the first lawyer to call back. As the attorney is interviewing the employee, the employee will be interviewing the attorney as an individual and as a representative of his or her firm. Do they have experience in employment matters? Have they been to trial recently, or frequently in the past, so that it is evident to the employer that they've got what it takes to go all the way, if need be? Is the attorney prepared to take the case on a "contingency basis" only getting paid if the Target wins? Will they "front" the Target the costs for depositions, which can run into the tens of thousands of dollars, or will the Target be required to pay for them? Will they promptly return the phone calls? Will they mail the Target copies of the paperwork traded by the two sides of the litigation in order to keep him or her up-to-date? Do the Target and attorney "click?"

Of course, the attorney is going to be checking the Target as well. Does he or she have provable damages and has not yet collapsed into the unattractive role of "victim" that's unlikely to appeal to a judge or jury. Will the Target be responsive to the attorney's needs, such as collecting and providing him or her with the relevant documents and the particulars of witnesses in a timely manner? When actually testifying, is he or she likely to exercise restraint in their delivery, yet have what it takes to back off the opposition's lawyer when need be. Did the Target wear a suit when he or she first visits the attorney's office?

Private practitioners have bills to pay both at the office and at home. Sure, they sometimes get to take on a progressive cause, but unless that's their life's devotion, they have a living to make. Their time is valuable. Whatever a Target does to save time is to the Target's advantage. Before Targets call prospective attorneys, they should compile their relevant documents and maybe draft a chronology, as already discussed. The chronology doesn't have to be to be long, and, for time considerations, it *shouldn't* be long. Instead of making their pitch hurriedly on the phone to an attorney or paralegal who doesn't know them, they can ask for the intake individual's name and mail him or her the written materials to brief the firm in advance of discussion.

A real lawyer, as opposed to a television one, is well versed in the current state of a large legal discourse and carefully follows procedural rules. The general thing sometimes called the *substantive law* is not something someone can know merely by looking up a certain point in a manual, like one might do so for a production question. Substantive law is an enormous, ongoing debate between different legislatures, executives, judges, and lawyers in different jurisdictions. It's always in motion. A good lawyer has to know how to fit cases into a debate that's already in progress. That's frequently a tricky call, and it's probably not at all personal to the prospective client.

Section Three

Aid and Support Groups

AID AND SUPPORT GROUPS

Locally and nationally there people who do the hard work of protecting people from oppression and exploitation. Generally, they are more interested in defending their cause and constituents than any particular person as an individual, but that can work for Workplace Warriors if they're not only personally dedicated, but also professional in their work and well connected in the community. Their staff and activists have experience, expertise, and resources.

They also have workable access to the press. As noted, even on a "slow news day," a Warrior getting a raw deal from a Bullying Boss is predictably not news, but professional and progressive organizations know how to use what's happening to a Warrior as an example of a larger problem.

A great many labor organizations that are not unions earnestly attempt to improve working conditions, such as those fighting against discrimination, for workers' health and safety and those seeking to reform the labor movement itself. There are also colleges and universities that have extensive labor studies programs that have evening classes and can also make referrals.

There are many organizations that focus on representing a special issue or population, such as women or a particular minority. In the process, they also defend that population's working people. Among the more notable organizations are The National Organization of Women, La Raza, NAACP, and the Asian Law Caucus. There are attorney groups like the National Lawyers Guild that represent multiple causes as well as the ACLU that specifically defends our constitutional rights, such as those associated with the First Amendment.

Warriors can consider approaching a group, evaluating it, and possibly integrating it as an asset into their strategic plan. They are dedicated defenders for their causes. Their experience prosecuting medium-to-large political campaigns can be of enormous help in mentoring a Warrior in their efforts. Some are so powerful that, in some cases, the mere utterance of their name could either get an employee fired or put on pedestal by the employer.

UNIONS

Workplace abused union members expect representation from their unions and many get it. AFSCME, CWA and UE are powerful unions that have taken stands against workplace abuse. In others, they may have to fight for their due. If they happen to have a bullying union, that will more than double their difficulties. But it's productive for Warriors to drop the "us vs. them" approach with their unions that place members in opposition to the institution. As union members, they may or may not have a "right" to representation from the union, but they absolutely do have the right to win leadership over some small corner of it as a shop steward or elected official. Employees in trouble do it all the time.

In the process, at least in the more democratic unions, Workplace Warriors receive invaluable training, experience and support in labor-management relations. They learn how to protect themselves as they learn to protect others. For non-union employees, there's a good likelihood that there exists similar training at a community college or by local labor activist groups. In these networks, employees make contacts with other employees suffering situations similar to theirs, as well as build connections with union members and officials. Meanwhile, the Warrior collects contracts, manuals, and phone numbers.

CHAPTER

12

GOLD SMELTING RETREATS

AS BETWEEN SWORDS AND SHIELDS,
RETREATS ARE SHIELDS.

Section One
Leave With Style

Under all circumstances when Warriors finally leave a workplace, it's critically important that they are as joyful and positive as possible about their impending future. A winning attitude kills the "credit" for a supposed conquest their Bullying Boss might otherwise claim. If circumstances change for the better and coming back becomes desirable, leaving as a winner makes that easier. Importantly, leaving a negative job as a joyful victor rather than victim maximizes their standing in their occupational field generally.

When Warriors leave, they're not vaguely planning "to just take some time off." Warriors might have a great job or a project they're going over to. They might be about to fulfill their life dream of going into business for themselves. A good severance agreement could go a long ways in financing their new enterprise. If their intention is to finish writing that book they've been working on, for at least face-saving purposes, it ought to have a title. They won't be singing "You Can Take This Job and Shove It," as this author once did in the foolishness of youth.

In their last days, they'll take time to make personal contact with every individual they can, friend and foe alike except, of course, the Bullying Boss. Ideally, that will include socializing with coworkers in more personal settings outside of work. If affordable, that could mean going out to lunch or for drinks with the people they truly cared about, along with those they previously couldn't have cared less about. With all sincerity, the Warrior should find at least one important thing to thank each person for. Warriors will be amazed at how receptive even their suddenly former enemies will be to their offerings. Whatever else they do or don't do, Warriors are better off not carrying any bad blood on their on their way out the door.

Section Two

Vacation Visions

Regularly leaving the workplace battleground for greener pastures to contemplate and experience the larger scheme of things is absolutely essential. In stark contrast to the inadvisability of taking sick leave except when medically necessary, taking vacations is critically important. However, vacations can be more difficult to initiate than sick leave. Warriors often fail to schedule and plan vacations when working furiously and living in the midst of battle. Just as frequently, Bullying Bosses may attempt to sabotage them. If Anna wasn't careful in securing her vacation leave, her Bully Wayne's shame might explode out of that scary place inside of him. He might even cancel an approved vacation at the last minute or attempt to undermine it. But she'd be careful. Finding some measure of *peace* in some place removed is more than worth the effort and, if need be, a fight.

Surely even from Warriors' traumatized state, they can remember long ago being on vacation in some amazing place, remarking on the largeness of the universe, and promising themselves to do more of that sort of thing in the future. Simply being removed from the stressors at work helped short-term but putting things in their proper perspective had longer-term benefits. It provided absolute truth of a sort that can't regularly be seen or understood from inside the confusion of a workplace nightmare. Bullying Boss problems were not even a speck compared to all they saw and felt out there. Gaining a larger view, and their good humor that came with it, may have been the most important step they could have taken to survive the abuse syndrome, and it still is. Even if Warriors can't actually feel that healing power after they've returned to work for a while, they can remember and honor the out loud promise they made to themselves to go back as seekers and to heal again.

Anna had largely survived Bully Wayne's intrigues, having grown politically larger than his Ring of Fire. Looking forward, she had been anticipating her annual vacation with great hopefulness. Wherever she eventually went and whatever she did, she was willing to spend extra in order to make it memorable. That way, later during the difficult patches, she could hold onto at least the vibrant memory of the special and positive feelings there. The photos she'd take would help.

Between vacations and to protect her good humor, she disciplined herself to spend every third Saturday at her favorite beach not far away. While driving there, she could almost literally feel workplace toxins sliding off of her. On each return, she was rejuvenated and better able to defend herself back at work. Her improved disposition was somehow enough to make negative incidents fewer. There was power in the experience of that quiet beach, with its mountains and cold, clean water. She brought at least some of that power back to work through feelings, memories, and pictures. She'd gotten to know a few people there. Healthy, sane people. On the rare occasion when she failed to go, there was an unhelpful, emptiness inside of her; one tainted by bullying.

Anna's vacations were also for healing and strengthening, except more so. Working under constant duress, she felt a poignant need to save money for her eventual and permanent "get away," but what she really needed right then was to save herself. In planning her escape, she hoped she could put herself as many time zones as emotionally and spiritually disconnected as possible from her "ground zero" time zone, and to soak up cultures and environments as different as possible than those that have supported abuse behaviors against her – even if that merely meant staying at her brother's cabin in the next state over. Wherever she would end up, she aspired for an emotional and spiritual makeover.

As with everything else, if she let her Bullying Boss, Wayne, get away with it, he'd make even her vacation time away from him, "all about him." Indeed, as they both well understood, the whole point of her vacation was to experience life somewhere removed, beautiful, and pleasing, specifically as an antidote to his toxic anxieties. For Wayne, the prospect of loosing control over Anna, for even a short time, caused him to be more sensitive than usual. His all-consuming concerns for his unique notions of status and sexual justice palpably predominated his end of the office. To the extent that any aspect of her vacation or relationship might become known to him, he'd would see it as a violation of himself and retaliate. In non-bullying environments, employees who periodically get out from under supervisory control are healthier, stronger and more productive all year long. In bullying environments, suppression through control is only thing that matters.

Being an odd and disconnected duck, the Bullying Boss Wayne only rarely had someone to take his vacations with but even when he did, it was unimaginable to Anna that he could share intimacy. He'd be alone regardless. To Anna's initial surprise, sharing quiet intimacy with another wasn't the most egregious "totally out of control" crime she could commit against Wayne. Dancing was. Upon reflection and knowing the tight-hipped Wayne—it made sense. *Dancing is the rhythm of "the personal" that is openly and sometimes exuberantly shared with others.* For people to dance was against Wayne's rules.

She understood she'd have to jump through some hoops to get away but she was getting good at it. The immediate goal was to get her Bullying Boss to adjust her workload and approve her time off. She was uncomfortably aware that to have a need was to have vulnerability. No longer naïve, she consciously pieced together a tactical plan leading to her healthful goal. Being technically legitimate under company policies, the vacation served as a political *cover* for what was really an escape attempt. The vacation itself was a personal and physical *flanking* maneuver to get around and away from the workplace battles.

And, she knew from experience that she'd be wise to paint a particularly bland picture of her vacation when discussing it at the office or with Wayne. Its purposefully low status profile was *camouflage* for the emotional, spiritual grandeur she anticipated. Whatever can remain unknown has no status to, and is safe beyond the Bully's challenge and control. As a profoundly anti-social man, Wayne had no clue about the nature, and thus full import, of her relationships with her man, friends or family. There was no need for him to know whom she would be spending her time with. Wayne's limited perspective on what is interpersonal, was not just her worst enemy on an everyday basis; it was ultimately her best protection as well.

It was imaginable that Wayne could experience happy moments on his vacations but not the profundity of joy. He was lost outside of work, stripped of his institutionally defined status and his political platform. His real self was all that remained and that picture didn't work for him—and not anyone else either. Anna was just his opposite. She was never more productive at work or happier in life than when her freedom to make choices and move with them was secure.

Most importantly, Wayne could never make out her core need to immerse herself in Nature, to pull into her chest and belly the Universe from its nighttime sky or to be passionate in her love. In that safe light, work consternations would dissipate without thought or effort. By being somewhere especially different and maybe a bit magic, she'd no longer feel bullying negativity. It would let go of her. She'd be free to consider fully what her priorities had actually been and how they should be different. If she came back, she might not come back to the place she left, and might not even be the same person. She'd come back sharp and strong. She'd *dance*.

ENDNOTES AND INDEX

Introduction

[1] Namie, Gary & Namie, Ruth, (2000, 2003) *The Bully at Work*. Sourcebooks. Corroboration as to the "thin" prospects for success, p. 239. Drs. Namie calculates an average exposure to bullying is 16.5 months. Names, p. 277.

[2] Herman, Dr. Judith, author of *Trauma and Recovery* (Basic Books 1992, 1997) as interviewed by Harry Kreisler UC Berkeley Institute of Industrial Studies (September 21, 2000) http://globetrotter.berkeley.edu/people/Herman/herman-con0.html

Chapter One

Work politics is not optional
[3] Hornstein, Harvey *Brutal Bosses and Their Prey* (Riverhead Books 1996).

[4] Keashly, Loraleigh, "A Year 2000 Scientific Survey of Michigan Residents" (2001) cited by Namies, P. 11.

Flight, fight, frightened
[5] Somer, Eli (2002) "Posttraumatic dissociation as a mediator of the effects of trauma on distressful introspectives" *Social Behavior & Personality: An International Journal.*

Chapter Two

Courting
[6] See also Futterman, Susan *When You Work for a Bully* (Croce 2004)

p. 9. Herman, (for the domestic violence version of courting) p 82.

Chapter Three

Several bullying boss definitions
[2] Namie (statistics) pp: 8, 11, 109, 275.

[8] Needham, Andrea *Workplace Bullying* (Penguin 2003). pp. 22-24.

[9] Namies, pp. 91-99 (international).

[10] Tracy, Sara (Arizona State University), "The Bullies Among Us" (Fourth International Conference on Bullying and Harassment in the Workplace, Bergen, Norway; Namies. (workplace Bullying and domestic violence), p. 50.

[11] Herberg v. California Institute of the Arts 101 Cal.App.3d 142 (*not* severe or pervasive).

[12] Rene v. MGM Grand Hotel 305 F.3d 1061 (9th Cir. 2002) (severe or pervasive).

[13] International Labor Organization (United Nations, 1998 ILO definition) cited by Susan Futterman in *When you Work for a Bully* (Croce 2004) p: 8.

[14] Hoel, Helge; Sparks, Kate and Cooper, Cary L. Cooper. "The Cost of Violence/Stress at Work and the Benefits of a Violence/Stress-Free Working Environment" (Report Commissioned by the International Labor Organization (ILO) Geneva.) University of Manchester Institute of Science and Technology, p. 14. http://www.ilo.org/public/english/protection/safework/whpwb/econo/costs.pdf

A businesslike definition
[15] United States Federal Register #61:4029-4067 (proposed OSHA workplace violence rule). "Injury or illness is any sign, symptom, or laboratory abnormality which indicates an adverse change in an employee's anatomical, biochemical, physiological, functional, or psychological condition." OSHA excluded from its definition violence "committed by family members or former spouses."

It's not about degree, it's about type
[16] Hornstein (targets in series).

Chapter Five

Four business irrationalities
[17] Needham, (models to analyze business costs for workplace Bullying) pp. 34-133. See also ILO study above and Futterman, pp. 192-196.

[18] Pearson, C.M., Anderson, L.M. & Porath, C.L. (2000) "Assessing and Attacking Workplace Incivility" *Organizational Dynamics*, 29, 123-137; see also Zellars, Kelly (University of North Carolina); Tepper, Bennet (University of North Carolina); and Duffy, Michelle (University of Kentucky) "A Study of 373 National Guard Members and Their Supervisors" *Journal of Applied Psychology* (December 2002).

[19] Pearson (*Assessing*)

Take it like a man
[20] Namie, (7% of Bullies "censored, transferred or terminated") p. 267.

Workplace confusion
[21] Bond, Frank W. and Bunce, David (Goldsmith College, University of London) "The Role of Acceptance and Job Control in Mental Health, Job Satisfaction, and Work Performance" *Journal of Applied Psychology* (December 2004): "Research has shown that negative affectivity and locus of control have the potential to bias, or distort, people's self-reports on a wide range of variables, from work characteristics (e.g., job control) to well-being (e.g. mental health, job satisfaction) and coping behaviors (problem- or emotion-focused coping." p. 1059.

[22] Namie, p. 47, 67. See also Herman (for the same syndrome in the domestic violence context: hypnotic trance, dissociation, witnesses can't see it all), pp; 1-2, 37 42-43.

Chapter Eight

Personal independence can isolate targets

[23] Carey, Benedict, *Fear in the Workplace* (June 22, 2004) New York Times.

Chapter Nine

General cultures determine reasonability
[24] Ellison v. Brady 924 F.2d 872 (9th Cir. 1991) (reasonable woman standard).

[25] Tannen, Deborah *Talking from 9 to 5: Women and Men at Work* (Quill 1995); and *You Just Don't Understand: Women and Men in Conversation* (Ballantine 1990).

[26] McGinest v. GTE Service Corp. 360 F.3d 1103 (9th Cir. 2004) ("reasonable person belonging to the rational or ethnic group" standard.

Personal doctrines in the workplace tend to be unreasonable
[27] Bodett v. Coxcom, Inc. 366 F.3d 736 (9th Cir. 2004) (personal doctrines in the workplace).

[28] Peterson v. Hewlett-Packard Co 358 F.3d 599 (9th Cir. 2004) (personal doctrines in the workplace).

Workplace attempts at justice tend to be unreasonable
[29] Varian Med. Sys. Inc. v. Delfino (2003) 6 Cal.Rprt.4th 325; ordered depublished, remanded on unrelated, procedural grounds on March 3, 2005 05 C.D.O.S. 1871 (the reasonability of angry, former employees v. reasonability as seen by the jury).

Chapter Ten

Some information must be shared
[30] State Department of Health Services v. Superior Court of Sacramento 31 Cal.4th 1026 (2003) (to follow internal complaint procedures).

[31] Allan v. Pacific Bell 348 F.3d 1113 (9th Cir. 2003) (ADA is an interactive process requiring the exchange of information.

[32] Barbee v. Household Auto. Fin. Corp. 113 Cal.App.4th 525 (2003) (rule requiring a supervisor report having an intimate relationship with a subordinate).

Chapter Eleven

Dollars and sense
[33] Futterman, pp: 73-104, 145-158.

Literature drops
[34] Needham, pp: 34-133; ILO, Hoel et al; Futterman, pp: 192-196.

Chapter Eleven

Speaking out or not
[35] Free speech, a few public sector cases: Pool v. Van Rheen 297 F.3d 899 (9th Cir. 2002); Shaarp v. City of North Las Vagas 320 F.3d 1040 (9th Cir. 2003); and Ceballos v. Garcetti 361 F.3d 1168 (2004 9th Cir.).

[36] Free speech, a couple private sector, labor law cases: Phoenix Transit System 337 NLRB No. 78 (2002) and Tradesman International 338 NLRB No. 49 (2002).

[37] See *West's California Digest.* (2 editions) Reference KFC 57 W47

Chapter Twelve

Workplace and community
[38] Barsade, Sigal (Yale University) Gibson, Donald (Fairfield University) "The Experience of Anger at Work: Lessons from the Chronically Angry" (1999).

[39] Bell v. Farmers Ins. Exchange 115 Cal.App.4th 714 (2004) (manager status).

Therapists and clergy
[40] Herman, (contact with abusers) p. 81.

Index